HOLLYWOOD INTELLECT

JAMES D. BLOOM

LEXINGTON BOOKS
A Division of Rowman & Littlefield Publishers, Inc.
Lanham • Boulder • New York • Toronto • Plymouth, UK

Published by Lexington Books
A division of Rowman & Littlefield Publishers, Inc.
A wholly owned subsidiary of The Rowman & Littlefield Publishing Group, Inc.
4501 Forbes Boulevard, Suite 200, Lanham, Maryland 20706
http://www.lexingtonbooks.com

Estover Road, Plymouth PL6 7PY, United Kingdom

British Library Cataloguing in Publication Information Available

Library of Congress Cataloging-in-Publication Data

Bloom, James D., 1951–
  Hollywood intellect / James D. Bloom.
      p. cm.
  Includes index.
  ISBN 978-0-7391-2923-4 (cloth : alk. paper)—ISBN 978-0-7391-2924-1 (pbk. : alk. paper)—ISBN 978-0-7391-4086-4 (electronic)
  1. Motion pictures—Philosophy. 2. Motion pictures—Social aspects. I. Title.
  PN1995.B4976 2009
  791.4301—dc22   2009021362

♾ ™ The paper used in this publication meets the minimum requirements of American National Standard for Information Sciences—Permanence of Paper for Printed Library Materials, ANSI/NISO Z39.48-1992.

Printed in the United States of America

HOLLYWOOD INTELLECT

What are intellectuals?

—PROFESSOR ROBERT HAVEN FRENCH (LARRY GATES)
IN *SOME CAME RUNNING* (1958)

[H]is next movie will include a bibliography at the end, to refer viewers to the copious research he does on every project. "We make movies that raise many questions that can't be answered. . . . Our idea is to do unpolished movies . . . in a movie, you can start a debate."

—2007 INTERVIEW WITH JOSÉ PADILHA (BARRIONUEVO)

CONTENTS

ILLUSTRATIONS

Intelligentsia Café

The Savage Eye

The Apartment

The Night of the Hunter

Love and Death

Raging Bull

Fredi Washington Award Poster

The Sidney Poet Heroical book cover

Annie Hall

★★Full array of illustrations available at www.muhlenberg.edu/depts/english/faculty.html#bloom

Preface: "Intellectual Fantasies"

It is a sad reflection of the limitations of intellectuals and artists all over the world to see history repeat itself in the contemptuous resentment with which they are greeting the arrival of the talking picture . . . between the incompetence of the commercial entertainer and the superior self righteousness of the intellectual, the talking picture is apparently doomed to grope blindly.

ALEXANDER BAKSHY, 1929

[E]veryone's "golden age of movies" is the period of his first moviegoing and just before. Sometimes we suspect—and sometime rightly—that our memory has improved a picture— that imaginatively we made it what we knew it could have been or should have been. . . . The educated person who became interested in cinema as an art form through Bergman or Fellini or Resnais is an alien to me. . . . There is a kind of young television watcher seeing old movies on for the first time who is surprisingly sensitive to their values . . . seems to have extreme empathy with the material in the box . . . but he may not know how to enter into a conversation.

PAULINE KAEL, 1967

Movies or Films

Movies made me. "Cinema" or "film" helped form me, intellectually, but much less influentially. For decades I identified myself with the intellectually sophisticated, self-conscious "cinema"-minded film generation Stanley Kauffmann heralded over forty years ago in his famous essay "The Film Generation," which—at least as caricatured in the 1950s—preferred discussing "the film" to any particular movie:

> When we returned to the table, Simp would be talking about "the dance" and her fiancé about "the film," until Brenda finally asked him, "Which film?" (P. Roth, *Goodbye* 56)

But long before I knew I was having a cultural experience and developing intellectually as I faced the screen, Hollywood pervaded my everyday little-boy world. Long before qualifying for Kauffmann's "film generation," circumstances had enlisted me, willy-nilly, in "the movie generation"—a generation Pauline Kael describes above as not bound to any particular span of years.

If it was raining on Saturday—*only* if it was raining—I was packed into a stationwagon "way-back" and dropped at one of several neighborhood theaters—some grandly christened the Embassy, the Palace, or the Hollywood, while others were more modestly named for towns and their main drags and cross streets, like Milburn, Sanford, and the Branford. I might watch a kiddy triple feature including a black-and-white war movie tracking a Marine platoon's retreat—"attacking in another direction"—over frigid Korean peaks (actually Orange County's "whitewashed hills") (Edwards 93) or the Third Infantry holding its beachhead under the guns at Anzio, a Francis the Talking Mule or an Abbott and Costello comedy, and a cartoon sequence; a Fess Parker Disney vehicle like *Davy Crockett* or *Westward-Ho the Wagons!*; a genre film like *The Fly* or *House of Wax*; or, during that halcyon interval between the full rigors of the Hays Office code and Jack Valenti's ostensibly transparent MPPA rating system, age-inappropriate classics like *The Apartment* and *North by Northwest*. Occasionally, blockbusters like *The Ten Commandments*, *Lawrence of Arabia*, *Exodus*, or *Around the World in 80 Days* would prompt a full-fledged family outing, maybe even a day "in the city." Day to day, though, movies mostly entered my life, after school, from the huge black steel RCA TV in the den. I gazed indiscriminately as Hollywood recycled thirty years of hits and misses on content-hungry emerging TV stations on such shows as *Movie Four*, *The*

ABC Saturday Movie, *The Early Show*, and *The Late Show*. *Million Dollar Movie*, which opened with the *Gone With the Wind* theme and showed the *same* movie each week, five nights in a row, on a New York station made it hard for me to avoid memorizing each song in *Yankee Doodle Dandy*. Little did I know at the time that I was participating in "a powerful social ritual for millions . . . experiencing and defining the shared values of peers and family" (Czitrom 59).

"There isn't much for the art-cinema person on television" (Kael, "Movies" 501). So in an entirely separate sphere, as a college sophomore, I was initiated into a more cloistered "ritual" about a decade later, finally joining Kauffmann's "film generation." My initiation was a class with a prominent film theorist who exposed me to the likes of Maya Deren, Stan Brakhage, James Broughton, and, most memorably, Polanski's *Repulsion*. At the risk of sounding philistine, the images and scenes with the most staying power for me—with the possible exception of Polanski's close-up of a rabbit corpse in *Repulsion*—have come out of Hollywood. The frisson prompted by the final shot in the 1958 version of *The Fly* (the camera looking down on the tiny human head faintly crying "help me") still hasn't entirely faded. So, too, the image in the more highbrow Americana classic *Night of the Hunter* that helps make this 1955 movie one of the most "visually fecund" and much "plundered" "movies of the 'Golden Age'" (Atkinson, "Houses"): the way Stanley Cortez's camera closes in on Shelley Winters's corpse wrapped in her wedding dress, sitting in her Model T at the bottom of the river with her hair billowing in the current like the surrounding weeds.

My personal image-canon reflects the extent to which Hollywood "movies" and "art-house cinema" lie along a continuum, rather than inhabiting separate spheres. Insofar as European imports created "art-house cinema" in the United States and so spawned Kauffmann's "film generation," it too needs to be seen as yet another Hollywood product. For the French *Nouvelle Vague*, most influential in making art-house erudition such a mid-century mark of class and generational distinction and in turning "cinephilia into a legitimate aesthetic discourse" (V. Schwartz 148), built their movement on a "love of Hollywood" by "applying Hollywood formulas" and looking to Hollywood movies as a "source of inspiration" (V. Schwartz 149; Brody 61).

Without my having made a single movie, they served as inspirations, cautionary as well as exemplary, for me as well, and, I'd wager, for millions of other kids my age. Some formative images have become resonant visual rhetoric and still haunt my understanding of what it means, for better and for worse, to be a man, especially an American man:

- Jean-Pierre Leaud constructing his identity by repeating his own name and those of his two true loves before a mirror as he girds himself for the picaresque adventure before him at the beginning of *Stolen Kisses*.
- Robert Mitchum strutting across the fields bellowing "Leaning on the Everlasting Arms" in the *Night of the Hunter*.
- Sinatra's insouciant one-handed hold on a lit cigarette and a tumbler of scotch in *Some Came Running*.
- Cary Grant lending a hand to Eva Marie Saint as their train enters a tunnel at the end of *North by Northwest* and Grant *safely* driving drunk at the beginning.
- Jack Lemmon using a tennis racket as colander to fix Shirley MacLaine a spaghetti dinner in *The Apartment*.
- Van Johnson in *Battleground* quizzing a suspected Nazi spy in a GI uniform about Americana.
- Burt Lancaster terrifying sinners in *Elmer Gantry*.
- Gregory Peck turning to address the courtroom in *To Kill a Mockingbird*.

A lifetime of formative movie images refract one another so recursively that the indelible impact on me of the image of the Grim Reaper playing chess in *The Seventh Seal* may owe as much to Woody Allen's parody of it in *Love and Death*. Finally, venue and memorable life events compound these images, so that my lasting recollection of the traffic and auto carnage in *Weekend* may owe more to the coincidence of my first viewing this movie, at the New Yorker theater, with my very first acid trip.

Movies and Films

Including the directors Wilder and Hitchcock and the writer James Agee in this grouping of memorable scenes confounds the difference between art-films and Hollywood movies, a difference once bluntly reduced by *All the President's Men* screenwriter William Goldman to "audience size" (*Which Lie* 275). David Mamet recently underscored the limits of this distinction, observing that all movie plotting depends on tapping into moviegoers' "intellectual fantasies" as a prerequisite for getting them "emotionally involved" (*Bambi* 124). As David Bordwell and Kristin Thompson have demonstrated, the art-film/Hollywood movie divide fell, at least briefly, to the Hollywood renaissance nearly realized in the 1970s when a "Hollywood art cinema" spurred by Robert Altman and Woody Allen, sustained by Francis Ford Coppola, George Lucas, and Steven Spielberg, and fully realized by Martin Scorsese took hold (*Film History* 520). This vaunted renaissance coincided with the dead end traditional, print intellectual work was approaching around 1970, when popular political historian Theodore White complained that "the job of intellectuals is to come up with ideas and all we've been producing is memos notes" (Flaherty 220). More boldly than Bordwell, Pauline Kael, perhaps the most influential arbiter of this renaissance, argued for a less chronologically confined understanding of the inadequacy of opposing films and movies, art and entertainment because "unlike 'pure' arts which are often defined in terms of only what they can do, movies are open and unlimited . . . a wonderfully *convenient* art" ("Trash" 346).

Kael's argument that movies may be as intellectually meaty as films, perhaps more so, has become less tendentious, due largely to the apparent "rise of" a "mass educated class" (Brooks "Segmented"). Hollywood reflects this leveling in its institutionalization of so-called indie moviemaking under the aegis of the Sundance Foundation and such major studio boutique production operations as Miramax, Fox Searchlight, Time-Warner/New Line, and Paramount Vantage. Nevertheless, this tension still holds influential tastemakers in its grip. A *Times* reviewer observed late in 2007 that "American cinema is in the grip of a kind of moribund academicism," which results in "fastidiously polished film[s] earning 'gushing praise from critics' at the expense of movies that 'reach beyond the obvious, push past' the moviemaker's 'and the audience's comfort zones' by offering 'more ideas, visual and intellectual, in a single scene than most American independent films have in their entirety'" (Dargis, "Apocalypse"). The distinction between "moribund academicism" and abundant "ideas, visual and *intellectual*," reflects not only the persistence of Kael's animus, but also an even longer-standing anxiety about the place and value of intellect in Hollywood movies.

The Conversation

Hollywood Intellect represents a bid to join in this conversation to promote a flexible egalitarian view of intellectual work, especially to demonstrate that much of the most influential, conceptually challenging and pleasure-providing intellectual work takes place in popular culture and that for the past century this place has, for the most part, been the movies.

With this debate now fully assimilated into the marketplace of ideas, movies play a more fully acknowledged and appreciated role in setting the standard for intellectual—discursive and artistic—depth. Urging video games to follow the evolution of the movies from mass diversion to an intellectually transformative medium, Daniel Radosh notes how "many games now aspire to be 'cinematic' above all else" and have become "successful as entertainment." By "appropriating the language of cinema," Radosh explains, "the best video games are more inventive, exciting and rewarding than most summer action movies. . . . But as much as everyone enjoys summer blockbusters, *Transformers* is not what we have in mind when we talk about the art of cinema." To overcome this limitation, Radosh importunes game makers to design games that "like cinema . . . embrace the dynamics of failure, tragedy, comedy and romance," that will "stop pandering to the player's desire for mastery in favor of enhancing the player's emotional and intellectual life," and that "develop the power to transform as well as to entertain" ("Play").

Questions

The assumptions governing the arguments throughout *Hollywood Intellect* include Radosh's claim for movies as the touchstone of intellect, Mamet's understanding of how movies we care about always engage us intellectually, Kael's appreciation of what movies, exclusively, "can do" for the collective life of the mind, and Wilder's simultaneously self-deprecating, self-aggrandizing view of moviegoers as idiot-geniuses. The movies, according to such assumptions, nurture the "genius" Wilder extols. With this aim in mind, *Hollywood Intellect* asks: How have many Hollywood movies worked—or at least demonstrated their aspiration to work—such a transformation of moviegoers into "geniuses"? Or, picking up on Mamet's cue, how have a number of Hollywood movies over the past century stirred our "intellectual fantasies"?

Addressing these broad questions prompts the following exploration of and argument for the way in which many Hollywood movies often do intellectual work as ambitious as and often more influential than the "art-films," as well as books, artworks, and other performances, that have also moved me and taught me. These reflections also speak to a broader hope that many readers, looking back on the movies in *their* lives, will also recognize their own "genius" and their own movie-made intellectual "fantasies" in order to begin composing their own movie-centered intellectual autobiography.

The Argument

My argument begins with a historical and political account of the title phenomenon—Hollywood intellect—and then examines three discrete challenges Hollywood intellect has grappled with. Stardom, chronologically the earliest of these intellectual challenges, predates Hollywood. It came to Hollywood as an inheritance from the nineteenth century and the modern promotional apparatus it developed. The second "take"—on what I call "civilization panic"—looks to early the twentieth century and some of the ways in which world wars, colonialism, and racial and ethnic strife preoccupied Hollywood. In her late-career on-screen demand "You tell me what it's like to be civilized," Bette Davis was speaking collectively for Hollywood, highlighting its most pressing, perennial intellectual challenge.

Attention to two perennial sets of intellectual questions caps my argument in *Hollywood Intellect*. In considering the relationship of language to the other senses and faculties movies appeal to. I track the uneasy place of poetry in the movies and how this very venerable, hard-to-pin-down intellectual aspiration has surfaced throughout the history of Hollywood, and some of the ways in which Hollywood writers and directors have aspired to make movies that work like poems. Finally, I take up the most fundamental intellectual impetus, curiosity, which has inspired and vexed writers and directors in every Hollywood genre for several decades.

Hollywood Intellect takes its title from and elaborates the argument sketched out in an article first published in 2004. The argument takes off from the controversy or at least the anxiety that peaked during the 1990s over the role, the fate, the purported absence or dereliction of so-called public intellectuals. As recently as 2006, an article in *New York* magazine reminded readers of the extent to which these concerns persist, with James Atlas declaring that "the death of the 'public intellectual' has been announced more often than the death of the novel" ("Ma and Pa"). Two years later a *New York Times* editor mourned the passing of "intellectual heavyweights" (Tanenhaus). He praised intellectuals who find "validation outside the intellectual establishment," but stopped short of casting his gaze beyond his own parochial "establishment" boundaries, beyond print media, or even beyond New York—toward Hollywood, for example. From this wider perspective, laments about the passing of public intellectuals look more self-congratulatory than elegiac. So much so, in fact, that one English observer has called the very phrase "irritating," one that Americans got stuck with, "for want of a better name," for an amorphous phenomenon (Wheatcroft).

Hollywood Intellect begins by looking beyond these boundaries in order to challenge some assumptions on which such discussions have rested. This challenge serves as a point of departure for arguing that such assumptions rest on a misleading inattention to the intellectual work that mass culture performs. Hollywood writers in particular have, for much of the past century, done the same kind of work as public intellectuals, often doing it more influentially than the print writers, the "higher journalists" and "crossover" academics normally identified as intellectuals.

The emergence in 2006 of "*South Park* Republicans" (Tierney), touted as an alternative to traditional think tanks, with their generously sponsored partisan agendas and academic trappings, provides one notable recent example. A year later a *New York Times* editorial elaborated, enthusing over the "explanatory power" of the Culver City *South Park* movie/TV/merchandise franchise ("Digital"), a provocative series aimed at teenage boys. Looking to "*South Park* to explain life's deeper mysteries," one right-wing pundit described the series as "possibly surpassing Milton Friedman's *Free to Choose* as the classic defense of capitalism" (Stephens).

In responding to this need, *Hollywood Intellect* prompts its readers to reflect on many Hollywood movies, and their impact, with some of the same assumptions, expectations, and questions we apply to writing by the likes of Irving Howe, Edmund Wilson, Walter Lippmann, Susan Sontag, Edward Said, or Stanley Crouch. *Hollywood Intellect* will consider in turn how literary writers over the past century have addressed—and even critically anticipated—the emergence of Hollywood as a shaper of the public mind. Such shaping has been variously characterized by cultural theorists as:

- "the political imaginary" (Buck-Morss, *Dreamworld* 11–12)
- "the political unconscious" (Jameson, *Unconscious* 20–21)
- "imagined communities" (B. Anderson 6, 7)
- "the public sphere" (Habermas 160–61, 175–76)
- "public opinion" (Lippmann 8, 11, 25, 29, 125; Schumpeter 149; Habermas 89, 236)
- "civil discourse" (Denby, "Balance" 81)
- Jung's "collective unconscious" (Shamdasani 235)
- "conventional wisdom" (Galbraith 9–13, 18–20)
- simply "what everybody's talking about" (Kael, "Trash" 363)
- what C. Wright Mills understood as "the cultural apparatus" whereby "learning, entertainment, malarkey, and information are produced and distributed . . . to small circles, wider publics . . . great masses" (*Power* 406, 376) harkens back to the hoariest of all such concepts for mass media spaces, John Stuart Mill's "marketplace of ideas" (May, *Big* 23–24).

Whatever conceptual tag one prefers, this public forum was claimed fifty years ago by the novelist and Hollywood chronicler Leo Rosten:

> Producers . . . give more space and time to minority views (which include the *avant garde*) than numerical proportions require. The popular media carry far more of this material than anyone would have predicted two decades ago. The democratic society must insure a viable public forum for the dissenter (343).

Warily welcoming the influence of the movies and other mass media into our "public forum," Rosten announced that "I, for one, do not lament the epochs in which 'high culture' flourished while the majority of mankind lived in ignorance and indignity" (343).

The opening chapter traces this alternative "public intellectual" narrative by showing how studio-sponsored writers functioned and conceived of themselves as public intellectuals. An overview and a working definition of the book's overarching concept, "Hollywood intellect," this chapter marks both Hollywood intellect's debts to and departures from established understandings of intellectual work. The next chapter examines the intellectual challenge posed by the growing impact of stardom in America by comparing literary rendering by James, Dreiser, Cather, Updike, Didion, Robert Stone, and Susan Sontag of the mass-cult star-is-born narrative with the three Hollywood versions of this staple narrative. In relation to the book as a whole, this chapter looks to representations by the earlier novelists in this group as laying the groundwork for a signature development in the growth of Hollywood's influence, one that also came to pervade critiques of Hollywood.

A two-chapter account of the movies as arbiters of what constitutes *civilization* begins by tracing the "civilization panic" stimulated by the Great War. Illustrating how the movies took over as the century's dominant culture arbiter, its "quintessential cultural form" (V. Schwartz 10), as more established arbiters maintained their authority, the centenarian memoirist Harry Bernstein remembers how, in the wake of the 1918 armistice, his family's leisure-time allegiance split between the majority who spent Saturday at "the picture show" and the minority who "preferred the library" (176). This split came to pervade work by such pioneers of modernism as Eliot and Faulkner, as did the widespread, readily exploited anxieties I label "civilization anxiety" (Pease 77, 79). "Civilization panic" rhetoric also fostered the emergence of Hollywood as the dominant mass medium in reflecting and refracting national aspirations and assumptions. Moving from the formative years of

Anglophone modernism and Hollywood's infancy during and after the war, the first of these civilization chapters traces Hollywood's representations and exploitations of "civilization panic" through the world wars and the Cold War up to its recent post-9/11 resurgence. A companion chapter views mainstream expressions of this anxiety during the twentieth century through the lenses provided by African American writers—Richard Wright, Ralph Ellison, James Baldwin, Toni Morrison, and Amiri Baraka—in challenging Hollywood's authority as the arbiter and guardian of civilization.

An inquiry into the kind of intellectual work screen adaptations perform and, perhaps more significantly, sidestep, a fifth chapter takes as its premise an obvious but barely explored fact: most of Hollywood literary adaptations draw on plays and narratives—novels, short stories, and reportage. This tendency has produced and reflects an implicit consensus about what makes a literary source "filmable" (as press coverage of Michael Winterbottom's 2006 adaptation of *Tristram Shandy* illustrates). Hollywood seldom looks to make movies from poems. In 1969, Robert Richardson contrasted the "countless novels and plays" with the "few poems" that "have been done into films." Thirty years later Timothy Corrigan stressed the staying power of this limitation, noting how, "of all the different literary genres that film has drawn on and influenced," poetry has proven "the most elusive," citing only three examples to come out of Hollywood since D. W. Griffith set up shop. The investigation in this chapter of this durable resistance and uneasily persisting attraction to poetry looks to the implications of Budd Schulberg's, Evelyn Waugh's, and Christopher Isherwood's depiction of script-writing poets in *What Makes Sammy Run*, *The Loved One*, and *Prater Violet*, respectively; John Collier's long-incubating, published but never-produced screenplay for *Paradise Lost* as an elaboration of Eisenstein's praise for Milton's epic as "a first-rate school" for "the study of montage and audio visual relationships" and the preparation of "a shooting script"; the quixotic, up-and-down career of Robert Frost and Howard Hughes protégé Joseph Moncure March; and the comically futile attempt to bring Whitman to the screen depicted in Richard Kwietniowski's *Love and Death on Long Island*, especially its recurring visual allusions to Whitman and to Henry Wallis's painting *The Death of Chatterton*.

Working from the axiom that poems, in comparison with other literary writing, tend to distill language more than most narrative and more often present words themselves as a central problem, I'll look at some of the more acclaimed Hollywood movies that explicitly offer themselves as efforts to draw on the work of canonic poets such as Kipling (*Gunga Din*),

Pope (*The Eternal Sunshine of the Spotless Mind*), Blake (*Chariots of Fire*), and Yeats (*Million Dollar Baby*).

Hollywood Intellect closes with readings of movies featuring what Parker Tyler, writing in the 1940s, identified as "agents of curiosity" (197). Tyler's characterization prompts reflections on the role of movies in what historian Barbara Benedict describes as the regulation of curiosity (27). These reflections rest on the premise that curiosity is the linchpin of all intellectual work and that all cultural production depends on channeling curiosity or regulating it. Hollywood's enduring interest in the effects and force of curiosity is reflected in generations of biopics about renowned inquirers such as Freud, Pasteur, Ehrlich, Edison, and John Nash. Conversely, in *Reds* and *Zelig* Warren Beatty and Woody Allen, "an auteur . . . obsessed with his role as an . . . intellectual" (Davis), turned the inquiry narrative upside-down. In movies that ran concurrently in the early 1980s, they critically refracted the biopic formula. Diffusing and parodying the biopic formula, they manipulated moviegoers' "intellectual fantasies" by punctuating otherwise straightforward biographical narratives with documentary talking-head interviews that often disclosed more about the interviewee than about the biographical subject.

About a decade ago, in my third book *The Literary Bent*, I began this inquiry into how novelists and poets have confronted such curiosity-regulators in a discussion of several contemporary writers' contention with Disney and the *New York Times*. (In 2006 the *Times* announced that it had retained a Hollywood talent agency to help shop film and television projects based on articles appearing in the newspaper [Manly].) In my most recent book, *Gravity Fails*, I extended this inquiry into the role of mass media in regulating curiosity in "Talking Heads/Shrinking Heads," a chapter treating our many thriving "explanation industries" as a staple source of comedy. The intellectual impact of popular comedy surfaced in the summer of 2007 with the release of the box-office record-setter *The Simpsons Movie*. This movie's opening scene prompted one reporter to explain this impact by characterizing Lisa Simpson as "the conscience of the liberal intelligentsia." In this scene (which chapter V examines), the cartoon prodigy provides a comic example of the "intellectual fantasies" David Mamet singles out as the impetus for getting movie audiences "emotionally involved." This approach to engaging moviegoers flourished in Depression-era screwball comedies, such as *My Man Godfrey*, *Bringing Up Baby*, *Ball of Fire*, *The Talk of the Town*, and *Sullivan's Travels*. Such movies figure prominently in my inquiry, since the plot in each of these movies turns on its hero's "research project" and implicitly, therefore, on broader questions about what merits interest and attention—what should the characters (and audiences) be curious about?—that this plot formula prompts.

All the movies discussed throughout *Hollywood Intellect* share and exhibit, for all their more obvious differences, a commitment Lary May identifies as having waxed and waned throughout Hollywood—and U.S.—history: the will to "bring a critical edge to mass art" (*Big* 213). On this commitment rests the "seriousness" Stanley Kauffmann embraced in 1966 in dubbing my cohort "the film generation": "the first generation that has matured in a culture in which the film has been of accepted serious relevance, however that seriousness is defined" (415). *Hollywood Intellect* joins a collective continuing effort to keep redefining and stretching the seriousness that Kauffmann welcomed.

Approach

Though *Hollywood Intellect* draws on nearly six decades of watching movies and films and its references and allusions range over a century of movies, it is neither a sequential narrative nor a cause-effect history. Readers intent on pinning a genre on *Hollywood Intellect* will have to settle for "genealogy" (Foucault, *Reader* 79–86; Lye). As defined by Michel Foucault, genealogy takes as its point of departure a wariness of explanations asserting origins and assuming orderly continuity, "cultivating" instead the details and accidents that produced and sustained Hollywood intellect over the past century when it came to both dominate and challenge what and how Americans thought and said. Following this genealogical approach, *Hollywood Intellect* cites many movies released over the past century—either briefly to establish contexts, or as focal points in more sustained discussions of particular instances of the various kinds of intellectual work Hollywood has done and aspired to do. Although considering these focal points entails looking closely at on-screen images (supplemented by illustrations), my approach remains primarily discursive—"logocentric," some readers might object—throughout.

Hollywood Intellect also belongs to a much older, less formal genre: the essay. Essays, as Montaigne explained half a millennium ago, *try out*, *test*, or *weigh* simple ideas, in this case the straightforward proposition that Hollywood—as an industry, an institution, and a mass medium—both produces and elicits much of America's influential intellectual work.

Identifying the collective anxieties and aspirations implicit in Hollywood's words and images, *Hollywood Intellect* aims to underscore attention on Hollywood's chronic engagement with public questions, note responses to these efforts, redress influential misunderstandings of and inattention to this engagement, and begin to enumerate the variety of discourses Hollywood has touched on and been touched by. Numerous references to sociologists, historians, poets, novelists, and literary critics—along with the expected film scholars, movie reviewers, and Hollywood writers, directors, producers, and performers themselves—serve as reminders of the controversial openness of such key terms as *intellect* and *intellectual,* Hollywood the city as opposed to Hollywood the idea and metaphor, and movie, film, art-film, and cinema (Robinson 116–19).

Acknowledgments

MGM Studios has graciously allowed me to print stills from *The Apartment*, *Love and Death*, *The Night of the Hunter*, *Raging Bull*, and *Annie Hall*.

My family, many staff and faculty colleagues at Muhlenberg College and elsewhere, and countless students over the years have helped make this book possible.

Shorter versions of chapters I and II first appeared in the *Canadian Review of American Studies* and the *Columbia Journal of American Studies*, respectively.

Intelligenti   I

> *Then there is what is called a too intellectual tendency. Can there be too much intellect? We have never met with any such excess. But the criticism, which is leveled at the laws and manners, ends in thought, without causing a new method of life. The genius of the day does not incline to a deed, but to a beholding.*
>
> —EMERSON "ON THE TIMES"

> *He said, "What do they write?" and we said, "Movies." He looked aghast and said, "You mean they write that stuff?"*
>
> —MILLARD KAUFMAN (MEAD)

I

At least since the introduction of talking movies, several Hollywood screenwriters and directors have done work ascribed to so-called public intellectuals. Thanks to talkies, movies "matured" intellectually and "first became the art form that we know today" (Radosh). "Developing the power to transform as well as to entertain," in "about 1930 . . . movies became more complex, more 'realistic,' more 'psychological'" and more open to "thematic complexity" (Radosh; Morin 9–10). Though obvious to many, influential agenda-setters purporting to speak on behalf of intellect have tenaciously resisted this narrative. The end of the twentieth century brought increasingly vociferous laments over the decline of public intellectuals and their influence. This nostalgia has made acknowledging the legacy of Hollywood intellect—and its persistence—increasingly difficult. Increasingly necessary, too, since intellectual work in Hollywood exerts more influence than more obvious venues for intellectual work: universities, museums, cultural journalism, editorial, and think tanks. The head of one of Washington's most successful think tanks, the American Enterprise Institute, acknowledged his organization's sense of itself as a popular medium, recalling that "when new arrivals from academia ask me whom they should write for, I tell them: for your Mom" (Demuth). At the same time, seizing the highbrow ground, he claimed to be rivaling, and in some ways surpassing, universities by "discovering new ways of organizing intellectual activity." The motives claimed for this intellectual activity coincide with the rhetorical motives apparent in such products of Hollywood intellect as *On the Waterfront* and *Bulworth*: "criticism and devotion to reform."

More than these less obviously populist, often less frankly commercial sources of inquiry and civic discourse, intellectual work coming out of Hollywood grapples with the central intellectual contradiction of modern life characterized a century ago by the German historian and founder of academic sociology, Max Weber. Commercial moviemaking manufactures and markets enchantment, while the modern intellectual's agenda, in Max Weber's resonant formulation, aims at disenchantment (155).

Budd Schulberg—an Oscar-nominated screenwriter and novelist, self-described "Hollywood Prince" (*Moving*), "self-appointed Hollywoodologist" ("Any" 55), and ever-aspiring intellectual—has embodied Hollywood intellect for the past seventy years. In *Raging Bull*, Martin Scorsese asserted the intellectual stature of Schulberg and other screenwriters of his era. He introduces the last act in the career of middleweight champion Jake LaMotta (Robert De Niro), his dramatic readings of great writers' works, with a closeup of a marquee announcing "An Evening With Jake La Motta featuring the works of Paddy Chayefsky, Rod Serling, Shakespeare, Budd Schulberg, and Tennessee Williams." Schulberg has repeatedly addressed the contradiction this position entails—the dilemma of the intellectual aspirant and principled disenchanter paid to enchant millions. Metaphorically echoing Weber's formulation, Schulberg maintains that pursuing a traditional intellectual's agenda in Hollywood means walking a "treadmill of disenchantment" (*Sanctuary* 159). Antagonism between Hollywood's commercial imperatives and any intellectual's aspiration, to disenchant the world and disillusion audiences, the very customers who bring Hollywood its profits, confronts all would-be Hollywood intellectuals.

To understand Hollywood intellect, as represented by Schulberg and his successors, it might help to replace the now overused noun "intellectual" and audition a replacement: Vladimir Nabokov's preferred Russian noun, *intelligenti*. Nabokov prefers this coinage because it has "more socially idealistic and less highbrow connotations than 'intellectual as used in America' has" (277).[1] This substitution may prove even more apt now than when Nabokov introduced this distinction. The Hollywood-seasoned playwright Theresa Rebeck laments an industry plagued by numerous influential players "who want to be *thought* of as intellectual" but, lacking the wherewithal actually to be intellectual, end up sabotaging the work of those "who perhaps actually *are*" intellectual (77–78). One veteran producer ascribes to these associates the mere desire "to look like those East coast . . . intellectuals" (Linson 175). The importance in Hollywood of at least *appearing* intellectual derives from its big-studio era image of itself as "pipe-smoking kind of place, tirelessly working for the moral improvement of America" (Kehr, "Big"). This aspiration has in recent years made "panel discussions" and "political provocation" integral to studio marketing campaigns (Cieply). In 2007 Hollywood's intellectual aspirations became even more visible along the storied Sunset Boulevard with the opening in Silver Lake of the immediately popular Intelligentsia Café (Dicum). Though less explicit than this café's name, on-screen visual cues announcing intellect at work are no less subtle than such storefront announcements. "Piles of papers and books," one debut novelist observed in 2008, have come to serve as visual shorthand for turning any "movie set" into "an intellectual's rooms" (Galchen 73).

The *intelligenti* Nabokov praises allows for distinctions between these self-styled intellectuals and writers and directors effectively doing intellectual work. Despite its Old World aura, Nabokov's coinage reflects the way in which the Hollywood *intelligenti* differs from both the European intellectual and the American wannabe: the *intelligenti* aims to identify with "a wider public," values "access" to the prevailing "civic idioms that press the moral questions embedded in political debate," and is "prepared to live, at least most of the time, with the give-and-take of political life" (Elshtain). Work by the *intelligenti* takes into account Orwell's little-heeded caution that the "intellectual *is* different from the ordinary man, but only in certain sections of his personality, and even then not all the time" and embraces—builds on—each "sign of the overlap between the intellectual and the ordinary man" (130).

Half a century ago, the French historian Raymond Aron reacted to the "egghead" crisis—the debates over the status of intellect in America.

Prompted by Adlai Stevenson's intellectually "ostentatious" presidential runs (Trilling 281) and by congressionally sponsored Red Scares, the egghead crisis peaked just before Stevenson's second loss to Eisenhower. *Time* marked this crisis with a cover story documenting how intellectuals were "taking stock" ("Parnassus"). Aron argued that among Americans even self-styled intellectuals who defensively "affect to despise" "the big public" implicitly "long to serve it" (322, 229–321). In the decades since the egghead debates, Hollywood's perennial aspiration, "to open the possibility of an alternative public . . . culture" (May, *Big* 77), may have even grown hardier than it proved at mid-century, when intellectual aspiration appeared conspicuously on the defensive. The "eggheads" in their proto– "think tank" in *Ball of Fire* (Smyth 339), the newly serious protagonist in *Sullivan's Travels*, and the jazz-aficionado aesthete challenged by teenage Philistines in *Blackboard Jungle* made easy targets in these critically and commercially successful movies.

One of the most influential late-century jeremiads on the death of the "public intellectual," Russell Jacoby's *The Last Intellectuals*, illustrates how far Hollywood has moved from this defensive position. Jacoby implicitly— apparently inadvertently—hints at Hollywood's role in sustaining American intellectual life by calling the New York print intellectuals whose passing he mourns "*publicists*" [Jacoby's italics] (26). In using a noun widely associated with Hollywood, and with the mass entertainment industries in general, Jacoby discredits his own laments about the disappearance of public intellectuals, even as he strives to recuperate and restore long-lapsed, high-minded connotations of "publicist" (Jacoby 235; Itzkoff).

In fact, Hollywood intellect had become entrenched enough by 2007 to appear on the other side of the mass-elite, popular-egghead divide so long a staple of cultural critique and consequently to be subjected to the more narrowly aimed "egghead" bashing of the 1950s. Such accusations took the form of "the ideologically convenient notion that Hollywood is out of touch with the American people, and also the economically convenient idea that people go to the movies to escape the problems of the world rather than to confront them" (A. O. Scott, "War"). Writing about Hollywood's intellectually demanding responses to the Bush regime's various anti-jihad crusades, *Times* reviewer A. O. Scott takes the part of those moviemakers he finds eager to grapple with the "touchy, serious political issues" these wars provoke. "This new crop of war movies" does intellectual work, in Scott's view, "not" because of "their earnestness or their didacticism—traits many of them undoubtedly display—but rather their determination to embrace confusion, complexity and ambiguity."

II

Budd Schulberg set the agenda Scott described both in print and on screen as far back as the 1950s. One of Schulberg's most renowned collaborators, the director Nicholas Ray, described him as "a vigorous, polemical writer, an anti-demagogical demagogue with a style derived from Hemingway" (Ray 216). Thanks to the vigor, animus, and craftsmanship Ray cites, Schulberg has played the part of a tough-minded, tenderhearted cultural combatant. His narratives on screen and in print show "powerful characters whose success depend[s] on pitiable humans who cower before the very forces that exploit(ed) them" (Hye 674). Career trajectories such as Schulberg's, when they lead to studio screen credits, confirm the humbling turn that Nabokov identifies with the *intelligenti*, the turn away from highbrow presumption. This turn demands a nonspecialist approach to civic discourse, which reflects a quixotic goal: to encourage the reading and moviewatching publics to reason rather than to merely emote (which entails contesting the enchantment that *both* mass entertainment *and* political oratory foster) and to distill articulated *knowledge* from proliferating information (D. Bell). The Hollywood *intelligenti*'s defining métier, the screenplay—a commerce-driven lowest common denominator—makes their task more demanding than do the favored forms of traditional print intellectuals: essays and reviews. In 1937, English actor Robert Donat challenged theatergoers to lose their snobbery toward movies by arguing that "commercialization" is "the most rigorous discipline" (20). *Some* egalitarian-minded print intellectuals, and *every* Hollywood *intelligenti*, must tool and often retool the vernacular style (Jacoby 235) with which they address a public with increasingly more schooling and increasingly unavoidable sense of the global multiplicity reflected in such recent releases as *Babel*, *In the Valley of Elah*, and *Syriana*, described by its star as the work of an "issues-guy director" (Parker 47).

In theoretical academic parlance, these movies engage in the postmodern practice known as "cognitive mapping": they provide "subjects"—audiences—"with some new heightened sense of its place in the global system" (Jameson, *Postmodernism* 54). Such movies participate in a literary movement academe has recently described as the "critical cosmopolitanism" that fosters a wariness toward the rhetoric of heroism and progress and a suspicion of "epistemological" authorities who claim to know for sure what's going on (Walkowitz 2). In narrating, dramatizing, and visualizing such concepts, Hollywood provides curious lay audiences with a service that intellectually ambitious mass media have long furnished, dating back to Joseph Addison in Georgian England or Thomas Paine in colonial Philadelphia. Both then and now, this effort calls for a vernacular "middle style." These styles aim to provoke discussions of ideas that intellectuals believe fellow citizens ought to consider. When it resonates, this style infiltrates the broader "style in which" nations "are imagined" (B. Anderson 6).

III

Early arrivals in the movie industry's nascent capital seemed to have construed their citizenship in these civic and stylistic terms. Raymond Chandler, as a founding father of the hardboiled posturing in prose and in performance (and in much adolescent coming-of-age) that constitutes one of Hollywood's profoundest influences, stands in the forefront of such infiltrators. Not surprisingly, Chandler, who cast the villain in *The Big Sleep* as a rare-books merchant before killing him off, claimed to look warily at the "little groups who thought they were intellectual used to call [Hollywood] the Athens of America" (Rayner R1, 4). Chandler nevertheless participated in these early neo-Athenian stirrings of Hollywood intellect and so assented to its aspirations to shape the mind of as well as styles in American culture. As a new Angeleno, "Chandler himself belonged to a little intellectual group, the Optimists," where "music was played, poetry declaimed, literature and philosophy were discussed" (Rayner).

Another, later infiltrator—screenwriter Howard Koch, who imagined various Americas in such movies as *Casablanca* and *Sergeant York*—expressly placed himself in the constellation of Hollywood intellect, comparing the intellectual ferment he found while working in Hollywood to the climate of Greenwich Village "in late teens" when *The Masses* and The Provincetown Players (and such writers as Randolph Bourne, Van Wyck Brooks, Waldo Frank, and Lewis Mumford) created America's first intellectual bohemia. Koch found that, contrary to persisting caricatures, studio moguls permitted writers "leeway" for their intellectual interests (Giovacchini 18–19). Walter Wanger, one of Hollywood's most influential and durable independent producers (from the Marx Brothers first movie, *Coconuts*, in 1929 to Joseph Manckiewicz's notorious fiasco, *Cleopatra*, in 1962), began his career when "screen writers had more . . . power than directors" (Smyth 118) and so stood out in his determination to "reconcile popular taste with elevated values" and treat movies as "the premier vehicle of enlightenment" (M. Bernstein 394, 74). This determination made Wanger so solicitous of the *intelligenti* he employed that he called in 1942 for "an entente between the intellectuals . . . and the motion pictures producers, directors, writers" because "they are not some tribe apart" from often and counterproductively "snobbish" intellectuals, but rather "men [*sic*] who have learned the technique of speaking to the world today."

Prominent directors in the following generation fulfilled Wanger's call for an "entente." Schulberg's collaborations with Elia Kazan and Nicholas Ray, along with contemporaneous work by Otto Preminger and Stanley Kubrick, starting in 1950s, raised civil discourse to the level of subtle entertainment (Denby, "Balance" 82) and melded "the sensibility of a literary intellectual with the technical expertise of a photographer/editor and the instincts of a showman," as argued by Kubrick's biographer James Naremore (Doherty). Soon before his death in 2006, Robert Altman characterized his lifetime oeuvre as "an *examination* of class" (Hoge—emphasis added). Altman's aspiration and achievements recall Joseph Schumpeter's argument that one distinguishing trait of intellectuals is the commitment to advancing "class interests other than their own" (146). Warren Beatty followed Schumpeter's prescription for intellectual aspiration in his 1982 epic, *Reds*. This study in "the irony of history" (G. Smith 36) depicted its hero John Reed's revolutionary aspiration—his fight for a classless utopia—through the retrospective, seasoned, and often ironic vantage points of surviving witnesses. This technique emphasized the contradictions in Reed's saga and the tensions between political action and artistic sensibility that Reed and his circle embody. At the same time, though, Beatty's approach honors conventional views of intellectuals as rebels and provocateurs in their intimate and domestic actions as well as in their public professions and partisan attachments (Smith 36).

In 1998, in *Bulworth*, Beatty revisited what W. E. B. DuBois had called the problem of the twentieth century (even as it augured to become the problem of the twenty-first century): "the color line" (vii). *Bulworth* vexed the right-wing press as a remnant of "old liberal Hollywood," which "passionately believes that entertainment film can be honorable, important popular art" that even "at its darkest . . . creates space for possibility" (Aufderheide 24). One disparaging review of *Bulworth* reflects the extent to which this "honorable" commitment positions Hollywood *intelligenti* in the same arena as traditional print intellectuals writing for the *Nation*, the *Weekly Standard*, or the gold standard of high-minded, high-brow intellectual engagement, the late *Partisan Review*, mourned on its demise as "a treasure from the past and a model for the future" (Birnbaum). Writing in the *Weekly Standard*, a foundation-supported opinion journal, *New York Post* editorial writer—and second-generation neoconservative—John Podhoretz judged *Bulworth* guilty by association with the *Nation*, the *Weekly Standard*'s philanthropically funded counterpart on the left. Podhoretz, who can't make his own movie and therefore can't exert anything near the influence Beatty can, charges Beatty with "bringing the domestic platform of the *Nation* magazine to the American moviegoer." Implicitly disclosing his own hermetic irrelevance and confessing his own intellectual impotence, Podhoretz switches the target of his attack from the celebrity Beatty to the newspaper and magazine reviewers who praised the movie, who all pose a threat from "the Left" ("Bull").

Podhoretz's fears, and his inadvertently self-indicting rhetorical tactics, illustrate to what extent Hollywood auteurs such as Beatty and Altman conduct the same kinds of provocative examinations of class and color, for example, as traditional print intellectuals. But what distinguishes a popular, well-funded, ambitious moviemaker such as Beatty should, if right-wingers held true to their own partisan principles, appeal to professed conservatives, for Beatty represents the ideal contemporary intellectual as entrepreneur. "Entrepreneur," writes philosopher Steve Fuller in *The Intellectual*, is "the ultimate compliment for an intellectual" in that it describes someone who "causes a change in world view" (40)—or at least strenuously aspires to. Despite Fuller's hopes and Podhoretz's worries, Beatty views the effect of his intellectual work more modestly than either. When Beatty explains his movies as intellectual work, he cautions that since he can "never know if" his movies are "going to have impact," that's not his goal. It is rather more narrowly intellectual: movies are opportunities "to think things through." Beatty adds that he's "lucky enough to be in a profession where I can express" the results of this process (Hirschberg).

Effective intellectual work, like entrepreneurial work, invariably faces the paradox that Schumpeter resonantly named "creative destruction." By 2007, marketers could expressly link Schumpeter's creative destruction to moviegoing, in particular to the "aspirational audience" of "ordinary people who comprise the mass audience" for "edgy, artsy, esoteric . . . cultural offering[s]" (P. Martin, 70). The aspirations of this "emerging strata of enlightened individuals" recall aspirations traditionally attributed to intellectuals: "to challenge the status quo, disrupt the marketplace, and transform society" (1).

Intellectual and entrepreneurial work both depend on, and challenge, a dominant system or discourse. Writing in the 1940s, Schumpeter didn't account for the way in which the difference between Hollywood intellect and traditional print intellectuals complicates this paradox. For Schumpeter, traditional intellectuals "wield the power of the written and spoken word" without "direct responsibility for practical affairs" (147). Schumpeter's equivocal phrase "practical affairs" stands out in connection with Hollywood because it begs questions about the "practicality" of any artistic or entertainment product. Likewise the questions of "responsibility" that Schumpeter raises sidestep the way Hollywood's necessarily collaborative moviemaking diffuses responsibility (far more than do the collaborations involved in producing quarterly journals or organizing an outfit such as the storied Cold War intellectual advancement program the Congress for Cultural Freedom or running a contemporary think tank). A *New York Times* movie reviewer recently highlighted the aptness of Fuller's view of intellectuals as risk-takers and Schumpeter's stress on their struggle with "practical affairs" by singling out Francis Ford Coppola. One of contemporary Hollywood's legendary risk-takers and most notoriously vexed budget managers, Coppola sustained his "intellectual ambitions" over a forty-year span, even though "everybody said," during Coppola's most productive years, "Francis is crazy," "more ambitious and less sensible," blessed and cursed with the "obstinate independence that routinely leads to ruin" (A. O. Scott, "Coppola"; Preissel 26; J. Lewis 80–81). Some sixty years ago, a decade before American cinephiles imported the *auteur* concept from France, novelist Harold Robbins observed that beginning with the advent of talkies

> a picture man had to be a financier, an economist, a politician, and an artist all rolled into one. He had to read balance sheets as well as scripts, market analysis as well as stories. He had to be able to forecast public tastes and preferences six month to a year in advance because that's how long it would take for the picture he was working on to reach the public. (404)

Such "practical affairs" often link print intellectuals and screenwriters. This parallel is a result of the supervisory constraints circumscribing both kinds of intellectual work. Martin Jay recollects his debut as a public intellectual, his election to the empyrean of "New York intellectuals" on receiving his first *Partisan Review* assignment. Jay recalls both elation and disillusionment—an exciting opportunity to intervene "in a general debate that resounded outside the walls of the academy" ("Force" 51) and the sort of letdown screenwriters typically bemoan (Dunne 7–8; Vidal, *Palimpsest* 274). "Rather than exercising sovereign control over his words," Jay found himself "in danger of becoming rather like the scriptwriter in the Hollywood cinema production process" (51). In contrast to typical print intellectuals, however, the Hollywood *intelligenti* conduct their examinations while addressing more heterogeneous and more capricious publics. Late in her career celebrity New York intellectual—probably the only one—Susan Sontag wryly recalled how she began her career with a "dream" to "write for *Partisan Review* and be read by 5,000 people" (Weinberger).

Seeking rather than disdaining a mass audience actually brings the Hollywood *intelligenti* closer to the ideal of the public intellectual. One aspirational view of the public intellectual's role features a "character on the public stage" who can, in contrast to many quarterly contributors and academic commentators, "intervene in a public setting" and "address the world . . . eschew[ing] all jargon" (Todorov 13). Early in the evolution of film theory, Erwin Panofsky registered this need to reconcile intellectual challenge and popular appeal: "While it is true that commercial art is always in danger of ending up a prostitute, it is equally true that noncommercial art is in danger of ending up an old maid" ("Style" 301). Panofsky presents intellect as a choice available to the producer of commercial art who requires and "allows the general public—or his idea of the general public—both to educate and pervert himself." Panofsky warns fellow traditional intellectuals that "[w]hether we like it or not, it is the movies that mold, more than another force, the opinions, the taste, the language . . . of a public comprising more than 60 percent of the population of the earth." Panofksy's understanding of the role of the commercial moviemaker who chooses intellect echoes the ideal envisioned by his Marxist contemporary Antonio Gramsci. The "organic intellectual," in Gramsci's memorable phrase, conveys through the media of culture what the populace experiences but can't or won't articulate themselves (Eagleton 119). With his quaint "old maid" metaphor, Panofsky exposed in the 1930s and 1940s what academe has only in the past few decades begun to consider:

> More often than not it [the high/low, art/life relationship] has appeared in the guise of an irreconcilable opposition. . . . Yet this opposition . . . has proven to be amazingly resilient. Such resilience may lead one to conclude that perhaps neither of the two combatants can do without the other, that their much heralded mutual exclusiveness is really a sign of their secret interdependence (Huyssen 16).

Even at its most meretricious and superficial Hollywood has long reflected this "interdependence," self-flatteringly envisioning itself as a marketplace of *ideas*. In 1942 Parker Tyler examined the role of the "idea department" in Hollywood's major studios. The problem of intellect in Hollywood has never been its absence; on the contrary, observers from Tyler to Woody Allen have noted an abundance and consequent institutionalization of "ideas" by the studios. Allen's 1977 Oscar "best picture,"

Annie Hall, shows Allen's alter-ego eavesdropping on two Hollywood players as one explains how project development works: "At the moment it's just a Notion, but with a bit of backing I think I could turn it into a Concept, and then an Idea." With this exchange, Allen, like all influential satirists, subjects his own preoccupation with idea-centered movies to scrutiny and even ridicule. A generation after *Annie Hall*, a reviewer saluted Allen's persistent commitment to making such movies: "While Mr. Allen may feel as if he's running out of time, he has scarcely run out of ideas" (Dargis, "In").

In his 1940 story "A Man in the Way," F. Scott Fitzgerald expressed an even more jaundiced view of Hollywood's paradoxical, simultaneous resistance to and respect for "ideas" in an exchange between a has-been contract writer boasting that "I got the germ I could be telling you all about at lunch" and a producer plagued by "story trouble" who asks the writer to "to bring" him a "full idea" because nobody gets paid "unless he's got an idea" (*Pat* 14–15). In the face of rejection, Pat Hobby, the writer, waxes nostalgic about how "in the old days he had just busted in sometimes and sold an idea, an idea good for a couple of grand because it was just the moment when they were very tired of what they were doing at present" (17). Forty years ahead of *Annie Hall*, Fitzgerald has unmasked Hollywood's bogus but apparently axiomatic distinction between *idea* and *notion* or between "the notion" that he's pitching to a producer "looking for ideas" and "just a flash—nothing really worked out." Whatever Hobby calls his thought, he's told: "That's no idea, Pat. I can't put you on salary for that" (18). The recurrence of such exchanges also illustrates why professing such a commitment to movie "ideas" warrants satiric scrutiny. Missing from these exchanges is the fundamental understanding of movies as sensory, especially as a visual forum for the ideas Fitzgerald's moviemakers bandy about—the understanding that came to advertising legend and "cultural provocateur" George Lois as an "art-school epiphany about how an image had better have an idea" ("George Lois" 9; Paumgarten).

A boast by Sherry Lansing, CEO at Paramount who supervised such facile or formulaic late-century hits as *Braveheart*, *Forest Gump*, and *Titanic*, reveals this tendency to downplay the possibilities for embodying ideas among both effective and lip-service promoters of Hollywood intellect: "Most people who got into the movie business wanted to make a certain kind of movie: movies that were character-driven, that affected the way you thought, that had social content, political content" (Waxman). In 2007 the *Wall Street Journal* reported that Hollywood moguls Steven Spielberg and Norman Lear keep consultants, who "can earn well into the six figures," on their payrolls to help them manage their "serious ideas" (Emshwiller). Six months later, the *New Yorker* reported that Brian Grazer, the Oscar-winning producer of *A Beautiful Mind*, advertised to hire an "idea curator," "a new cultural attaché," innately "curious," and "responsible for keeping Brian abreast of everything that's going on in the world; politically, culturally, musically" and doing "LOTS of reading . . . 4 or 5 books a week" on Grazer's behalf (Widdicombe).

Whether or not such commitments yield results or are even stated in good faith, the cost producers are willing to bear to maintain a supply of (intangible) ideas reflects a compelling aspiration and implicit homage to intellect. So successful have such efforts proven, at least in Spielberg's case, that, as J. Hoberman frets, "the most successful filmmaker in Hollywood" now holds "'expert' status on" at least one "controversial and complex social phenomenon": the Holocaust ("Film" 533). A more sanguine Pauline Kael celebrates this tendency, insisting that "what's so miraculous and expedient about" movies is that "they can take on some of the functions of exploration, of journalism, of anthropology, of almost any branch of knowledge" ("Trash" 346). In a recent example of the intellectual range Kael extols, a *Wall Street Journal* reviewer praised Charles Burnett's *Killer of Sheep* as "a mix of formal beauty, quasi-anthropology . . . a cinematic tone poem . . . about the blues" (Morgenstern, "Old"). On the very same day reviewers for the *New York Times* mentioned "philosophic and poetic implication," "clarifying insight" and "moral investigation," a "measure of artistic seriousness" as reasonable expectations in nationally distributed commercial movies (Holden, "50"; A. O. Scott, "Rage"). A review in the *New Yorker* of the same movie, Brian DiPalma's *Rendition*, describes it as an exploration of the question that had long preoccupied Susan Sontag, the most eminent public intellectual of her generation: "the morality of visual representations of atrocity" (Denby, "Obsessed" 103).

IV

A revealing but less appealing example over the past decade or so of the allure of belonging among the Hollywood *intelligenti* while laying hold of a capricious public has been the career of Joe Eszterhas. After writing scripts for such lowest-common-denominator hits as *Willard*, *Showgirls*, and *Basic Instinct*, Eszterhas made a bid for intellectual status with his millennial memoir *American Rhapsody*. This study of the Clinton presidency, especially the impeachment scandal, features Eszterhas as gonzo intellectual. Eszterhas claimed to be doing nothing less than examining the "national ethos" (*American*, Author's Note xiii), tracing his own growth as "a public man" (Hertzberg, "Basest"), and working as a "genuine scholar" (Kinsella). Despite Eszterhas's donnish observations on his generation's defining reading habits—Bukowski, Kerouac, Miller—and an explanation of how Hollywood evolved from blacklisting to "fervently militant liberalism" (145–6), the buzz *American Rhapsody* generated centered on its celebrity gossip, accounts of glitterati drug use and sexual escapades, and what Eszterhas admitted were his fantasies of Clinton and Monica Lewinsky's intimacies. *New Yorker* columnist Hendrik Hertzberg acknowledged Eszterhas's intellectual aspirations and characterized their failure, dismissing *American Rhapsody* as a movie "treatment" spliced with a "numbingly long op-ed piece." When Eszterhas set out—and apparently failed—to establish his intellectual credentials, he already had what any Hollywood *intelligenti* covets: widespread public interest in his work. Ironically, though, Eszterhas's work met mostly with derision, not critical acclaim.

In contrast to Schulberg, Altman, and Beatty, Eszterhas has been quick to signal his contempt for his audience. In his most recent book, *The Devil's Guide to Hollywood*, Eszterhas approvingly cites B. P. Schulberg, Budd's father and Paramount production chief during the 1930s, reminding associates that "we can't afford to alienate our audience by telling them the truth about themselves" (287). Filial affection notwithstanding (Schulberg, "Two"), B. P.'s warning represents the Hollywood Budd Schulberg fled as a young man, the milieu he skewered in *What Makes Sammy Run*. With this implicit acknowledgment that his disdain for the moviegoing public trumps his intellectual aspirations, Eszterhas outs himself as an antagonist of movie-industry workers "who actually *are* intellectual" (Rebeck 77–78). Eszterhas's stellar success should serve as a reminder to treat Hollywood intellect as a chronically endangered aspiration. Like all such worthy aspirations, it has been honored and attained as well as thwarted and even hijacked by its assailants and by run-of-the-mill charlatans.

V

Along with their allegiance to "the liberalized modern consciousness" (Kael, "Movies" 500), the Hollywood *intelligenti*'s aspirations to converse with, not simply exploit, moviegoers dates back to the dawn of talkies. This "sound revolution"—so dubbed by playwright-turned-screenwriter and cofounder of the Hollywood Writers Guild John Howard Lawson

(106)—coincided with an increasingly acute concern among Hollywood screenwriters for what intellectuals then called "the masses." Arguably, the burgeoning around 1930 of a Marxist American Left contributed as much as did the sound revolution to the advent of the Hollywood *intelligenti*. The technological transformation of the movies into a talking medium coincided with the mainstreaming of Communist and socialist sentiments among educated Americans. With its call for a revolution-provoking "cinema in words," Mike Gold's 1930 manifesto "Proletarian Realism" sums up this convergence of utopian ideology and mass-media technology (207), a convergence spawning the triumph in movies and broadcasting of what Murray Kempton came to call the "social muse" (139). Lawson recalls that these "stirrings of new social consciousness" proved compelling enough to convince even "producers that social criticism is inherent in any honest story" and hence "their problem lay in controlling"—not simply banishing—"social criticism" (116). The advent of sound, Lawson argues, strained the studios' capacity to exercise such control. This strain spurred Lawson to become the top Communist in the Writers Guild, more of a commissar than an artist (Schulberg, "Two" 120), at once embodying and promoting Hollywood's sharp left turn during the 1930s.

Even though Hollywood intellect came of age with the "sound revolution" and the institutionalization of "the social muse," Hollywood intellect surfaced as an influential ideal at least as far back as 1915 with the publication of *The Art of the Motion Picture* by Vachel Lindsay. Lindsay envisioned a complementary relationship between movies and "the arts" as traditionally understood, especially Lindsay's own art: poetry. More grandiosely, he argued that the rise of Hollywood represented a development comparable to the Boston-based American literary renaissance of the nineteenth century (1: 307). He urged intellectuals to "lay hold of the motion picture as our national textbook in Art as Boston appropriated to herself the guardianship of the national text-books of Literature," to become "new romanticists . . . artists as indigenous" to Hollywood "as Hawthorne was to 'witch-haunted Salem or Longfellow to the chestnuts of his native heath,'" so that Hollywood might 'become the Boston of the photoplay' or 'better to say the Florence.'" However utopian Lindsay's design, by holding up such canonical figures for emulation, Lindsay ends up looking back, relying rhetorically on the status of traditional literary practice rather than looking forward and envisioning a transformation, or at least a new departure.

This nostalgic, if not retrograde, impulse would come to color Hollywood intellect throughout subsequent generations. In 1920, for example, Charlie Chaplin reached for the patina and authority of cultural tradition when he told a *New York Times* interviewer that "he want[ed] only to retire to an Italian lake with my beloved violin, my Shelley and Keats" into "a life purely imaginative and intellectual" (quoted in Maland 62). Seventy-four years later, *Star Wars* mastermind George Lucas told another *Times* interviewer that he left Malibu pursuing "quality of life" in a Marin County neighborhood where "most of my friends are college professors" (Weinraub). Denzel Washington's more recent homage to intellect pairs the importance of hiring "a very good agent" with "reading a lot of material until something strikes you. Reading a lot. Reading books. Reading" (Little).

Lucas, Chaplin, and Washington seem to lend credence to analyses by Thorstein Veblen and Pierre Bourdieu, which bracket the twentieth century, of cultural capital as a means of conspicuously displaying one's importance or "distinction." This joint campaign for distinction, this alliance between the stars and the poets, has become as much a cultural commonplace as its converse: explaining "the movies" and proposing cultural generalizations on the basis of the movies. A short list of intellectuals, poets, and novelists who have looked at the movies and see America or even "the human condition" (Bordwell and Thompson, *Film Art* 76, 425) would includes F. Scott Fitzgerald, William Faulkner, Norman Mailer, Nathanael West, Dwight MacDonald, Frank O'Hara, Jane Smiley, Gore Vidal, John Updike, Theodore Roethke, and Robert Stone.

VI

Several of the novelists in this group not only wrote about Hollywood, its allure as well as its corruptions, but also wrote scripts *for* Hollywood. Like Schulberg, they produced influential insider critiques of what, arguably, has long been America's fundamental industry. Schulberg's unusual position as a resident insider, whose livelihood and reputation rest on intimacy and even complicity with Hollywood and who at the same time exhibits aspirations of traditional print intellectuals, has come in the last decades of twentieth century to belong to Joan Didion.

Since the 1960s, Didion has kept a sharp eye on what she regards as the diminished status of ideas in our collective conversation and disenchantment with the inflated idea of status that the U.S. movie industry cultivates. In Didion's Hollywood, it has become impossible to utter the very noun "ideas" without surrounding it with irony-stressing quotation marks, because "such 'ideas,' when explored, typically tend toward the general" (*After* 162). In Hollywood, Didion observes, a vaporous sentence fragment, like "the relationship between men and women," might pass for an idea. Even in the 1930s, when the "social muse" was ascendant, Lawson recounts how the legendary MGM production chief Irving Thalberg earned his renown, in part, by being a rule-proving exception: the only studio chief with a "genuine respect for ideas" (104). Lawson's portrait of Thalberg contrasts him with a nameless director, who only "glanced at the script and then tossed it aside." Lawson recollects how Thalberg, by contrast, "read every word slowly" and then announced "there's an *idea* in it." Convinced that "the studio cannot live without ideas," Thalberg "used to call all the writers together" and then, anticipating Didion's scathing judgment, demand, "Why are there so many writers and so few ideas?" (104). Lawson answers that there are so few ideas because in Hollywood, except in a shop like Thalberg's, substantial ideas can never count on a fair hearing, let alone a hearty welcome. The relationship between this resistance to "ideas" and Hollywood's contradictory dependence on those who produce them defines Hollywood intellect. These workers both aspire to shape civic discourse and alter public consensus. The continuum linking Schulberg's and Didion's careers encompasses both this aspiration and what limits it.

The most memorable phase of Schulberg's career is the decade bookended by his 1941 novel *What Makes Sammy Run* and his screenplay for Elia Kazan's 1951 movie *On the Waterfront*. This multiple Oscar winner, widely viewed as an allegory about resisting totalitarianism, has become a perennial political lightning rod, a prime example of mid-century movies as invitations to "intellectual brawling" (Maslin). A vivid example of Daniel Dayan's view of popular movies "as the ventriloquist[s] of ideology" (117), *Waterfront* provoked Columbia Pictures chief Harry Cohn to denounce it as "communistic" while liberals and leftists denounced it as Schulberg and Kazan's rationalization for testifying—"ratting out their friends"—before the Red-baiting House Un-American Activities Committee (Tallmer). Surviving and newly committed subscribers to this view protested the Motion Picture Academy's decision to award Kazan its Lifetime Achievement Award in 1999. Splitting these differences, Victor Navasky recognized that this movie's importance lay in its intellectual ambition as "a valiant attempt to complicate the public perception" and in the controversies *On the Waterfront* at once evoked and provoked (209).

On the Waterfront also signaled for Schulberg the convergence between careerism and intellectual ambition, prompting his realization that "you can do the same thing in a film you can do in a book" ("Two" 111), demonstrating how tensions between the status of ideas and the idea of status color Schulberg's writing. Schulberg's coda to *Waterfront*—the post-movie novel version of Schulberg's script—melds his narrator's voice with that of Father Barry, the story's heroic Catholic priest (played Karl Malden on-screen and earning him an Oscar nomination for best supporting actor). Presenting this character as sounding less doctrinaire than the priestly vow of obedience obliges him to be, Schulberg endows the narrator's reflections with ecclesiastical authority. Recalling a recent visit from a parishioner, he finds himself glad that "she had changed" and had become "older . . . less of the onward-Christian soldier . . . I-want-it-to-be-just-as-it-is-in the missal" kind of Catholic. Barry regards her as one of his pastoral success stories because she ends up "apologizing for expecting him to solve everything overnight now" that "she had a taste of the complexities" of the refractory ideological quandaries that vexed Schulberg (*Waterfront* 315).

In a 2002 interview, Schulberg accounted for his relationship to "ideas" genealogically ("Two" 101, 107, 111). Though the son of Hollywood giant B. P. Schulberg, studio head at Paramount during its formative years, Schulberg *fils* pictures his "Hollywood Prince" childhood and the Schulberg home as being more *in* Hollywood than *of* Hollywood. Recalling a home life no one "would associate with the habits of Hollywood tycoons," Schulberg came "always [to feel] himself an outsider, always looking in . . . nose pressed against the glass" and to characterize his surroundings, warily, as simply another "company town" (Schulberg, *Moving* 189, 125; Gross 93). Schulberg summed up this stance toward Hollywood in a *Playboy*-sponsored exchange with James Baldwin in 1966: "God knows I have never been a champion of Hollywood—I'm certainly better known as a critic of the place. I think I've tried to write more effectively about what's wrong with that world [Hollywood] than anybody who ever came out of it" (Papers).

Marveling at the distance his parents traveled from Manhattan's Lower East Side ghetto to become "instant Americans," Schulberg recalls that "they not only spoke English, they were literary. They loved the English language. Melville . . . Galsworthy" ("Two" 111). His father, in particular, Schulberg revered as one of Hollywood's two "top intellectuals." "A profound reader" and an "original mind," blessed with a "literary bent," Schulberg senior seemed "never at a loss for words or clever phrases" (*Moving* 304–5).

Schulberg once boasted that, thanks to this legacy, he could write "anything." Flouting genre hierarchy, he enumerates "anything": "I could write a movie; I could write a novel; I could write a play; I could write lyrics, which I did for *a Face in the Crowd*" in 1957 ("Two" 111). Schulberg *pere's* influence proved decisive during his son's most crucial career crisis. Despite B. P.'s prominence and career investment in Hollywood's studio system, he counseled Budd not to heed the attacks that *What Makes Sammy Run* provoked, most notably L. B. Mayer's threat of "deportation." To write with artistic integrity and intellectual rigor, B. P. assured his son, means to "say 'to hell with Hollywood'" ("Two" 101).

Schulberg's account of his intellectual patrimony extends beyond his family. He recounts his discovery as a Dartmouth undergraduate of a climate and a mentor representing for him all that Hollywood *wasn't*. To write *What Makes Sammy Run*, Schulberg returned to this atmosphere after a brief, postgraduate, Hollywood stint, during which he worked with F. Scott Fitzgerald on a script for the 1939 United Artists' release *Winter Carnival*. More than the college itself, Schulberg singles out one mentor, Sidney Cox, as his reason for returning to Dartmouth to write (99). Schulberg has praised Cox as a "wild man" who made "the Dartmouth English department . . . afraid of him" and who "drove his students kind of crazy." Cox's "intensity," though, left his students feeling "that when you came out of that classroom, you couldn't wait to get back to your desks and write—to go deeper into yourself" (98).

A decade after Schulberg's graduation from Dartmouth, this "inspirational," superlatively "important" mentor published a guide for writers, titled *Indirections*, that Schulberg would later, temperately praise as "very interesting" (99). Not a guide in the same way as Strunk and White's *Elements of Style*, Cox's *Indirections* reads more like a manual for becoming a man-of-letters or an intellectual, along the lines of some examples Cox cites, such as Edmund Wilson or Lewis Mumford (113). Cox opens *Indirections* succinctly specifying the motive for writing as the will to "change the composition of ourselves and of the world" (vii). Spelling out the difficulties that an aspiring Hollywood *intelligenti* faces, even one with Schulberg's double Ivy League and Paramount pedigree, Cox warns young writers that "as a chance taker you are one of the hoi polloi" who risks having his work "stigmatized as 'popular'" by "custodians of the higher taste" who mistake "everydayness for triviality" (33). The two-step goal of such risk-taking, Cox maintains, is to achieve "detachment with attachment" in order to maintain "a far perspective" (30). Cox envisions the intellectual's vocation as requiring incessant mental traveling: "moving between the ordered world of current and classic dogma specialists and the dangerous changeful world that is always grassing over roads and deflecting compass needles" (36). During the (more than usually) ideologically vexed war years, Cox warned circumspectly against the allure of mass movements, such as the

Communist Party that briefly held Schulberg's allegiance. Don't, he warned, treat "organized thought more trustingly than" one "takes organized business, politics, or religion" (36).

At the same time, though, Cox instructed would-be intellectuals not to peremptorily dismiss prevailing group-think since intellectuals need to "keep connection with organized thought at least as much as [do] potential readers" busied by daily tasks (36). Cox offsets this "daily routine" with a recommended routine of his own, practically a checklist for intellectual work. When Cox urged readers to "fend all supervision off" (45), he anticipates by over half a century Alan Wolfe's summation of what it means to be an intellectual: Wolfe realized that "I became an intellectual the day I decided that no one was looking over my shoulder as I sat down to write" ("Point"). Cox then encourages aspiring intellectuals to "find . . . conflicts" of their own (64). His menu of "conflicts" includes such favorites as individual-versus-society and freedom-versus-equality, along with a question about whether "skepticism should menace faith" (64). Familiar, but undeniably durable, these conflicts and questions have figured prominently in the work of Hollywood *intelligenti* since the 1930s. To the extent that Cox articulates a credo in *Indirections*, it lies in his pronouncement that "democracy and art both gamble on order not established but in the making"; to the extent that Cox articulates an aesthetic, it reflects the constraints of trying to make movies do intellectual work: "[E]xplanation should follow aroused interest" (12, 77).

Whatever their demerits, Schulberg's two most memorable movies, *On the Waterfront* and *A Face in the Crowd*—both collaborations between Schulberg and director Elia Kazan—reflect both of these aspirations. Toward the end of *On the Waterfront*, for example, Terry Malloy, the movie's hero-martyr, argues with his older brother Charlie, a mob henchman who has betrayed Terry. Not merely a fraternal, personal spat, the exchange stages an ideological conflict. It pits an agent of coercive, "organized thought" against a convert to and ultimately a promoter of democratic openness. It also ends with Terry's cry for an explanation. "See, you don't understand," Terry protests, as he identifies Charlie as a traitor to both kinship and freedom.

Three years later, *A Face in the Crowd* even more explicitly followed this trajectory from ideological strife to explanation. Director Kazan describes *A Face in the Crowd* as the deliberate work of intellectuals, telling an interviewer that he and Schulberg set out to produce an essay on "the dialectic" of politics and broadcasting and stressing the extensive "research" this project entailed (Kazan 234–5). This collaboration depicts the

meteoric rise and precipitous self-destruction of a charismatic TV demagogue named Lonesome Rhodes. Rhodes believes that "this whole country's just like my flock of sheep! Hillbillies, hausfraus . . . they're mine!"
and regards himself as "not just an entertainer" but "an influence, a wielder
of opinion . . . a force . . . America's answer." His calling: to "sound off
about everything . . . from the price of popcorn to the hydrogen bomb."
The team of "understated network eggheads" (Patricia Neal and Walter
Matthau) who invented Rhodes finally helps destroy him, recognizing in
him "a crystallization of every right-minded intellectual's worst fears about
mass civilization" (A. O. Scott, "Week").

While the Rhodes character (played by Andy Griffith) recalled the
rabble-rousing Depression-era radio bigot Father Coughlin, he also presages current talk-show stars like Rush Limbaugh and Sean Hannity just as
the movie itself anticipates media exposés such as Sidney Lumet's *Network*,
Spike Lee's *Bamboozled*, Tim Robbins's *Bob Roberts*, Barry Levinson's *Wag
the Dog*, Mike Nichols's *Primary Colors*, and Stacy Title's "Swiftian" *The
Last Supper* (Ebert). Unlike these successors, though, Schulberg's script
closes with the on-screen intellectual taking over the narrative. The seasoned reporter played by Matthau appears on screen to get the last word
and pronounce on the significance of what, in naming the book he's
working on, he calls the *Demagogue in Denim*. His demeanor, rumpled and
pipe-smoking, signals his credentials as the intellectual conscience of the
media milieu the movie depicts. His closing lines, counterpointed by the
fallen demagogue's maniacal raving, summon the wisdom and strength
needed to resist the blandishments of mass media demagoguery. Though
a commercial disappointment, *A Face in the Crowd*'s harsh analysis of mass
media prompted the Communist Party organ, *People's Daily World*, to
grudgingly acclaim it "one of the finest progressive films we have seen,"
even though it had been produced by "two stool pigeon witnesses" (alluding to Schulberg's and Kazan's obliging testimony before the House
Un-American Activities Committee in 1951) (Billingsley).

Schulberg's less memorable work after these two movies demonstrates
the pitfalls of intellectually ambitious progressive moviemaking. Perhaps
none more than Schulberg's misbegotten collaboration *Wind Across the
Everglades* with the famously dark *Rebel Without a Cause* director Nicholas Ray. This collaboration highlighted Schulberg's traditional literary
and intellectual commitments more starkly than did *Waterfront*. In *Wind
Across the Everglades*, these commitments take the form of overtly staged
debates between equally sympathetic characters over the competing claims
of preserving the wild environment and effecting progressive, economic

"improvement" of Florida's undeveloped wetlands, together with a more abstract contest between quixotic "masculine" romanticism and "feminine" realism (*Across* 84).

This proclivity for staging idea contests surfaced first and most durably in Schulberg's novel, *What Makes Sammy Run*—his only novel that has remained in print. The entire plot of *What Makes Sammy Run* turns, in fact, on the stacked contest over the soul of the movies. Schulberg modeled his title character Sammy Glick partly on Columbia Pictures chief Harry Cohn (Tallmer) and partly on writer-producers Jerry Wald and Norman Krasna (*backstory* i). Now regarded as the prototype for DreamWorks studio cofounder David Geffen (Sawhill), the triumphantly status-seeking title character meteorically rises the through ranks of contract writers, becoming a major producer by secretly exploiting Julian Blumberg. This self-effacing, script-writing genius championed by Schulberg's narrator ghostwrites Glick's scripts and remains under his thumb. Schulberg avenged Blumberg a decade later in *On the Waterfront*, which Schulberg expressly envisioned as furthering this campaign to thrust the screenwriter to the intellectual forefront. Sharing Schulberg's goal, Kazan recalled how he sought in *On the Waterfront* "to upset the traditional balance and make the writer more important than" such on-screen stars as Marlon Brando and Karl Malden, so as to "disturb, stir up, enlighten, and offend" America (Schulberg, "Writer" 136).

Schulberg looked, as mid-century U.S. intellectuals often did, to Europe for validation of his aspirations, to the cinematic Italian Renaissance fostered by Rossellini, De Sica, and Fellini (134). Long after Schulberg's reputation crested after *A Face in the Crowd*, he sustained an overtly politicized, European understanding of *engagé* intellectual struggle by probing union violence in *Everything That Moves* (1980) and U.S. domination in Latin America in *Sanctuary V* (1969). During the 1960s, he shored up his *engagé* credentials by establishing a writing workshop for teenagers in Los Angeles' insurrection-devastated Watts neighborhood.

These polemics, inquiries, and initiatives dovetailed with Schulberg's lifelong, seven-decade attention to the relationship between movies and world-historical violence, to the social dislocations that have inspired and threatened Hollywood, and to contradictions between the way Hollywood's products have at once reflected and sidestepped political strife. Edmund Wilson's 1941 homage to Nathanael West has become even more applicable to Schulberg, if for no other reason than the durability and versatility of his engagement. Even more than West, Schulberg has "not slipped . . . into relying on . . . Hollywood values in describing Hollywood" itself (E. Wilson 69).

VII

Wilson's characterization of West may more aptly describe the perhaps the only Hollywood *intelligenti* to match Schulberg for durability and versatility: Joan Didion. An established screenwriter and novelist, like Schulberg, Didion spent her career probing and skewering Hollywood insider culture in her 1968, 1979, and 1992 essay volumes, *Slouching Toward Bethlehem*, *The White Album*, and *After Henry* and in her fiction, especially her first novel *Play It As It Lays* (1970). Didion's characteristic distancing stance, articulated in *The White Album*, entails assuming the role of an anthropologist, a participant-observer of the circulation of "totemic significance" throughout Hollywood's superlatively "stable . . . rigid, intricate" subculture. Didion seeks such "significance" in familiar entertainment rituals and in the movie industry's must-read "trades" like *Variety* and *Hollywood Reporter* (*White* 159–60, 157, 152, 156).

In the later essay collection *After Henry*, Didion aims a binocular gaze at America's most influential elites, counterpointing Hollywood and the Washington, D.C., beltway so that they converge. This convergence recasts a Ronald and Nancy Reagan Sunday church photo-op as an *I Love Lucy* episode (*After* 41). Citing this scene as a "perfect" paradigm of the Reagan regime, Didion looks at national politics through the lens of stardom. This emphasis analytically elaborates the point Kazan made a generation earlier, boasting that *A Face in the Crowd* served as a harbinger of Reagan's ascent (Kazan 566). In this respect *A Face in the Crowd* belongs to the most influential cultural transformation of 1950s; Schulberg and Kazan paradoxically refracted the "obsessive" fear on the part of many "intellectuals of culture manufactured for the masses," which "they associated . . . with totalitarian propaganda," by contributing to the emerging "'adversarial' commercial culture" that came of age a decade later (Menand 127).

This emerging understanding of Hollywood as a political power center facilitated Schulberg's and Didion's carving out unusual niches as Hollywood insider *intelligenti* by demonstrably cultivating a dialectical intimacy with movie making and its social repercussions. Schulberg, for example, stages Sammy Glick's rise against the rise of European fascism almost as a sideshow to the triumph of Old World totalitarianisms and an impediment to the intellectual aspirations of the screenwriter-journalist narrator, the allegorically named Manheim. Throughout the narrative, Schulberg revisits Manheim's attempts to pitch his pet project: a biopic about Czechoslovakia's founding president-liberator Tomas Masaryk. Manheim regards the anti-clerical, democratic nationalist as "a natural for pictures"

(*Sammy* 158), such a paragon that Manheim finds himself "wondering what Masaryk" (182) would do when faced with the crises of conscience inescapable among Hollywood *intelligenti*. Schulberg presents Manheim's Masaryk project as the antithesis of what the studios want. The consummate Hollywood know-it-all Sammy Glick scoffs at all "that anti-fascist stuff": "it hasn't got a prayer" because the moguls "don't want to get Hitler and Mussolini sore" (185). As a writer, Manheim moves between journalism and screenplays, a mix that has also marked Didion's career. This parallel also encompasses a critical fascination with showbiz climbing. This emphasis drives *What Makes Sammy Run*, which has over seven decades turned Sammy Glick into an American byword (and a "long dormant" and "haunting project" trapped in the same development hell as Manheim's idealistic Masaryk project) (Kohn; Dargis, "War"). A generation later showbiz climbing would later serve as the focus of *Play It As It Lays*, Didion's first novel.

Play It As It Lays also tracks, darkly, the career trajectory of a Hollywood wannabe. Instead of eliciting the sympathy, the identifying with Manheim Schulberg prompted (Kohn), Didion depicts her sometime narrator and protagonist as complicit in her own disaffection. *Play It As It Lays* opens by counterpointing this bit player's perspective with that of a third-person narrator's intellectually and morally commanding voice asking an intellectually weighty, doubly allusive question. This intractable question alludes to one of the most resonant moments in Shakespeare criticism, the 1812 lecture in which Samuel Taylor Coleridge inquired into the "motive hunting of" the apparently "motiveless malignity" of the hero- and heroine-destroying antagonist in *Othello*. This question also reverberates with the "motive hunting" question that the title of Schulberg's famous novel raises about its protagonist Sammy Glick. "'What makes Iago evil?' some people ask," the third-person narrator muses. "I never do," snaps back Didion's other narrator, her first-person Hollywood narrator, a wannabe star named Maria Wyeth, who becomes at once the antagonist as well as protagonist of Didion's inconclusively motive-hunting narrative (2).

Didion's subsequent screenplay collaborations, on the 1970s remake of *A Star is Born* and the 1990s biopic adaptation titled *Up Close and Personal*, about the star-crossed network newscaster Jessica Savitch, also reflect a preoccupation, like Schulberg's, with showbiz ambition and power. When Didion's collaborator, her husband John Gregory Dunne, published a studio-damning account of their work for Disney/Touchstone on the *Up Close and Personal* screenplay, one reviewer referred readers to Schulberg's 1951 novel *The Disenchanted* for a more insightful and informative account of the same issues—yet another measure of Schulberg's lasting role in sustaining Hollywood intellect.

In contrast to Schulberg, Didion has long cast a relentlessly skeptical eye on the consolations of liberal or progressive humanist rhetoric, reflected, for example, in the way Schulberg has his *Sammy* narrator honor Masaryk or in Schulberg's own Watts project. This severity never becomes crudely cynical, as Didion's books on Central America—the reportage in *Salvador* and the fiction in *The Book of Common Prayer*—and her Henry Adams–inflected novel *Democracy* demonstrate. Nevertheless, Didion's skepticism can make her agonizingly complex politics seem as close to Sammy Glick's recoil from "that anti-fascist stuff" as to Manheim's—and Schulberg's—concern for the oppressed.

This departure from the familiar liberal narrative that Schulberg promotes—and Tomas Masaryk embodied—was most pronounced early in Didion's career, in the 1967 *Slouching toward Bethlehem* essay "California Dreaming," and in another collaboration with Dunne, the screenplay for the 1981 movie *True Confessions*. "California Dreaming" derides the "rhetoric" of Santa Barbara's Center for the Study of Democratic Institutions. Didion derided the work of this liberal proto–think tank as "real soufflé and genuine American *kitsch*" (*Slouching* 75). The institute rests, in Didion's account, on the "conviction that everything said around the center mystically improves" the common weal.

True Confessions, a neo–noir account of corruption in the Los Angeles archdiocese, elaborates this critique of well-meaning, but securely entrenched, eleemosynary institutions. One reviewer read this movie as "a practical guide in worldly affairs," a reproach to "Americans in public life . . . who have behaved as if they could abolish sin" (Grenier, "Our Lady" 83). Even Didion and Dunne's less appreciated screenplay, for *Panic in Needle Park*, impressed a *New York Times* reviewer by offering a "nightmare world-view" (Greenspun), which "never pretends" that to scrutinize unsettling perspectives obliges us to "subject" them "to moral condemnations" or render them susceptible "to easy cure or to the insights of urban sociology." This jaundiced conclusion sharply challenges the mission of both the Center for Democratic Institutions and the Catholic Church. The resistance to bromides characteristic of Didion's scripts, novels, and commentary sets the bar high for what distinguishes public intellectuals from earnest policy theorists and spiritual leaders, self-important pundits and mercenary publicists.

One Schulberg alter-ego, the first-person narrator of his 1969 novel *Sanctuary V*, an *à clef* account of the Castro revolution, characterizes this stance as that of the "diffident, self-doubting" opponent of "the agents of certainty" (64). Didion's 1979 critique of Woody Allen savages the effect of these agents' influence inside popular movies. Didion equates Allen's and his fans' sensibility with the certainty, the smugness, she ascribes to the exhibition-istically angst-ridden self-scrutinizers who populate Allen's movies. What Didion treats as their self-glorifying navel-gazing appeals to the moviegoers Didion earlier castigated as "the rote middle intelligentsia" (*Slouching* 151). Allen, in Didion's view, colludes with his audience in an insidious form of late-century pseudo-intellectual and hence anti-intellectual posturing. This posturing, Didion argues, recalls the "false and desperate knowingness of the smartest kid in the class." All "their smart talk"—about Strindberg, Hitler, Flaubert, and Kafka, as well as about Hollywood's reigning couples—aims, Didion scoffs, "to convey the message that the speaker knows his way around Lit. and History, not to mention show biz" ("Letter").

Three years later, in her introduction to *The White Album*, Didion re-fined this dour iconoclasm, observing that "we live entirely, especially if we are writers, by the imposition of narrative line upon disparate images, by the 'ideas' with which we have learned to freeze the shifting phantasma-goria" of "actual experience" (11). Didion ratchets up her skepticism with quotation marks around ordinary but abstract words—*ideas*—the meanings of which we all think we know. But despite the pyrrhonic caution her quotation marks advocate, this observation nevertheless reflects a deter-mination to shape public opinion. It also reaffirms a 1922 pronouncement by Walter Lippmann, who formulated the concept of "public opinion" for Americans and whose book of that title popularized the very phrase. Lippmann explained how all "public opinion" rests on presenting ideas as images—as "the pictures" we make ourselves or are "given . . . pictures which are acted on" (25, 29). Didion's long preoccupation with such "images" and "pictures," moving ones in particular, marks her narrative work as a novelist and scriptwriter perhaps even more than it figures in her reportage and commentary. Her metaphoric view of writing as "freezing" reinforces this alignment by recalling such cinematic devices as "freeze frame" and "stop action." Didion's pronouncements on experience, ideas, images, and narrative imposition also reflect the extent to which Didion's observational iconoclasm and reportorial skepticism are inseparable from her wariness of the very possibility of any narrative cohering or resolv-ing, let alone explaining, what it evokes. Didion's articulation throughout her career of tensions between these intellectual scruples and her many commercial-studio writing credits have made her the late twentieth centu-ry's most exemplary instance of Hollywood intellect.

Note

1. As I was completing *Hollywood Intellect*, I attended a lecture by Spike Lee, who was introduced by his student host, presumably part of a generation untouched by any "where are the public intellectuals?" anxiety, as one of America's leading "popular intellectuals" (Moravian College, March 11, 2008).

Stargazers

II

per un pertugio tondo e quindi uscimmo a riveder le stelle *(through [hell's] round aperture we emerged to see again the stars)*

—DANTE

We are all of us in the gutter, but some of us are looking at the stars.

—OSCAR WILDE

[T]he hunger artist had not forgotten his sense of the way things really were, and he took it as self-evident that people would not set him and his cage up as the star attraction somewhere in the middle of the arena, but would move him outside in some other readily accessible spot near the animal stalls.

—KAFKA

I

During the 2004 Democratic convention, a Pennsylvania newspaper recounted how a delegate used his cell phone, during a speech by Illinois Senate candidate Barack Obama, to announce to his wife back home that "a star is born" (Micek). A week later syndicated columnist Clarence Page upped the ante, proclaiming that as a result of this speech a "superstar was born." Three years later Senator Obama found himself vying for his party's presidential nomination with a fellow senator committed to becoming "reconciled . . . to the fate of not being the star" (Leibovich). The durability of this same tried, if not assuredly true, narrative became particularly pronounced four years after pundits anointed Obama when an editorial headline in the *New York Times* heralded the selection of Alaska governor Sarah Palin as the GOP vice presidential candidate by asking "A Star Is Born?" (Kristol).

This broadly compelling narrative became part of an encompassing public discourse along with the movies themselves as

> names like Paramount Pictures, Metro Pictures, Famous Players, Vitagraph were beginning to be bruited around. . . . The public was beginning to recognize players such as Mary Pickford, Charlie Chaplin, Clara Kimball Young, Douglas Fairbanks, and Theda Bara. The newspapers woke up quickly to the news value in those names. . . . Reporters were assigned to chronicle daily every action, every statement they made. (Robbins 167–68)

Nowadays this discourse reaches beyond political reporting and tabloid celebrity voyeurism and extends beyond its passing "news value." The "star is born" formula, and the concept of stardom in general, has also come to preoccupy highbrow intellectual discourse. During World War II one of Hollywood's most influential producers wrote that "it is impossible . . . to mention the star system to an intellectual without causing pain" (Wanger). Nowadays these once-wary intellectuals belong to this formerly upsetting system.

Obama himself exemplifies this transformation. His own public persona evolved, according to press reports, from that of an intellectual to that of a star. Before his rebirth as a star, in one opponent's view, "Obama was seen as an intellectual, 'not from the 'hood'" (J. Scott). At about the same time that Obama was morphing, the death of America's preeminent nonacademic intellectual, Susan Sontag, and especially the response to her death, confirmed her star status. (Weinberger, "Notes"). Sontag's last novel *In America* confirms moreover the status of stardom itself as a problem addressed repeatedly in Hollywood movies themselves and "intellectualized" by such prominent Kulturtragers such as Sontag, Simome de Beauvoir, and Roland Barthes (V. Schwartz 104, 129). Sontag's narrative not only retells the classic star-is-born narrative. Sontag also doubles the "star is born" formula by showing a European stage star, a Polish countess, as she's reborn on the boards of Gilded Age America, where she comes to costar with Edwin Booth.

In preparation for surmounting the "obstacles between her and stardom in America" (228), Sontag's Bernhardtesque heroine becomes the earth mother for a utopian émigré commune in Anaheim. With this southern California pastoral interlude Sontag suggestively prefigures the utopian mass promises, of mobility, transformation, and pleasure, that Hollywood stars would come to embody (Buck-Morss, *Dreamworld* 149). Recalling this era while melding three stock narratives—an immigrant's self-making, the pioneers' struggle with a recalcitrant wilderness, and the birth of the star—*In America* harkens back to origins of Hollywood stardom.

> In Hollywood melodrama, the popular form of the cinema inherited from the stage of the late nineteenth-century becomes the ideal vehicle for stardom. It simplifies, it exaggerates, it intensifies. It is designed to put a stranglehold on the viewer's emotions. (J. Orr 44)

Sontag's narrative parallels her career, which culminated in her becoming the subject of a leading fashion photographer. Already Sontag had long been subjected to the celebrity gossip her rumored intimacies, especially with this photographer, provoked. These circumstances of Sontag's reputation highlight how stardom, formerly a mass obsession disdained by supposedly educated elites, now stands on its own as a legitimate intellectual concern. Perhaps the most influential theorist of stardom, Richard Dyer, has argued that stars have become culturally significant, ideologically charged, and consequently integral to thoroughgoing intellectual reflection because of "the political value that has been claimed for them" (*Heavenly* x). In Dyer's view, "being interested in stars is being interested in how we are human" (15). Though intellectuals' acceptance of this conclusion may have come slowly, even grudgingly, Dyer's point has held now for over a century, since the era Sontag evokes in *In America*.

As a perennial mass-market favorite and now a respectably entrenched up-market commonplace, this star-is-born trope has proven hardiest at the movies. This obviously irresistible Hollywood formula has yielded three major-studio releases in Hollywood's brief and in the talkies' even briefer history. In 1937, 1954, and 1976, major studios used the pronouncement that "a star is born" as the title of a star vehicle, with the first incarnation winning its sole Oscar for best original screenplay. The 1938 awards ceremony showed exactly how much this narrative belongs to Hollywood rather than to the two credited cowriters Robert Carson and director William Wellman. After accepting the prize, Wellman descended from the podium and brought the statuette over to the table belonging to producer and studio chief David O. Selznick. Wellman "offered it to the producer, saying, 'Here you deserve this—you wrote more of it than I did'" (Schatz 187).[1]

The *A Star Is Born* movies' narratives all present the gestation of stardom rather than highlighting stardom as an achieved status. As causal narratives, such movies provide a lens—or a *stellar optic*—for examining American cultural transformations. Under this lens, these changes can seem, paradoxically, to be underwritten by a concept of stardom that has remained more or less fixed now for several generations. Even more than the three studio versions spanning forty years, the rote familiarity of the very phrase "a star is born" and the very phrase's ubiquity in the marketplace of ideas demonstrate the appeal of the concept. Long part of the public domain, the stellar optic evolved decades ago into one of Hollywood's most durable and flexible products, in part because it encapsulates a deep-seated, usually unexamined consensus about the qualitative relationship between performance and fame.

II

This stellar optic and representations of star-making predate Hollywood, notwithstanding Wellman and Carson's 1938 Oscar for *originality*. This continuous stargazing has resulted in recurring revisions of, and critical narratives about, the "star is born" formula dating back to fiction by such novelists as Henry James, Theodore Dreiser, and Willa Cather. These largely pre-Hollywood writers helped establish stardom as "a distinctive feature of modernity" broadly considered, not simply of Hollywood and the entertainment industries (Shumway 527). Each novelist provides "a rumination in narrative form" (P. Roth, *Exit* 200–201*)* scrutinizing how "a star is born." Writing either before the advent of or during the very infancy of Hollywood, James, Dreiser, and Cather didn't simply censure the allure of stardom from the lofty heights traditionally preferred by elite cultural arbiters. Neither did they, like fans or flacks, uncritically buy into stardom as typically mass-marketed and as promoted in each Hollywood version of *A Star Is Born*. Before it became apparent to the rest of us, they demonstrated the insight that novelist Steve Erickson had a cinephile Cannes courtesan speak well over a century after James showed a star being born in *The Tragic Muse*: "Directors, they make the art, but stars, they make the culture" (Erickson 203), especially the "great star . . . who embodies a cultural moment while nudging us on to something new, to feelings not yet explored and contradictions not yet expressed" (Kehr, "Appraisal").

The kind of appreciative curiosity toward and critical distance from stardom these novelists exhibited has increasingly colored each subsequent iteration of *A Star Is Born*. With each "new" release, the recycled title *A*

Star Is Born has ironically come closer to undermining and darkening the perennially popular success story the formula, for the most part, embraces. With each retelling, this narrative increasingly casts doubt on the promise this narrative makes. The most recent version came from the screenwriting team of Joan Didion and John Gregory Dunne (see chapter I). Their script stresses even more than its predecessors the extent to which stars aren't born but uneasily made (Dunne 7–8). Didion and Dunne's approach reflects the aspiration by the female lead, Barbra Streisand, to star not only on-screen but in the executive suite as well. As executive producer, Streisand also took on the role of star *auteur*—as "interventionist . . . author"—in order to control the representation of her career and "the meaning of her image" as well as of her scripted character (Dyer, *Stars* 38, 175; Pierson).

In contrast to the earlier *A Star Is Born* movies, both depicting movie stars, Streisand's "vanity project" remake depicts a romance between a rising and a fading rock star (played by Kris Kristofferson, then a popular singer in the process of becoming primarily an actor) (Haglund). Underscoring the extent to which stars aren't born but made, Kristofferson's—Didion and Dunne's—lines also implicitly and acerbically ask why should we care about any performer's aspiration to stardom. In encouraging Streisand's character Esther Hoffman to *make* herself a star, Kristofferson's character John Norman plays the mentor role played under the name of Norman Maine by Frederic March and James Mason in the earlier movies. Unlike his predecessors, though, John Norman's advice to Esther highlights at once the durability and triteness of the "star is born" narrative by counseling her to "reach for every cliché you ever heard."

More obliquely and despite its Oscar for originality, William Wellman's initial version repeatedly acknowledged, in both its opening and closing sequences, that his movie would be telling a twice-told, even an oft-told tale. Wellman opened with a process shot showing the first and last pages of the shooting script, which begins with the following instructions:

Screenplay

A Star is Born

In the next shot, a man's hand descends into the frame with a rubber stamp designating the sheet the cover page of a

FINAL SHOOTING SCRIPT

Then a spinning camera zooms in on these three words. The next page offers the conventional disclaimer about the fictitiousness of what follows, but then, instead of the action beginning, another page keeps delaying the on-screen action, with a camera instruction, to "fade in" to

MOONLIGHT. A LONG SHOT EXPANSE OF SNOW.
In the foreground a wolf silhouetted in the moonlight.

The background image shows an "isolated farmhouse" as the soundtrack instructions indicate "the melancholy howling of the wolf."

Though indicated on the script page, this scene never appears on screen. The action opens instead inside a crowded farmhouse as the aspiring star Esther Blodgett and her kid brother return from the picture show in town. This opening at once stresses the extent to which this "original" narrative is itself a revision, a response to whatever appeared on a small-town movie screen and fueled Esther's stellar ambition. The phrase "final shooting script" implies many precedents and the usual serial revisions while omitting the opening shot that the script calls for assures moviegoers that we don't need to see the exterior of the farmhouse or to see and hear the wolf, presumably because we already have—time and again.

III

This collective knowledge of the "star is born" narrative belongs not only to Hollywood. By the time of the first *A Star Is Born* movie stardom had already become densely embedded in American fiction, in pre-Hollywood narratives by James, Dreiser, and Cather, and elaborated after the rise of Hollywood in novels by Nathanael West, Joan Didion, Gore Vidal, Norman Mailer, John Updike, and Robert Stone. In much American fiction, stargazing does double duty. Beyond embodying and examining the concept of stardom, these writers also prompt readers to gaze through the stellar optic as a way of reflecting on the novelist's own status, resources, and desired effects as yet another performer in the cultural marketplace: the "semantic importance" the performance produces and "the possibilities for" achieving such desired effects by publicly performing private identities (King 46; Austin and Barker 265). Novelists and movie stars, like all culture industry competitors, vie for public attention. A sage reclusive novelist reassures a protégé in Philip Roth's 1979 novel *The Ghost Writer* by urging him to consider his place among these rivals:

> [P]eople held up for our esteem everyday: movie stars, politicians, athletes. Because you happen to be a writer doesn't mean you have to deny yourself the ordinary human pleasure of being praised and applauded. (40)

Roth's sage continues, though, to distinguish novelists and stars from mere celebrities such as "athletes and politicians." The difference lies in their commitment to transformation, to troping: turns of phrases on pages and turns of voice, affect, and appearance on-screen. Elia Kazan saw the "star turn" as the linchpin of both the American stage and screen (Simon 10). Likewise, the novelist's essential move, in Roth's alter-ego's view, is to

> turn sentences around. That's my life. I write a sentence and then I turn it around. Then I look at it and turn it around again. . . . Then I get up and throw them out and start from the beginning . . . found himself turning sentences around. . . . I turn sentences around, that's it. (*Ghost Writer* 17–18, 19, 51, 66)

This will to turn or to trope, a preoccupation in recent "literary theory," spurs "the effort to earn [the] right of expression" to keep turning—transforming—one's medium and available identities: to keep moving from one "meaning" to the next, from one "conception" to another, from "notion" to "notion," and to acknowledge that what appears on the page, stage, or screen can always be "expressed otherwise" (White 2–3; H. Bloom 93–94).

James's *The Tragic Muse*, Dreiser's *Sister Carrie*, and Cather's "Coming, Aphrodite" all highlight this effort to earn an audience and to keep moving from meaning to meaning. Each narrative depicts a featured star, near the end of the nineteenth century, as conquering the stage rather than the soon-to-be more publicly accessible movie screen. *The Tragic Muse* and *Sister Carrie* demonstrated, well before Hollywood started manufacturing them, the extent to which "stars are narrative characters" (Dargis, "Hot"). In showing stardom as an irresistible yet unexceptional literary preoccupation these novelists anticipated Manny Farber's enthusiastic homage to novelist, screenwriter, and movie-reviewer James Agee, whom Farber honors as "the most intriguing star-gazer" among his peers (84). This homage stresses how much the stellar optic has meant to American literati and intellectuals. During the reign of the big studios, Agee mastered the stellar optic, proving himself "a virtuoso who capped a strange company of stars on people's lips and" at the same time "set up a hailstorm of ideas for other critics to use."

As Hollywood's star system reigned most triumphantly during the interwar wars and the stellar optic became a mass-culture staple, modernist critics of mass culture, appealing to a narrower, more literate readership, appear to have been similarly fascinated by stars as a lens for examining cultural behavior. F. Scott Fitgerald's 1934 novel *Tender is the Night*, for example, attributes the fall of its intellectually precarious hero Dick Diver mostly to alcoholism and his obsession with his wife and wealth. Almost as crucial, though, is his fascination with a rising starlet named Rosemary Hoyt. Readers of Fitzgerald's previous novel, *The Great Gatsby*, who know from the name of its narrator, Caraway, that Fitzgerald's name-play had botanical tendencies, might be tempted to bear in mind the folkish association of rosemary with persistent memory, the basis for obsession. Remembering Fitzgerald's connection with New York City and lowlife characters, as depicted in *Gatsby* and in early stories like "Mayday," readers will also hear *hurt* as once pronounced in many parts of the city in the name Hoyt. While treating Rosemary Hoyt as Dick Diver's painful obsession, which leads to erotic humiliation, Fitzgerald also stresses her stardom as an economic phenomenon and a product of modern imaging technology (40, 24).

Nathanael West's 1939 novel *The Day of the Locust* focuses more narrowly on Hollywood as a star-spawning, fan-breeding culture. In evoking these conditions, West demonstrates what made the "star is born" narrative both appealing and appalling. West not only depicted, in excruciating detail, the pursuit of screen stardom, but he also violently skewed and so entirely discredited the "star is born" narrative.

The Day of the Locust ends with a shift of focus from the would-be stars in the foreground throughout the narrative to the crowd that views its circumstances through a mass-manufactured stellar optic. The stars they gaze on at once infatuate and enrage this crowd. With this shift, West indefinitely and so abortively defers the longed-for star birth. Featuring a would-be-star-turned-prostitute and the male entourage that fosters her "star is born" fantasy, *The Day of the Locust* turns the narrative of stellar aspiration against itself and highlights the capriciousness with which star careers are dreamed of, made, and aborted.

IV

Moving from stage to screen and from page to celluloid, the concept of the star has become so much a part of the way we speak as to entirely obscure the metaphoric origins of the concept. Hollywood intellectuals, such as Didion, who have done much to foster this star aura, have at the same time worked to call it into question and disclose some of its more disturbing implications, and its monstrousness.

Didion's view of the entertainment industry as a "monster" (*Slouching* 150) echoes Henry James's description, in *The Tragic Muse*, of the consummate theatrical star whose rise the novel depicts. James aligns this understanding with the perspective of a painter who becomes fascinated by and sets out to "capture" this emerging star.

It came over him suddenly that so far from there being any question of her having the histrionic nature, she simply had it in such perfection that she was always acting; that her existence was a series of parts assumed for the moment, each changed the next, before the perpetual mirror of some curiosity or admiration or wonder—some spectatorship that she perceived or imagined. Interested as he had ever been in the profession of which she was potentially an ornament, this idea startled him by its novelty and even lent, on spot, a formidable, a really appalling character to Miriam Rooth. It struck him that a woman whose only being was to "make believe," to make you believe that she had any and every being that you liked, that would serve a purpose, produce a certain effect, and whose identity resided in the continuity of her presentations . . . lived in a high wind of exhibition, of presentation, of figuration . . . was a kind of monster. (147–48)

This passage moves from treating Miriam's performance affect as part of her "nature" to an emphasis on "ornament," "making," "producing," and "exhibition." These shifts track the transformation of the observer's understanding of Miriam as a born star to his recognition of Miriam as a made star, partly self-made and partly remade by her mentor Madame Carre, who equates the construction of Miriam with producing "cuisine" (152). This figurative equation here between the glamour of star-making and the domestic routine of cooking underscores the jaundiced view that links James's novel to the successor narratives, which over the next century tracked "the star system" as it "emerged" from the nineteenth-century transatlantic theatrical milieu and, as the movies took hold as the prime mass medium, came to dominate mass culture (Boorstin, *Image* 154).

Like *The Tragic Muse*, Dreiser's *Sister Carrie* unmasks stardom as artifice rather than fate or endowment. Like James, Dreiser never entirely relinquishes faith in the enchanting, albeit slight, possibility that the "monster" star depicted might turn out after all to be a sport of nature rather than an interchangeable and marketed artifact. Dreiser links his heroine Carrie's initial affection for the stage to "theatrical paraphernalia": "the matter of make-up . . . the flare of the gas-jets, the open trunks, suggestive of travel and display, the scattered contents of the make-up box—rouge, pearl powder, whiting, burnt cork, India ink, pencils for the eye-lids, wigs, scissors, looking-glasses, drapery—in short, all the nameless paraphernalia of disguise" and their transformative power (128). To all this backstage machinery, Dreiser adds Broadway's promotional apparatus—"the names upon the bill-boards, the marvel of the long notices in the papers"—as a catalyst in Carrie's discovery of her opportunity for achieving the "perfect

state" of stardom and the passage "into Aladdin's cave" that stardom promises (334). Once Dreiser has positioned Carrie as a star, evoking the thrill
and wonder of this transformation, he subjects Carrie's ascent to critical
scrutiny. As Hollywood's insider skeptics would do later in the twentieth
century, Dreiser prompts wariness of both the consensus that makes her
a star and the supposedly intellectual discourse intent on questioning and
complicating this consensus:

> [A] critic called to get up one of those tinsel interviews which shine with
> clever observations, show up the wit of critics, display the folly of celebri-
> ties, and divert the public. He liked Carrie, and said so, publicly—adding,
> however, that she was merely pretty, good-natured, and lucky. (335)

Dreiser signals the formulaic banality of Carrie's supposedly Aladdin-like
entry into the charmed circle of stardom with the interviewer's pointedly generic reference to "such entertainments as the one in which she
was the star."

V

"Coming, Aphrodite," a 1920 novella by Dreiser's contemporary and
James's professed disciple Willa Cather, offers a more compressed and
jaundiced account than either *The Tragic Muse* or *Sister Carrie* of how
stardom begins in fascination only to turn stale, if not sclerotic. Cather's
would-be star Eden Bower appears early in this novella "like someone
standing before a great show window full of beautiful and costly things,
deciding which she will order." Cather shows Eden discovering her
calling "to be admired and adored"—to become a star ("Coming" 436,
444). Cather aligns both narrator and reader by means of the pronoun
we, as the audience of Eden's ascent and eventual stardom. Like James,
Cather foregrounds the stellar optic and conjures complicit "spectatorship." Like Dreiser, she tracks both the promise of stardom's metamor-
phic magic and then its souring. Cather's heroine begins with the prosaic
name Edna Bowers, but nevertheless appears "at twenty, very much the
same person that we all know her to be at forty, except that she knew a
great deal less. But one thing she knew: that she was to be Eden Bower"
(436). Cather seems here at the outset to be endowing her would-be
star with perpetual youth. Ultimately, however, she fouls this apparent
blessing and casts the same sort of cold eye on stardom as did James and
Dreiser a generation earlier.

Leaning back in the cushions, Eden Bower closed her eyes, and her face, as the street lamps flashed their ugly orange light upon it, became hard and settled, like a plaster cast; so a sail, that has been filled by a strong breeze, behaves when the wind suddenly dies. Tomorrow night the wind would blow again, and this mask would be the golden face of Aphrodite. But a "big" career takes its toll, even with the best of luck. (458)

Simply by moving Eden from the idolizing footlights into the prosaic glare of street light, Cather highlights both the monster and the common product into which Eden has transformed herself and so comes to embody what Ewan Kirkland pinpoints as the star's "attraction": her "ability to unify competing discourses" in a gesture of "ideological reconciliation" confirmed by how she appears beyond her public performance space (243). Remaining "still steadfast, still unchangeable," like Keats's "bright star" (195), Eden turns "ugly," not because of any move or choice she makes, but because of the technological presentation with which any stage or screen director or novelist decides to frame and light characters.

Like Gloria Swanson as the faded star *par excellence* in *Sunset Boulevard*, Eden may feel, with her fixed "mask," superciliously "ready for my close-up," though willfully oblivious to the "toll" such readiness takes. For such stars "the readiness" may be "all," as Hamlet insists (v.2), but it's not enough. Cather stresses this quandary in her very title. Cather identifies Eden with an Olympian goddess, and then with Lilith as rendered in "Eden Bower," an 1869 poem by Dante Gabriel Rossetti. "Eden Bower" features Lilith as Satan's sponsor and, like Swanson's character in *Sunset Boulevard*, a banished star intent on a comeback. Though known from the apocryphal Book of Tobit as the reviled "filth"-bearing first wife of Adam, Rossetti makes her the star of the paradise-lost narrative in Genesis, a star who promised "human bliss past hearing or seeing," though like a deity, "not a drop [of] her blood was human" (312, 308). With this double (Hellenic and Hebraic) allusiveness, Cather indicates both the overpowering allure and the inevitable corrosiveness of stardom.

VI

Naming the Greek goddess in her title Aphrodite, a reference to the play that stars Eden, Cather anticipates the extent to which the "fabrication" of stardom parallels ancient pagan polytheist cult formation or "mythification" (Morin 29, 82–83). In thus associating her heroine with a goddess of sexual desire Cather homes in on the familiar dependence of stardom on sexual allure and the freedom to make the most of one's sexual attractive-ness. Robert Stone's 1986 Hollywood novel *Children of Light* highlights this dependence. Stone shows a director and his entourage in his location trailer screening Hollywood classics. The group singles out the first *A Star Is Born* production as the best (179–80). The director's father, a legend-ary Hollywood director, extols the male lead Frederic March for showing what makes him "the greatest actor of all time." Then the conversa-tion turns to March's costar, Janet Gaynor. A real-life tabloid-touted—"adorable, warm, and real"—Galatea during the silent era, Gaynor made her mark as "the perfect example of" the on-screen persona who "combines the virgin and the whore" (Basinger 4; Haskell 50–52). Stone's Hollywood elder seconds Molly Haskell's perception. In lauding Gaynor for appearing "ultra-feminine" on screen, he attributes her singularity to having "started before sound" and so reduces Gaynor's star-power appeal to her audience's gaze, to being seen—and objectified—but not heard. His son, the director on the set, complicates his father's stellar optic even as he sets out to further simplify his father's view of on-screen "ultra-femininity." This simplifi-cation, though, embraces the "contradictory attitudes" that male gazing at the movies, an amalgam of "glorification and disparagement," entails (Kaplan 30–31; Chandler; cf. Mulvey, *Visual* 20): As the younger director "studied the images on the screen," he boasted of pinpointing "the pri-mal element in female sexual attraction" that "can explain" Janet Gaynor: "Her face looks like a cunt" (180). This coarse candor echoes, crudely, that of *auteur* theorist Andrew Sarris, who once confessed "that what really kept him going to the movies was the girls." Stone's senior *auteur* com-pounds this candor with a complicit, audience-embracing second person pronoun, bluntly illustrating Raymond Durgnat's observation that "the star communicates by a personal, even physical, language—face, gesture, build" (*Film* 145, 152): "You look at her face and it makes you think of her pussy" (Stone, 180). The male gazer's tendency that Stone evokes, to turn women's faces "vaginal," Richard Dyer suggests, "can be read as the analogue for a basic [masculine] conception of female sexuality" (*Heavenly* 54)—a conception long prevalent in Hollywood-made star images.

Stone's moviemakers' bluntness underscores the degree to which aspir-ing to be a (woman) star entails appreciating and exploiting "the primal element in female sexual attraction" (Kaplan 30). More decorously and more circumspectly than Stone, Cather traces the eros of stardom to books and words rather than confining it to the star's body. Early in "Coming, Aphrodite," Cather contrasts Eden's illicit adolescent aspirations with the licensed fantasies allowed middle-class girls in nineteenth-century Illinois:

When she was thirteen, and was already singing and reciting for church entertainments, she read in some illustrated magazine a long article about the late Czar of Russia, then just come to the throne or about to come to it. After that, lying in the hammock on the front porch on summer evenings, or sitting through a long sermon in the family pew, she amused herself by trying to make up her mind whether she would or would not be the Czar's mistress when she played in his Capital. (436)

By pointedly showing Eden as unconcerned with historical and geographic details—the dates of the czar's reign and the name of his "capital" city— Cather highlights the narrowness of her aspiration and thereby establishes Eden's status as self-made and self-directing sex object. This difference between what Eden "knows" as a star and what she knew back when "she knew less" (458) indicates that only Eden's sex appeal as a hardened "plaster" star at the end of "Coming, Aphrodite" marks her progress from an attractive aspiring neophyte.

Cather registers the reaction to Eden's pre-star sex appeal in the figure of the apparent author surrogate in the story, an avant-garde "experimental" painter named Hedger with whom Eden shares a partitioned Washington Square flat. Hedger begins, fortuitously, spying on Eden through a peephole in the partition dividing their apartments soon after Eden moves in. This arrangement recalls the primitive early movie technology, the peephole "protocinema" (Czitrom 38, 37), popular during the period in which Cather sets "Coming, Aphrodite": the Kinetoscope. Cather evokes both the solitude and spatial confinement reminiscent of this small cabinet with a peephole designed for solitary viewing in her account of Hedger's discovery of his clandestine visual access to Eden, "in the closet that was built against the partition separating his room from Miss Bower's" (428).

> When he took his overcoat from its place against the partition, a long ray of yellow light shot across the dark enclosure, a knothole, evidently, in the high wainscoting of the west room. He had never noticed it before, and without realizing what he was doing, he stooped and squinted through it. Yonder, in a pool of sunlight, stood his new neighbor, wholly unclad, doing exercises . . . before a long gilt mirror. Hedger did not happen to think how unpardonable it was of him to watch her. Nudity was not improper to anyone who had worked so much from the figure, and he continued to look, simply because he had never seen a woman's body so beautiful as this one, positively glorious in action. As she swung her arms and changed from one pivot of motion to another, muscular energy seemed to flow through her from her toes to her finger-tips. The soft flush of exercise and the gold of afternoon sun played over her flesh together, enveloped her

in a luminous mist which, as she turned and twisted, made now an arm, now a shoulder, now a thigh, dissolve in pure light and instantly recover its outline with the next gesture.

Thus "groping in the dark for the eyehole" that "makes *everything* other-worldly" "enchanted . . . remote," Hedger experiences what the Turkish Nobel laureate Orhan Pamuk would later describe as the primal moviegoing experience (301). More broadly, "the darkened room" and the "framing" effect of the "peephole" as an analogue of the "movie camera" combine, according to prevailing feminist film theory, as Hollywood movies have done perennially, to "produce the woman as object" (Walters 56, 54, 58).

Cather looks back on the pre-Hollywood 1890s from the vantage point of 1920, when this moviegoing experience was already widely familiar, when moviegoers were discovering that "cinema wished to leave nothing hidden, to throw nakedness up on the screen" (Updike, *Beauty* 147). At the same time, Hollywood's studio system and its production of movie stars had become an entrenched fact of American life; hence, Cather portrays Hedger as a stock moviegoer, initially besotted by Eden's star quality, just as Rossetti described Adam in "thrall to Lilith" (308). Just as his confining closet space mirrors and mocks this thralldom to what he watches, Hedger's limited but exhilarating peephole perspective concretizes the stellar optic.

By the time she published "Coming, Aphrodite," Cather had already established her fascination with the star-is-born narrative. This interest dates back at least to her early-career journalism and to her 1915 novel *The Song of the Lark*, which she would come to write off as apprentice work (Woodress 272–73). Notwithstanding her 1914 magazine article announcing the decline of stardom in favor of character acting, Cather closes *The Song of the Lark* by "generously" making peace with the enchantments of stardom, reconciling stardom with rather than alienating stardom from "the growth of the artist" and her pursuit of "some exalted ideal" (Woodress 255; Cather, *Early* 699).

Unlike Cather's narrator's enchantment with the heroine star in *The Song of the Lark*, Hedger's beguilement with Eden, his surrender to a limiting stellar optic, proves shortlived. As Cather's narrative unfolds, Hedger's artistic convictions come to trump his affections as a lover and besotted stargazer. In describing Hedger's profession as a painter and even his social pose as a raconteur, Cather associates him with a modernist view of the artist's calling as experimental antagonizer constantly "outliving a succession of convictions and revelations about his art" and "getting rid of ideas" he once embraced ("Coming" 423). Cather pits this position against the preference for stardom as a "marketable product" and the commercial "success" that Eden embraces and then presses futilely on Hedger as a desirable aspiration (423, 451). In the closing passage of "Coming, Aphrodite," Cather shows Hedger's resistance: he has achieved artistic "success" without stardom and without the "monstrousness" associated with stardom. A generation after Eden and Hedger's abrupt parting, Eden asks a carriage-trade Fifth Avenue gallery owner whether Hedger "had great success."

> "Certainly. He is one of the first men among the moderns. That is to say, among the very moderns. He is always coming up with something different. He often exhibits in Paris, you must have seen." . . . M. Jules pulled at his short grey moustache. "But, Madame, there are many kinds of success," he began cautiously. Madame gave a dry laugh. "Yes, so he used to say. We once quarreled on that issue. And how would you define his particular kind?" M. Jules grew thoughtful. "He is a great name with all the young men, and he is decidedly an influence in art. But one can't definitely place a man who is original, erratic, and who is changing all the time." (457)

In upholding the dissident option that she identifies with Hedger, Cather prefigures what would become a recurring stance in Hollywood critiques of stardom.

VII

Cather's choice of a painter's perspective as a vantage point for critically observing stardom, as both a complement and counterpoint to the star herself, in "Coming, Aphrodite" raises a question that Emerson never could have anticipated in 1836 when he proclaimed the stars "preachers of beauty" (*Prose* 28). A generation after "Coming, Aphrodite" and a decade after Nathanael West had mocked Cather as "catheter" (*Miss* 14), West put even more pressure on this question by elaborating this dissident painter's perspective in *The Day of the Locust*. The first, the most *outré*, and now "the touchstone for every myth-shattering Hollywood novel" (C. James, "Hollywood"), *Locust* inaugurated the classic trio of Depression-era Hollywood novels, which also includes Schulberg's *What Makes Sammy Run* and Fitzgerald's unfinished *The Love of the Last Tycoon*.

Like "Coming, Aphrodite," *The Day of the Locust* takes the perspective of a painter who seeks to work against the grain yet finds himself susceptible to blandishments made irresistible when viewed through a stellar optic. Teased for discouraging fellow Hollywooders from "cherishing their

illusions" (71), West's viewpoint character bears a name—Tod Hackett[2]— fraught with an allegorical suggestiveness. Despite the similar thrusts
of their critiques, West's Hackett contrasts, pointedly, with Cather's "successful" autodidact Hedger. West shows Hackett's failure as strikingly overdetermined thanks to his unchanging neophyte status, his lack of a mentor,
the Yale education that equips and burdens Hackett with "the tricks in the
very full bag of the intellectual" (141), and his need to settle for commercial
work, which distracts him from his artistic calling.

Tod's failures as a suitor compound these intellectual and artistic
shortfalls. In contrast to Hedger, Hackett's desire for *his* lascivious muse
remains thwarted throughout the novel and she, unlike Eden Bower, fails
to achieve the stardom she craves. As with Hedger, though, Hackett's
male-gaze preoccupation with this muse and would-be model, Faye
Greener, becomes less professional and more prurient, less identified
with professional aspiration and increasingly violent, over the course of
West's narrative. Hedger begins casting his gaze on Eden "crouching on
his knees, staring at the golden shower . . . on a faded Turkish carpet"
("Coming" 429). What Hedger sees soon becomes an "enchanted spot"
like "a vision out of Alexandria, out of the remote pagan past . . . bathed
. . . in Helianthine fire." This hyperbolically evoked inspiration soon
yields to the disenchantment Max Weber described as the inevitable
effect of modern intellect (155). On becoming Eden's lover, Hedger's
"enchanted" gaze turns bestial, demolishing for a spell the wall that had
kept him from Eden, a material reminder of the "mediation" on which
stardom rests (Shumway 531).

> Hedger was not trying to please her . . . but to antagonize and frighten
> her by his brutal story. She had often told herself that his lean, big-boned
> lower jaw was like his bull-dog's, but tonight his face made [Hedger's dog]
> Caesar's most savage and determined expression seem an affectation. Now
> she was looking at the man he really was. Nobody's eyes had ever defied
> her like this. They were searching her and seeing everything; all she had
> concealed. (447)

The very trajectory of Cather's narrative implicitly discloses not only
how the aspiration to stardom corrupts the would-be star who "enjoyed
being stared at" (N. West, 94) but also how stargazing can deform a rapt
audience.

Muted in "Coming, Aphrodite," this trajectory becomes superlatively
pronounced in *The Day of Locust*, where the violence in the male gaze starts

with Hackett's first sighting of Faye as "an invitation that wasn't to pleasure but to struggle, hard and sharp, closer to murder than to love" (68) and ends with Tod's image of her as "a deer on the edge of the road when a truck comes unexpectedly around the bend" (174). These images reflect Tod's "impulse . . . to throw her down in the soft warm mud . . . keep her there," do "nothing less than violent rape," and "crush her" (107).

VIII

West's novella extends this rage beyond the individual gazer. West complements the gaze of the desiring artist with that of the crowd whose gaze upon both the fading and rising stars pervades each *A Star Is Born* movie. George Cukor's 1954 musical remake, for example, opens the way *The Day of the Locust* closes, with a blockbuster Hollywood premier: "a dozen great violent shafts of light moving across the evening sky in crazy sweeps . . . fiery columns . . . lit . . . the rose-colored domes and delicate minarets of Kahn's Persian Palace Theater . . . to signal the world premier of a new picture" (175–77). But instead of the scripted spectacle and familiar ritual that Cukor stages, West shows a mob—"demoniac . . . pugnacious . . . savage . . . bitter." Egged on by a radio announcer and out for a glimpse of Gary Cooper, the mob rampages homicidally through the streets of Hollywood. West's stress on this mob's star obsession in 1939 illustrates Joseph Roach's account of "mob scenes" as the very matrix of stardom (180).

West's mob scene also presages Leo Braudy's account of how the ideological function of the star metamorphosed in the interval between Wellman's and Cukor's versions of *A Star Is Born*. Judy Garland's and later Barbra Streisand's off-screen identities—in contrast to Janet Gaynor's less flamboyant off-screen image (Bird)—both illustrate this change:

> The star system of the 20s and 30s encouraged more worship than imitation. But the 40s and 50s ushered in a preoccupation with film actors as social symbols, Rorschach tests by which individuals could connect their dreams across the American landscape. This search for emblematic stars, for admiration and for psychic support, became central to postwar culture. (Braudy 279)

In Streisand's 1976 musical version of *A Star Is Born*, the mob outburst that threatens in the opening scene turns out to belong to the star's routine.

Part of a familiar love-hate ritual between the rock-star protagonist and his fans, the outburst contains rather than ignites mass passions, in striking contrast to the two earlier movies.

Both Wellman's and West's Depression-era evocations of mobs presented staged fan-rousing events at the *end* of their respective narratives to illustrate the failure or even the impossibility of such containment. These failures of crowd control uncover the substrate of fan violence that usually passes for passionate attachment. HBO's Golden Globe and Emmy-winning BBC import *Extras* illustrates week after week what turns fans' passionate attachment to enraged rioting. This series tracks the career aspirations and misadventures of a corpulent, fortyish Robert De Niro wannabe named Andy Mellman. Played by the popular British comedian Ricky Gervais, who had already become a star on *The Office*, Mellman makes a living as a perennial extra—or "background artist." When his luck turns, precariously, he gets a regular TV series gig as "the face of Britain's stupidest sitcom" universally reviled for its offensiveness: the "former humiliated movie extra" becomes "the humiliated star of a stupid, smutty sitcom" ("Week"; N. Smith). Each episode depicts another of his career failures. Each failure yields yet another excruciating rationalization that keeps him on track in pursuit of stardom. To underscore that Mellman's ambition will forever prove a dream deferred, occasional guests appear, such as David Bowie, Ian McKellen, Daniel Radcliffe, Kate Winslet, and Ben Stiller. Playing themselves and often parodically savaging their own identities as stars, their presence sparks encounters that invariably push Mellman to humiliate himself with bumbling obsequiousness or self-sabotaging candor.

During its first season, Mellman asked—and got no answer to—the question that fuels the violence in both Wellman's version of *A Star Is Born* and *The Day of Locust*. Looking across the set at the star of a movie he's working on, Mellman asks, "Why is 'e a star and not me?" Wellman's original *A Star Is Born* shows what happens when this question is left to fester and pinpoints the moment attachment turns to rage, the moment the veil between star and nonstars falls, with a shot of the newly minted star of the title swarmed by a mob as she leaves the church after her fading-star husband's funeral. This sequence ends when one assailant rips off her veil as the camera zooms in on Gaynor's shrieking face. This Munch-esque view, through a stellar optic darkly, calls to mind Robert Ray's view of *A Star Is Born* as a "*noir* musical"—one instance of Hollywood's perennially "*noir*-ish" genre inversions (159), even though Ray was referring to Cukor's seemingly less *noir*-ish 1954 version. In marked contrast to Wellman's production, Cukor's McCarthy-era rendering screens out this violence by foreshortening Garland's grimace and eliding her scream.

Cukor and chief screenwriter Moss Hart's evasion of what Wellman highlighted seventeen years earlier serves as an illuminating counterpoint to West's rhetorical agenda in *The Day of the Locust*. West evokes both the mob's narrow violent gaze—the dark side of the stellar optic—and the artist's conflicted wide-angle gaze: his artist-protagonist's relationship with crowds or mobs as well as with his muse. With this double exposure West expressly presents the dilemma that intellectual observers of Hollywood always face: the Hobson's choice between identifying with the star or with the fan, with the knowing system or with its impressionable customers. With his close-up of gazing and gazed-on crowds, West complicates the question of how to gaze upon a star: of whether to see her with the masses' eyes or through the artist's. *The Day of the Locust* partly addresses this problem by telescoping the distance, evoked in "Coming, Aphrodite," between the enchanted gaze and the rapacious glare.

In both narratives the artist-protagonist sees the star, his muse, mediated through frames. By signaling the inescapability of mediation, these various "star is born" narratives raise questions about which agents or institutions get to control this mediation. In *The Day of the Locust* Hackett's first reported observation of his muse leaves him "grunting with annoyance" and shows her, not through a hole in the wall (like Hedger's), but in a photograph, "a still from a two-reel farce in which she had worked as an extra" (67). Showing Hackett thus annoyed at his own attraction to this mass-produced muse and at his susceptibility to the stellar optic, West shifts the work of fabricating fantasy from the gazer to the gazed-on.

Whether produced by star or stargazer, their stock fantasies draw on a similar body of lore. Faye first appears, in contrast to Eden's "unclad" state (428), "wearing a harem costume," as did Sister Carrie in launching her career (N. West 67; Dreiser 314). Faye's "Turkish trousers," in particular, evoke the same "oriental" mystique as did the "Turkish carpet" that framed Eden and the "rich, oriental appearance" that helped draw Carrie to the stage (280). Faye's appearance in this scene from a "lost in the seraglio" tale raises questions about parallels and contrasts between the role of their sexuality in Faye's and Eden's stellar aspirations. Does the kind of kept woman Faye played, for example, mirror or counterpoint the kind of kept woman Eden dreamed of becoming, "the czar's mistress"? Playing himself being played by John Cusack in *Being John Malkovich*, the actor sums up this carnal core of stardom for men as well as for women by exclaiming, "I look really amazing. I'd fuck me!"

IX

Equating stardom with prostitution has become so commonplace that by the middle of the twentieth century, as the studio system waned, Saul Bellow's *Seize the Day* shows its protagonist, a male wannabe star, beguiled and corrupted by an agent who promises to make him "a name like Roosevelt, Swanson. From East to West, out to China and into South America . . . a lover to the whole world." Instead of stardom, though, the agent gives Tommy Wilhelm (born Wilky Adler) "the kiss of death" and turns out to have been exploiting his studio "connection to operate a ring of call girls" (22)—a Hollywood talent agency as a front for pimping. Bellow follows West's and Cather's view of stars as whores. While Cather obliquely counterpoints Eden's "czar's mistress fantasy" with the nonjudgmental quasi-anthropological observation that "women who bore that relation to men were called by a very different name" than mistress in Eden's prairie hometown, West makes the connection expressly lurid with Tod's realization that his muse moonlights in a high-end Hollywood brothel, information that precipitates the novel's cataclysmic plot turn. When Tod tells Homer Simpson, Faye's only fan as well as her guilelessly besotted sponsor, who subsidizes her quest to "become a star," that "she's a whore!" (135, 162), Homer turns violently inconsolable and launches a homicidal riot-inciting rampage.

In exposing these would-be stars as whores, both Cather and West debunk the extravagant rhetoric and imagery with which wannabes launch their star fantasies from humbling, if not humiliating, points of departure, so that the conditions in the musty, disheveled closet from which Hedger discovers Eden and the beer bottle Faye clutches in the otherwise "exotic" orientalizing still she gives Tod (67) mock the hyperbolic overreaching that stirs each aspirant to stardom. Both the 1937 and 1954 *A Star Is Born* movies show studio executives stressing the rising star's repudiation of her birth name of Esther Blodgett[3] in favor of the stage name Vicki Lester, redolent of victory and luster. This move recalls Edna Bowers's self-christening as Eden Bower, a name evoking primal bliss.

However much West tarnishes Faye Greener's quest for stardom, her pursuit scrupulously follows the script that Didion and Dunne wrote into their *A Star Is Born* screenplay. Faye follows the advice Didion and Dunne had Esther's mentor offer: she "reaches for every cliché ever heard" in Hollywood:

> "I'd like to do a show on Broadway . . . that's how you get to be a star nowadays." . . . She went on telling him how careers are made in the mov-

ies and how she intended to make hers. . . . She mixed badly understood advice from the trade papers with other bits out of the fan magazines and compared these with the legends that surrounded the activities of screen starts and executives. (158)

Faye "reaches" when she asks Tod to collaborate with her in scripting the scenarios bound to make her a star (105–6). Faye instructs Tod that because he's "educated," he should "write up" her "swell ideas" to "sell to the studios" as she predicts that her (ghosted) "success as a writer" will complement her imminent screen stardom and will result in the executive and *auteur* control that Streisand claimed when she remade *A Star Is Born*.

Tod pictures Faye "manufacturing dream" after dream and promising "hundreds more." Tod watches Faye find her inspiration in the Tarzan poster facing her bed as she scripts a story about a rich girl yachting in the South Seas getting rescued by and marrying the handsome sailor who, before the shipwreck, had "refused to be toyed with." Faye also proposes turning her hand—and Tod's "education"—to a script about a Cinderella chorus girl "who gets her big chance when the star falls sick." Faye's hackneyed fabrications recall Eden Bower's seizure of equally generic pre-Hollywood mass-market fantasies. Eden's ambition of becoming a "czar's mistress," for instance, was what she seized on and adapted after encountering the "fascinating word" *mistress* "in the novels of Ouida" (Cather, "Coming" 436). Thanks to their scandalizing "reputation for daring" (Greene, *On Film* 92), Eden's "hard-worked little mother kept" these volumes in "a long row . . . in the upstairs storeroom, behind the linen chest" along with the other pulp fantasies, "books like *Sappho* and *Mademoiselle de Maupin*, secretly sold in paper covers throughout Illinois."

X

Women pursuing stardom, successes like Cather's Eden or chronic wannabes like West's Faye, see themselves liberated and even masterful in identifying with characters they play. In *Play It As It Lays*, Didion illustrated this will to displace the quotidian with one's screen persona by showing her heroine watching herself on screen. At first, she had no "sense that the girl on the screen was herself" (18). After Didion's narrator points out that her protagonist Maria is viewing the upbeat studio version, rather than the darker, open-ended director's cut, Maria appears lulled, "watching the picture" and supposing that "the girl on the screen seemed to have a definite knack for controlling her own destiny" (19).

Literary renderings of this aspiration, from James's to Didion's, implicate stardom in a broader cultural critique. James set the precedent in *The Tragic Muse*. Throughout the narrative Miriam Rooth's stardom faces the "critical spirit" and "urbane skepticism," all the baggage of "a skeptical age" and its "cynical science," that James ascribes to the male gazers at the center of the narrative: a painter and a theater aficionado (409, 167). Assigning them "day jobs," as a British MP and a diplomat, respectively, for whom "the arts and the aesthetic part of life are night work," James framed the novel as a "show of social realities" (*Art* 91)—as a "picture of the 'artist-life' and of the difficult terms on which it is secured and enjoyed," an effort "to 'do something about art'—art, that is a human complication and a social stumbling block" (79).

Like its literary counterparts, each Hollywood retelling of *A Star Is Born* also renders stardom in a context that extends beyond the protagonists' individual aspirations. The Hollywood versions foster the fantasy of the more encompassing transcendence that stardom promises: promises of surmounting "social stumbling blocks" and "controlling destiny." Literary star-is-born narratives, however, engage at length the temptations of such promises only to chasten them by confronting stars, would-be stars, and stargazing readers with the "stumbling blocks" about which James cautioned in his preface to *The Tragic Muse*.

XI

The end of *The Tragic Muse* singles out one such stumbling block. "In glancing about the little circle of interest I have tried to evoke," James's narrator finds himself "suddenly warned by sharp sense of modernness" that "renders it difficult for me to do much more than . . . allude to the general impression that" his star Miriam Rooth's "career is even yet only in its early prime" (575). Signaling this "difficulty," this narrator averts his and his reader's gaze from the star whose rise he has tracked over some six hundred pages and attributes this evasive shift in focus to a fear of "modernness."

"Modernness," or modernity, also vexes the star's rise or the gazer's appreciation in Cather's, West's, and Didion's narratives. Early in "Coming, Aphrodite," Cather intimates the advent of modernity with attention to the increasingly immigrant coloration of Bower and Hedger's Greenwich Village neighborhood (424–25). Cather describes Hedger doing his routine "marketing on West Houston Street, with a one-eyed Italian woman who always cheated him" before returning home to dine on "beans and scallopini, and . . . half a bottle of Chianti." Cather registers this shifting demographic coloration with a more expressly cultural reference to the ambient wafting of "Pagliacci, which rose ever and anon on hot evenings from an Italian tenement on Thompson Street, with the gasps of the corpulent baritone who got behind it" and "the hurdy-gurdy man, who often played at the corner in the balmy twilight."

This sharpening "sense of modernness" culminates in Cather's parallel between technological change and the corrosive impact of stardom on Eden. Cather sets Eden's "early prime" in Washington Square during "almost the very last summer of the old horse stages on Fifth Avenue" where "shining horses and carriages" stood next to "an automobile, misshapen and sullen, like an ugly threat in a stream of things that were bright and beautiful and alive" (422). The close of the narrative shows Eden "going down Fifth Avenue in her car," pointedly replacing *automobile* with the more modern noun *car* (456). This car trip takes Eden to a tony art gallery where she discovers the consequences of having once spurned Hedger. Unwittingly she had embarked upon a "hard and settled" life and had run the risk of appearing "an utter fool." Since their affair a generation ago, Hedger had become "one of the first men among the moderns" (457). While Cather exempts neither Hedger nor Eden from "modernness," Hedger's approach to modernity—"original, erratic, and . . . changing all the time" (458)—promises the artistic "success" Hedger's dealer claims for him. In contrast to Hedger's success, Cather describes Eden's success—stardom—as it shows in her face, as resembling "a hard and settled plaster-cast." Eden attained stardom by employing the apparatus of modernity—cars, telephones, spotlights—while barring modernity's opportunities for experimentation and liberation, which drove Hedger's success.

In *The Day of the Locust*, West telescopes this divide between Hedger's convictions and Eden's calculations in his single protagonist Tod Hackett. While holding down a day job as a studio illustrator, Tod sets out to paint the American future as he sees it emerging among his fellow newcomers to "the land of sunshine and oranges" (177). After tiring of "watching the waves come in at Venice," these future-hungering newcomers discover, in Tod's view, that if "you've seen one wave, you've seen them all." Turning from eternal nature, these wary seekers look and listen for what James called "the sharp sense of modernness." They look to "the airplanes at Glendale" and the hyperbolic mass-media promises of the thrills they've been denied: "If only a plane would crash once in a while, so they could watch the passengers being consumed in 'a holocaust of flame,' as the newspapers put it" (178).

Tod's calling as an artist, in contrast to his studio duties, is spurred by this collective mass betrayal. He sees this thwarted promise reflected in the ad hoc costumes, the "monstrously" heterogeneous architecture, and the death-besotted faces surrounding Tod both on the streets of Hollywood and on his studio's back lots and soundstages (59–61, 68, 80–81, 130–33). Cassandra-like Tod aspires to paint as his magnum opus "the burning of Los Angeles," the apocalypse that comes to obsess him: "He would paint their fury with respect, appreciating its awful anarchic power . . . to destroy civilization" (142). Janus-like, though, Tod also looks back. West repeatedly observes Tod conjuring painters from the seventeenth, eighteenth, and nineteenth centuries—Desiderio, Salvatore Rosa, Magnasco, Guardi, Goya, and Daumier. Tod paradoxically looks to this distant European past to help him repudiate his own more recent, American past, to move beyond "his race . . . his heritage" as well as the "training" that schooled him to produce "illustration or mere handsomeness" and earned him his job in Hollywood in the first place (60–61, 131, 142).

Didion also opens up this gap between what her would-be star protagonist came to Hollywood for and "the sharp sense of modernness" that vexed her as a Hollywood creature. In *Play It As It Lays* Didion sets a narrative challenge for both herself and her reader. Though linear, the narrative tracks Maria's course toward total paralysis and records her reactions to endlessly occupying the space between "plans" for the future and the constraints of "as it was" (6–7). Didion met this challenge, in part, by drawing on the formula that launched and framed the narrative in the 1937 release of *A Star Is Born*, even though Didion and Dunne omitted this sequence from their screenplay for the 1976 version of *A Star Is Born*. Just as Wellman and Carson's 1937 script begins in a frontier cabin, in *Play It As It Lays* the protagonist and would-be star also claims a frontier pedigree, one of several ways in which Didion conducts throughout the novel an "examination of nothing less than our heritage as Americans" (Wolff 481). Maria's American heritage includes her hometown: the frontier boomtown hamlet of Silver Wells, Nevada, with its "three hundred acres of mesquite," and coming-of-age on a now defunct cattle ranch (3–4). Countering the Hollywood cliché, Didion voids the guarantee of virtue such frontier origins conventionally imply in American narratives. After a family friend reminisces about Maria's father's unfulfilled plans for this "home," which revolved around "the ghost-town scheme, the midget golf, the automatic black jack concept," Maria bluntly hits him with the Turner thesis.[4] She reminds him that "there isn't any Silver Wells today. It's in the middle of a missile range."

By contrast, Hollywood's star-is-born formula maintains its aspirant's tie to her prairie home, soothing and smoothing the disturbances of "modernness" with the bromide of tradition. The opening frontier cabin scene in Wellman's version achieves this effect by pitting the orphaned would-be star Esther's grandmother against her custodial aunt and uncle. The aunt and uncle disparage both Esther's stellar aspirations and Hollywood in general. The grandmother (played by May Robson) encourages Esther and even surreptitiously subsidizes Esther's pursuit of stardom. Her argument equates Esther's quest for stardom with her own pioneer trek across the continent as a new bride. She recounts a familiar array of pioneer hardships including burying her young groom along the trail and moving on. The narrative comes full circle when the grandmother arrives in Hollywood—the end of the pioneer trail, geographically speaking. Grandma brings a booster shot of inspirational pioneer spiel to dissuade Esther, now a tragically bereaved widow like Grandma herself, from abandoning her dream by leaving Hollywood. Esther's embrace of perhaps the most "traditional values"—her grandmother's frontier pluck—deflects the impact of the modernness—the spotlights and radio microphones—that surrounds her at Grauman's Theater. By showing Esther arriving at a Hollywood benefit and awards ceremony with her frontier grandmother to protect her from modernity, this scene has all the trappings of the Hollywood Boulevard premiere scene that closes *The Day of the Locust*, plus the safety and comfort that Hollywood endings customarily guarantee.

The very representative of modernity, a radio announcer, stops Esther and her grandmother for comments as they enter the auditorium. Entering the future but bringing her reassuring pioneer virtues to keep the future as pure as our imagined frontier past, Esther's grandmother announces that she's in Hollywood to stay and that, like that of her granddaughter, her own example ought to inspire everyone else who dreams of Hollywood. Even more attached to tradition, her granddaughter simply tells the radio listeners her name, neither her given name Esther Blodgett nor her studio-invented stage name Vicki Lester, but her spousal name. With the star proudly proclaiming "Hello everybody, this is Mrs. Norman Maine," the script diffuses the sting of modernness that James identified as inextricable from the phenomenon of stardom. Esther/Vicki surrenders to tradition with her emphatic affirmation of "family values," a reminder that this self-made woman is as much a creature of her mentoring self-sacrificing husband as she is of her studio.

This affirmation of tradition also ends subsequent *A Star Is Born* remakes, despite the absence in them of framing frontier backstories. The

1954 and 1976 versions also move to tie the emerging star's rise to a pre-sumably stable past. These versions also bind the rising star to her tragically flawed mentor and spouse who embodies a stabilizing tradition without the girlhood tie to tradition in the form of a pioneer matriarch.

In the 1954 version the mentoring fading star husband, the Pygma-lion figure Norman Maine (played by James Mason), inspires his Galatea (Garland) by bequeathing to her his legacy as an actor. Harkening back to the Victorian stage (in an English accent) "for credibility" (Basinger 3), he assures her:

> You've got that little something extra that Ellen Terry talked about. Ellen Terry, a great actress long before you were born. She said that that was what star quality was—that little something extra. Well, you've got it.

The Mason character establishes his legitimacy as the spokesman for the legacy of the London stage with recurring, familiar snippets of Shake-speare—"my kingdom for a horse" and "once more unto the breach." The authority of the tradition that Norman Maine represents and this tradition's power to withstand the triumph of modernness, which James linked to stardom, persists posthumously. Maine's death-by-drowning confirms an axiom of stardom that poet-screenwriter Joseph Moncure March pronounced upon his departure from Hollywood: "taking 'a beating' has come to be regarded an essential factor of stardom" ("Star Gazing"). The mercenary studio flack and Maine's nemesis throughout the movie (Jack Carson) grudgingly eulogizes the dead, definitively "beaten" star. Pouring a scotch, he turns to his secretary with an (uncredited) line from T. S. Eliot's "The Hollow Men" (customarily read as a lamentation against "modernness") in linking Maine's death to "the way the world ends, not with a bang but a whimper."

A show-business tale but not strictly speaking a Hollywood story, the 1976 remake of *A Star Is Born* shows its attachment to tradition by displacing Hollywood lifestyle clichés. Instead of frontier pioneers and Shakespeare, the Didion-Dunne script harkens back to an ostensibly more venerable and authentic indigenous American tradition. While the first two versions located the star couple's romantic hideaway where fans ex-pect Hollywood luminaries to go (on the beach at Malibu), the Streisand and Kristofferson avatars set out to build, with such helpful manifestations of modernness as a personal backhoe and bulldozer, a pueblo-style desert retreat in Arizona. Didion and Dunne's screenplay has the couple envi-sioning their life in this retreat as placidly and conventionally domestic:

baking bread and bearing children. Director Frank Pierson recalls instructing Streisand to stress domesticity, to play her scene in the pueblo kitchen "out of an old *I Love Lucy* show" (Pierson). To highlight the star couple's affinity for frontier desert purity and their adopted pueblo heritage, the Didion-Dunne script also changes the beneficiaries of their Hollywood benefit performance, the spectacle that ends all three movies. In the 1937 and 1954 versions, the star couple performed at benefits for movie-industry charities. The 1976 adaptation substituted an American Indian relief organization. Literary renderings of stardom, from James through Didion, by contrast, never depict stars, recognized or aspiring, as "playing benefits" for any charities or eleemosynary causes. This omission leaves open questions about the *benefits*, social as well artistic, of stardom itself. Such questions about the benefits or ravages of stardom implicate audiences as well as star-makers and star-aspirants.

As he determines to kill himself at the end of the 1954 *A Star Is Born*, Norman Maine resigns himself to belonging to a passive audience, to having become another interchangeable male-gazer and stargazer. He asks his wife, the newly constellated star, one last rhetorical question: "Mind if I look at you one more time?" This question speaks to the uses and the value of the stellar optic. A staple of mass culture and "literary" fiction for over a century now and an indispensable gambit among Hollywood's self-critics, such open questions about stardom have also come to preoccupy Hollywood intellect.

Notes

1. *Internet Movie Database* lists a total of eleven writers for this script, including such luminaries as Dorothy Parker, Ben Hecht, Ring Lardner Jr., and Budd Schulberg.

2. Tod as *Todt* (German for dead) and Hackett as in the noun "hack," a synonym for violently cutting to pieces as a verb.

3. Changing the last name of the title character from Blodgett to Hoffman seems an accommodation to the public perception of Streisand as distinctly Jewish, a perception emphatically affirmed and exploited three years earlier in Sydney Pollack and Arthur Laurents's *The Way We Were*. Nonetheless, Didion and Dunne kept the given name, Esther, used in the earlier versions. A common name among both Jews and American Protestants, the name *Esther* bears a scriptural resonance especially apt in the context of "star is born narratives," because the name alludes to the story of a Ms. Nobody from Nowhere whose beauty, talent, integrity, and deferential demeanor made her the queen of Persia and the rescuer of her people.

4. The most influential "thesis" in American historiography: in 1893, Frederick Jackson Turner argued that the conclusion contained in the 1890 census that "there can hardly be said to be a frontier line" in the American West "marks the closing of a great historic movement. Up to our own day American history has been in a large degree the history of the colonization of the Great West. The existence of an area of free land, its continuous recession, and the advance of American settlement westward, explain American development."

Civilization: The Movie

George, we're trying to have a civilization here.

—JERRY SEINFELD

It ain't easy civilizing this motherfucker.

—THE WIRE

From the living room comes the sound of the television. Gabriel is attacking civilization. Now we shall lose him again.

—A. B. YEHOSHUA

I

Modernism and the movies grew up together. Between the world wars, the impact of literary modernism peaked at the same time movies established themselves as a dominant form of mass entertainment and as an influential artistic practice (Goldstein 7–8; North 62). The coincidence of the "moment of high modernism . . . between 1914 and 1925" and "cinema . . . in its infancy" (J. Orr 2) has become a commonplace of cultural history. Movies had already "become commercially important" by "around 1910" (Boorstin, *Image* 149) and as culturally powerful as "cathedrals" had once been (Gabler 50). By World War II, Hollywood intellect reached maturity as the influx into Hollywood of New York writers and refugees from Hitler began to meld the intellectual aspirations of modernism and Hollywood's necessarily market-driven populism as "the center of mass writing" (Stead 115). This influx resulted in an intellectual climate many newcomers found as intellectually vibrant as what they had been accustomed to in New York or Berlin (Giovacchini 5, 72).

As an emerging mass medium, movies became influential, as many modernist writers aspired to do, by mediating "the change from Victorian to modern life . . . at once so hopeful, so problematical, and so fearful" (May, *Screening* xii). Film historian David Thomson has argued that as Anglo-European literature "soars free in 'modernism,'" modernist writers looked to movies, and still photography before them, "for a new philosophy . . . a record of the past, in an obliging and patient form [of] memory" (*Whole* 53). Most sweepingly, Geoffrey O'Brien adds to this broad consensus by tracing the very birth of modernity to the emergence of movies as "a cultural currency permitting everyone to transcend the tribal, a global lingo penetrating . . . ethnic and professional enclaves," resulting in "the birth of cosmopolitanism" (*Phantom* 41).

Sharing a formative era and reacting to the same historical transformations, modernism and Hollywood also shared an anxiety that has persisted into the twenty-first century. Tom Gunning associates this anxiety with Hollywood in describing the movies as the emblem of modernity that at once provoked and inspired "both apocalyptic and millennial" expectations of "destruction and renewal" (301–2). Notwithstanding facile equations of aesthetic innovation and revolutionary iconoclasm, modernist writers and Hollywood moviemakers bear a similarly divided relationship to modernity, its promises, and its vexations.

Writing in the middle of the twentieth century and laboring in the shadow of modernist orthodoxy, the English novelists Margaret Drabble and John Berger noticed two prevailing yet countervailing tendencies among twentieth-century artists. They refract "traditional means for radical expression" (Drabble 40) and, conversely, they often "accept the realities of modern life . . . even make a dream of modern reality." Moreover, they respond to the imperative to grapple with the "complexity of . . . mass civilization" while repudiating "modern technics" (Berger 181). Embracing these contradictions, both elite-culture modernists and mass-culture entertainers have managed to experiment formally and spur technical innovation while, at the same time, promoting traditionalist nostalgic, even retrograde rhetorical agendas, and vice versa, often within the same work. These producers and performers, artists and theorists, at once embrace and look askance at what Yeats, in a late poem, called the "manifold illusions" with which "civilization is hooped together" (299). Such hooped illusions include Ezra Pound's freewheeling translations from classic Chinese, Provencal, and Anglo-Saxon; Eliot's worldly, cosmopolitan, eclectic, modernity-resisting *Waste Land* (Walkowitz 7); nostalgia-colored yet custom-questioning fiction by Fitzgerald, Hemingway, Faulkner, Cather, Lawrence, and Woolf; and popular yet provocative Hollywood movies ranging from *Birth of a Nation, Modern Times, The Wizard of Oz, Carnal Knowledge,* and *Raging Bull.* These affinities have prompted one scholar to argue for extending what academics call "high modernism" to embrace movies as "vernacular modernism" (Hansen 65; Rabinowitz 6). Beyond such matters of scholarly taxonomy, this mass-elite convergence illustrates Milan Kundera's observation that to be modern means to "be both progressive and conformist, conservative and a rebel, at the same time . . . the only modernism worthy of the name is anti-modernism" (35).

This dissonance links the bohemians and the intelligentsia who made modernism with the entertainment merchants who made popular movies. They all voiced, sustained, and exploited the apocalyptic apprehension Tom Gunning has described. They packaged this anxiety for the marketplace of ideas, establishing—and exploiting—over the course of the century a permanent *civilization panic,* which has become such a rhetorical commonplace and widespread topic of discussion that an influential French theorist has, without further specification, recently referred to civilization panic as the core business of intellectuals. "The crisis of civilization," Julia Kristeva recently stressed, is the "task" with which "the intellectual is confronted" simply by virtue of inhabiting "what we call—too often disparagingly—modernity" (15, 17). Like the weather, this "crisis of civilization" has apparently become the condition everyone likes to talk about but never does anything about.

Since emerging about a century ago, civilization panic—perennial mass media provocations over "the future of civilization" (S. Cohen 7, 44; K. Thompson vii, 31)—seems to have spawned several of the popular "moral panic" narratives that have become a chronic feature of modern public discourse. Studs Terkel's reminiscence about one of the vagrant tenants in the low-rent Chicago residential hotel his family ran during the 1920s points to the prevalence of this preoccupation. Nicknamed "Civilization" by fellow tenants, all he talked about was the "doom" of civilization along with crank cures for some its maladies (55).

During the same decade, early film critic Clive Bell (L. Marcus 99) warily questioned civilization panic. Though sheltered by the illustriously civilizing climate of Bloomsbury—at once a "shrine of" and an "experiment in civilization" in Bell's view (Frouda 5)—Bell became so "startled" by his compatriots' civilization panic—the "fear and force" with which they advocated "civilization"—that he silenced himself for fear of being "sent to prison" simply for asking the question implicit in their heated advocacy: "And what is civilization?" (13, 157). Though perhaps overstated to suit the rhetorical occasion, Bell's fear of incarceration delayed by a decade the completion of his book, *Civilization*. *Civilization* addressed what Bell took to be the century's chronically urgent question.

The power of "civilization panic" to silence even the voluble, privileged Bell illustrates its impact in legitimating forceful reactions to perceived threats or pathologies—as in the long-familiar phrase "sick civilization" (Marcuse 43, 245; Schuman 467). Such reactions range from the allegedly remedial Reconstruction Klan violence depicted in Griffith's *Birth of a Nation* to Woodrow Wilson's justifications for entering World War I and the ensuing "hatred of the Hun" movie subgenre (Young) to the Bush administration's so-called Patriot Act and the civilization-defense narratives that issued from Hollywood in the wake of 9/11. These include stories about troubled singleminded protectors of all we supposedly—and unanimously—value such as *American Gangster*, *The Departed*, and *Munich* as well as the cathartic solo vigilante quests depicted in David Cronenberg's *A History of Violence* and Clint Eastwood's *Mystic River*.

As invoked and conjured by statesmen and entertainment-merchants bent on arousing civilization panic, "civilization" doesn't refer to a set of fixed, explicitly set-forth standards, but rather to an array of self-congratulatory narratives, no matter how dark the writers' ultimate prophecy or prognosis. Gertrude Stein highlighted this self-congratulatory spin, generously reminiscing that "in the period between 1900 and 1939 . . . there really was a serious effort by humanity to be civilized" (38), which, as Stein and her readers knew, had collapsed catastrophically by 1939. The popular English novelist Elinor Glyn also offers a telling contrast to the ubiquitous gloom-and-doom rhetoric that "civilization" as a concept tends to provoke. In her 1937 recollections of her silent-era Hollywood sojourn (during which her 1927 novel eponymously inaugurated the durable mystique of the "it girl" first embodied on screen by Clara Bow), Glyn reassures readers that even "Hollywood" has "moved forward many steps along the path of civilization" (*Romantic* 308). With an irony perhaps more inadvertent than Stein's, Glyn thanks the Depression for restoring Hollywood's "soul" and its commitment to civilization.

More typically, though, Hollywood's Depression-prompted civilization panic took a more progressive turn. Mervin LeRoy's Oscar-nominated 1932 adaptation of the muckraking autobiography *I Am a Fugitive from a Chain Gang* turns on its hero's recapture. A holding-cell press-conference scene shows the wronged captive (Paul Muni) denouncing Georgia's penal system and agreeing to write a first-person exposé. LeRoy follows Muni's vow to get "this rotten chain-gang system exposed," with a process shot of headlines flashing on the screen, including one that asks: "*IS THIS CIVILIZATION?*"

This rhetorical question had two diametrically opposed *obvious* answers during the 1930s. The first, *no*, came from the perspective of LeRoy's docudrama. But a more powerful consensus about Dixie, Georgia, in particular, home of the exposed chain-gang system, became the basis for Hollywood's most enduring spectacle by the end of the decade. Likewise invoking civilization as an ideal, a far more popular Georgia saga, *Gone With the Wind*, opened in 1939 with a title card proclaiming its subject as "a civilization gone with the wind."

Civilization's enemies in *I Am a Fugitive from a Chain Gang* appear as the "brutes" in charge of the penal system. Elsewhere in the movies they appear as "barbarians," "savages" (Raphael, *Personal* 77), "primitives," or "heathens." In opposition to such foes, civilization-panic narratives customarily claim—ideologically, invidiously, or at best aspirationally—to represent, variously, "Christendom," "the West," "Europe," and especially the powerful nation-states and superior "races" (Aryan, Nordic, Anglo-Saxon) that made them. Their self-legitimating rhetoric typically entails asserting what the French call their *mission civilisatrice* or what Rudyard Kipling infamously proclaimed the "white man's burden." While also promoting such narratives, both Hollywood and several modernist works also distinguished themselves by probing, elaborating, and questioning these self-congratulatory public consensuses, implicitly acknowledging Walter Benjamin's famous observation that every "document of civilization" is also a "document of barbarism" (256).

As the ubiquitous anxiety over the fate, meaning, and the very possibility of defining what we loosely and uneasily call *civilization* became an overriding reflex among influential cultural guardians and insurgents alike, voices in both camps vied to "damn . . . Hollywood . . . as a threat to civilization" (Wollen 10). The curator of Berlin's Cinematheque museum recently confirmed the view of Hollywood as a participant in the long modern battle over civilization, of Hollywood's status not simply as the native home of American movies but as a durable world civilization in its own right: "Hollywood is not America. Hollywood is like Mecca. It's not considered only American, it's considered the cinema of the world" (Reesman).

Even the most facile journalistic accounts of this battle stress how the events roughly book-ending the twentieth century, the so-called Great

War—"the crash of civilization," as Henry James fretted (*Letters* 251)—and the 9/11 al-Qaeda attacks in 2001 reflexively invoke civilization panic. The end of the Great War not only failed to quell civilization panic, it also heightened fears that, in Winston Churchill's words, the West faced a "world-wide conspiracy for the overthrow of civilization" set to "pulverize . . . what is left of civilization" (Baker), so that such rhetoric became a staple of public discourse for generations to come.

This chronic anxiety prompted American presidents from Wilson (63, 511) to George W. Bush (Stevenson) to assume the mantle of the defender of civilization, championing "all civilized people" or standing firm "between civilization and chaos." In 2005 British Prime Minister Tony Blair (Cowell) and director Steven Spielberg upped the ante by claiming to speak on behalf of "all civilizations"; with the help of screenwriters Tony Kushner and Eric Roth, Spielberg championed "every civilization." Ventriloquizing Israeli Prime Minister Golda Meir at the beginning of *Munich*, Spielberg established civilization anxiety as "at once the film's precipitating event and its subject of study" (C. Orr).

> People say we can't afford to be civilized. I've always resisted such people.
> . . . Today, I am hearing with new ears. Every civilization finds it necessary
> to negotiate compromises with its own values.

Rhetorical flourishes like the Meir speech in *Munich* have become so commonplace as to become subject to derision. David Mamet's 1988 play *Speed the Plow* shows two Hollywood producers who aim in their movies to "drop a dime on western civilization" (24), while Jane Smiley's 2007 novel *Ten Days in the Hills* quotes a producer announcing that to succeed in Hollywood you need to "question the nature of civilization" (21).

This familiar century-old rhetoric that Spielberg exploits shows the powers-that-be, both Hollywood and a militarized nation-state, claiming "civilization" as their *mission*, as the cause *we* (on-screen, behind the cameras, and in our seats) represent and "our" antagonists threaten. Almost a decade after 9/11, the "civilizational struggle" narrative and "civilizational imperatives" continued to shadow the national elections from the United States to Russia to Australia, underscoring the rhetorical durability and versatility of civilization panic (Bai; Chafets 73; Hertzberg, "Follow" 42; C. Levy). Civilization panic has become such a handy ideological trigger that less dramatic developments than war and terror can prompt the resort to such rhetoric. Diplomatic, economic developments such as the expansion of the European Community can pique these anxieties and provoke heated exchanges over who embodies and what constitutes civilization. For example, the perennial debate over Turkey's suitability for membership in "Europe" prompted one Turkish official to protest that "we're as civilized as they are" and to sigh about being "so bored with all this back and forth about whether they're going to accept us or not, whether we are Asian or whether we're European" and about the way formally designated Europeans "talk as if we come from a completely different world," while overlooking the degree to which Turks see themselves as "descendants of ancient civilizations" (Sachs).

Reading preferences throughout the twentieth century also illustrate the durability of this preoccupation, the stimulus for *civilization panic*. Some widely read or at least much-discussed transatlantic modern "classics" illustrate both the prevalence and, for some more caustic observers, the fatuity of this preoccupation. Widespread interest in Oswald Spengler's 1923 tome *The Decline of the West*, and the enduring interest in Freud's elegiac, psychosexual 1929 account of civilization panic, *Civilization and Its Discontents*, resonate pithily and metaphorically in Anglophone modernism. Wyndham Lewis lamented a "dreary boiling anger at the contradictions of civilized life" in his 1918 novel *Tarr* (10). Two years later Ezra Pound pictured the modern West as "an old bitch gone in the teeth . . . a botched civilization" with its signature image the "accelerated grimace" disseminated by a poetry-usurping "prose kinema" ("Mauberly"; Goldstein 21). Even as crabbed and dogmatic a civilization champion as Pound ranged eclectically across continents and millennia in envisaging his ideal civilization (Zhu 57, 70). For all his hyperventilating about "civilization" and *Kultur*, Pound's heterogeneity is, at least rhetorically, representative of the intellectual limitations of civilization panic. Among modernists and Hollywood moviemakers civilization has always denoted, at most, an amorphous aspiration. Though widely and enthusiastically embraced, civilization as an ideal seems constrained by the unwillingness or inability of its champions—from D. W. Griffith to Will and Ariel Durant—to set a definitive standard by singling out only one historically and geographically demarcated civilization.

II

In contrast to the expatriate Pound's "bitching," stay-at-home American writers following the Great War addressed this anxiety more warily than did Europe's darker prophets. Such wariness encompasses some of the most memorable verse and fiction of the 1920s. Harlem Renaissance luminary Countee Cullen's agonized epiphany at the close of his 1927 poem "Heritage" illustrates this wariness. Despite the way this poem itself deftly affiliates the poet with the supposedly civilized practice of highly wrought stanzaic English verse, the poem ends insisting that the poet's relationship to civilization and his grasp of civilization endlessly elude him (see chapter IV): "Not yet has my heart or head / In the least realized / They and I are civilized."

Two years earlier, and much more famously, F. Scott Fitzgerald, probably the American modernist most associated with Hollywood, evoked both the amplitude and inanity of civilization panic. A scene early in *The Great Gatsby* shows Tom Buchanan—a bully, an adulterer, and arguably a prototype for civilization champion George W. Bush (F. Rich)—holding forth. Spokesman for "the idle rich"—the "careless people" who "smashed up things and creatures and then retreated back into their money" (180–81)—Buchanan pontificates, Cassandra-like, and postures as the champion of civilization. With a "profundity" that his wife attributes to his "reading deep books with long words in them," he prophesies (17):

> "Civilization's going to pieces," broke out Tom violently. "I've gotten to be a terrible pessimist about things. Have you read *The Rise of the Colored Empires* by this man Goddard? . . . a fine book, and everybody ought to read it. The idea is if we don't look out the white race will be—will be utterly submerged. It's all scientific stuff; it's been proved. . . . This fellow has worked out the whole thing. It's up to us, who are the dominant race, to watch out or these other races will have control of things. . . . This idea is that we're Nordics . . . we've produced all the things that go to make civilization—oh, science and art, and all that. Do you see?"

With such phrases as "scientific stuff" and "science, and art, and all that," Ftizgerald exposes Tom as no more a bearer of the fruits of civilization than the allegedly "lesser races" whom he stigmatizes (Hitchens 285). Fitzgerald clinches his ridicule of this rhetoric by interrupting Buchanan's rant and so turning his question "Do you see?" into a question unworthy of an answer. This interruption comes from a prosaic material token of civilization—of "all that." A ringing telephone summons Buchanan to talk with his current mistress (whose nose this paragon of civilization later breaks with a punch in the face). Though Fitzgerald renders him as a heedless buffoon, Buchanan's rhetoric, his identification of himself and his "kind" with civilization, was a perennial, familiar, and all too often respected stance over the course of the twentieth century. For example, a generation later, one of Sinclair Lewis's civilization champions, a wounded World War II veteran, bluntly echoed Buchanan ("Yessir, if we want to preserve our standards of civilization, we got to be firm and keep the niggers in their place") in *Kingsblood Royal* (16).

The beginning of *Gatsby* also links modernity—newness and change, disruptive as well as redemptive—with yet another everyday modern technological phenomenon: the movies. When the narrator envisions himself as a "pathfinder" newly endowed with "the freedom of the neighborhood," he announces, "just as things grow in fast movies, I had that familiar conviction that life was beginning over again" (8). Later this narrator finds that "the movies" incarnate the source of much of the disconcerting verve, the "raw vigor that chafed under the old euphemisms," of Gatsby's parties and associates this vigor with the moviemakers among Gatsby's party guests: "Newton Orchid, who controlled Films Par Excellence, and Eckhaust and Clyde Cohen and Don S. Schwartze (the son) and Arthur McCarty, all connected with the movies in one way or another" (114, 66).

At the truncated end of his career Fitzgerald revisited civilization panic, shifting from "deep books with long words in them" to Hollywood movies as the arena for contesting the meaning of civilization. Fitzgerald's last novel, the never-completed *The Love of the Last Tycoon*, tempers the pontification of civilization's self-styled guardians. It also shifts decisively the burden of this guardianship to Hollywood. Instead of a sinister buffoon like Tom Buchanan, the champion of civilization appears in *The Last Tycoon* as a more appealing and complex hero: "Like Lincoln . . . a leader carrying on a long war on many fronts" (107). A legendary studio production chief named Monroe Stahr, this Lincolnesque hero harbors an unrealized ambition to film the Russian revolution (an aspiration Hollywood finally realized forty years later with Paramount's release of auteur-minded Warren Beatty's labor of love, *Reds*). Stahr "knew there were many stories about Russia" but he thought "not so much about Russia as about the picture about Russia" (60): about the revolution as a Hollywood production.

This fascination of Stahr's notwithstanding, the last section of the narrative shows Stahr combating the "Reds" on behalf of Western civilization as he understands it. Stahr doesn't merely insist on a private meeting at his luxurious home with the Communist union organizer representing his employees. He also instructs him to "bring one of his books along" (118). With this request, Fitzgerald stresses Stahr's view of himself as a champion of ideas and not merely an executive with labor costs to control. Fitzgerald deepens Stahr's view of himself as the intellectual champion of Western civilization by detailing his preparation for this meeting. Stahr's perspective broadens—turns global—with the movies he orders to be sent to him for screening—unnamed postrevolutionary Russian films (presumably Eisenstein's and Pudovkin's), *The Cabinet of Dr. Caligari*, and *Un Chien Andalou*, along with instructions that his studio's "script department get him up a two-page 'treatment' of the *Communist Manifesto*" (119).

Fitzgerald's apparently paradoxical juxtaposition of Stahr's affinity *for* Eisenstein and his aversion to the Bolshevism that inspired Eisenstein reflects the extent to which revolutionary upheaval and the authority of a civilization often occupy the same aesthetic ground (Benjamin 256). A view like Stahr's, of the movies as an antidote to, antagonist of, or refuge from revolutionary upheaval, surfaces in *Blood and Oil*, Lev Nussimbaum's 1934 memoir of escaping the Russian Revolution. Nussimbaum recalls how his family found themselves refugees in what is now Tajikistan and settling into the only "civilized lodging" available: "the lodgings into which we moved are the most beautiful of my boyhood. We rented the motion picture theater, perhaps the only one between the Caspian Sea and the grave of Timur . . . we settled down in the large cool place, the only house in the city that had an almost European toilet" (137). Although "performances had to be discontinued" at first, when the Nussimbaums moved in, they eventually "bowed to the will of the people." They agreed to permit their home to offer "public amusements" in order to forestall the "disturbances" that "the governing body" feared and so to help maintain civilization while also enjoying it.

What Nussimbaum discovered became firmly entrenched farther west during the interwar years. Movie theaters now fondly remembered as movie "palaces" became fixtures in cities across Europe and North America. These palaces often imitated legendary architectural monuments from past and "exotic" civilizations and drew on an array of canonized architectural styles such as Moorish, baroque, and pharaonic. Evoking European "models of social hierarchy" (May, *Big* 102),

> the palaces had names like the Alhambra, the Luxor, the Roxy; the auditoriums were evocative of pagoda pavilions or Persian courts or some celestial paradise with flocks of fleecy blond cherubim suspended in blue ether. They were uninhibited American kitsch, the product of a commercial culture dizzied by fantasies of European or Eastern magnificence. (Denby, "Big" 56)

Hollywood's extravagantly exotic set design also reflected Stahr's faith in Hollywood as the curator of civilizations and "custodian of . . . heritage," a role also ascribed to intellectuals ("Parnassus"). Fitzgerald illustrated this faith early in *The Last Tycoon* when he set in motion the novel's romance plot with a flood engulfing Stahr's studio. The flood arrives bearing movie-set flotsam, including a head of the Hindu god of destruction, Shiva. "Immense and imperturbable . . . oblivious," adrift on an "impromptu river," this remnant was large enough to serve as a rescue raft—a refuge for a pair of stranded studio employees (26, 54). This scene recalls and illustrates Austrian novelist Joseph Roth's 1925 remark that "the orient is a movie" (167), and the degree to which for Hollywood not only "the orient" but *all* civilizations had become a movie by 1940.

III

The Last Tycoon and Fitzgerald's career end just at this point where both Western civilization as a stabilizing concept and Hollywood's investment in this concept falter. This coincidence seems to countenance Fitzgerald's preoccupation with this concept throughout the interwar years (J. Bloom, "Occidental"). This preoccupation yielded to the realization that evolves over the course of his three mature novels and of a career increasingly enmeshed in the friction between the ideal of a Medician renaissance Hollywood, with its civilizing mission that Vachel Lindsay envisioned in 1915 (1: 307), and the company town that sheltered the dying Fitzgerald and enabled him to pay his last bar bills. Walter Benn Michaels recently summed up this realization, which accompanies a preoccupation, like Fitzgerald's, with civilization as a concept and underlies an investment, like Stahr's, in civilization as a fixed ideal. The recognition Michaels cites of Western "civilization as something one remembers instead of learns" (80) was reflected in Hollywood's commitment to assuming this burden of collective remembering as eagerly as and perhaps more successfully than museums, libraries, colleges, and universities.

This understanding of civilization as mnemonic confection has become axiomatic and, like many concepts become axiomatic, meets increasingly with resistance. This understanding and the resistance to it manifest themselves nowadays as a tacit imperative among intellectuals and academics to maintain "implicit quotation marks around the word" *civilization*, argues Andrew Delbanco. This move serves to keep open the question of the primacy of so-called Western civilization (xii). Over the past century, though, resistance to a normative endorsement of Western civilization has gone hand in hand with conceptually assenting to it. Reportedly asked in 1930 about the status of Western civilization, Mohandas Gandhi mischievously demonstrated the need for the "implicit quotation marks" that vex civilization's self-proclaimed guardians: "What do I think of Western civilization? I think it would be a very good idea" (Mishra 129–30).

Soon after the 2001 al-Qaeda attacks Edward Said highlighted the extent to which a central modern argument turns on this question of whether we ought to maintain or drop the ironic quotation marks around "civilization" that Gandhi's quip countenances and Delbanco favors dropping. Said's post-9/11 critique of Samuel Huntington's expediently influential 1994 essay "The Clash of Civilizations" finally takes to task the legacy that Huntington inspired and the 9/11 attacks exacerbated: "an anxiety about the will and the coherence of the West" and "whether the West will remain true to itself and its mission" (Ajami 10). Said challenges not only the demagoguery civilization panic fosters but also the effect civilization panic has in both blinding and binding us to the way civilization works. It works, in Said's view, not by boundary-setting but by boundary-blurring, in particular the boundary between our understanding of the word *civilization* as signaling a fragile aspiration as opposed to offering a matter-of-fact description:

> The major contest in most modern cultures concerns the definition or interpretation of each culture . . . the unattractive possibility that a great deal of demagogy . . . is involved in presuming to speak for a whole . . . civilization . . . Conrad . . . understood that the distinctions between civilized London and "the heart of darkness" collapsed quickly in extreme situations, and that the heights of European civilization could instantaneously fall into the most barbarous practices without transition or preparation. (11–13)

In citing *Heart of Darkness* as a founding scripture of both civilization panic *and* the critical resistance it calls for, Said harkens suggestively back to the era when movies first exerted a cultural impact. Midway chronologically between *Heart of Darkness* and *Gatsby*, not only did the Great War rage but, even before the U.S. entry into the war, Hollywood volunteered to adjudicate on behalf of civilization and so exploit the civilization the war inflamed.

Most suggestively, proto-auteur and studio-system originator Thomas Ince made the study of civilization a vital Hollywood preoccupation, perhaps its first sustained intellectual challenge, with a 1916 spectacle that he modestly titled *Civilization*. Variously subtitled "an epic of humanity" and "the greatest production of modern times" in publicity posters, *Civilization* opens with a prologue announcing that "civilization has been misnamed in modern times" and that thanks to war and greed neither "can we hope for civilization" nor "call ourselves civilized." Ince ends his fable by showing Jesus come to earth and to the screen to take the place of a Junker admiral turned militant pacifist in the middle of World War I.

When, a century hence, posterity looks for the 9/11 analogue to the lost Ince fable, critics will turn to Manoel de Oliveira's *Um Filme Falado* (*A Talking Picture*). A reflection of the director's commitment to "grappling with the death throes of . . . civilizations" (Lim 15) and set, like Ince's movie, largely at sea—on a cruise ship—this narratively spare fictional travelogue follows a polyglot Portuguese history professor and her eight-year-old daughter during the summer of 2001 en route from Lisbon to Bombay. Before cutting the cruise short with a terrorist attack, Oliveira keeps the promise his title makes. Both shipboard and during shore visits, the characters entertain explanations and utter affirmations of the ideal of *civilization*. The most sustained of these takes place in Giza, in the following (subtitled) mother-daughter catechistical exchange:

> Can you see those magnificent monuments?
>
> What are they called?
>
> They're known as the pyramids of Egypt. They're famous for their great importance and because they represent the greatest civilization of antiquity.
>
> What does civilization mean?
>
> Civilization is what man creates and develops over the course of time by using his intelligence.
>
> How?

At this point the camera backs up to show the characters in the foreground and both the Sphinx and pyramid rising behind them. Then the exchange continues:

> Like the pyramids for their great size and for the surrounding method of construction.
>
> If it was so difficult, why did they do it?
>
> They built it precisely because they were civilized people.

Just the before the terrorist threat surfaces, the cruise ship's captain (John Malkovich) leads his celebrity tablemates in a polyglot surrender to the global triumph of English and nostalgic paean to Greece as "the cradle of civilization."

Both this nostalgia and this triumphalism recall Hollywood's earlier civilization sagas. Ince's storied friend and rival D. W. Griffith not only brought the Hollywood feature to maturity as a distinctive art form and commercial product, but also was the first director to realize how "compelling" a "mix of beauty and intellect" and what a shaper of "national consciousness" the movies could become (Blum 8, 158). With his 1916 saga *Intolerance*, Griffith also established Hollywood as an arbiter—a "custodian" ("Parnassus") and "rememberer" (Michaels)—of civilizations. As early as 1907, the movies were heralded as lifting "the sentient life of the half-civilized" Americans "at the bottom" socially and those economically "closer to the civilized beings at the top" (Czitrom 48). The now-mythic proponent of this ideal, Griffith inaugurated the "single fundamental film" that "the American cinema constantly shoots and re-shoots": "the birth of a nation-civilization" (Deleuze 148).

Maintaining this tradition, in 1920, Elinor Glyn—English émigré novelist, screenwriter, and Hollywood "courtier"—took on the burden of leading Hollywood's charge on behalf of civilization. Rallying moviemakers, armed with "the glorification of romance," she urged resistance to the Bolshevik threat of a "terrible eclipse of civilization" and defense of "the whole beautiful culture of our modern world" (Glyn, *Romantic* 292–93, 297; Roach 60–61). During the next decade, John Ford, an influential bearer of this legacy among first-generation talkie-directors, "constructed" in movie after movie "a scale model of all he wished to preserve of civilization" (O'Brien, *Phantom* 125).

In first assuming this role for Hollywood, Griffith was pursuing the agenda set forth a year earlier in Lindsay's manifesto promoting *The Art of the Motion Picture* and its hopeful claim that the rise of Hollywood constituted a cultural renaissance comparable to the mid-nineteenth-century flourishing of American letters in New England. Lindsay cites Longfellow as the poetic exemplar of this renaissance. Laurence Goldstein's reminder that Griffith's familiarity with Lindsay's manifesto prompted the auteur to invite Lindsay to attend the premiere of *Intolerance* (21) makes it seem less than pure coincidence that lines from Longfellow's *The New England Tragedies* appear in a pamphlet advertising *Intolerance*, indicating its ideological and rhetorical agenda.

> "Why touch upon such themes?" perhaps some friend
> May ask, incredulous; "and to what good end?
> Why drag again into the light of day
> The errors of an age long passed away?"

I answer: "For the lessons that they teach:
The tolerance of opinion and of speech."
　　　—Longfellow 302

The understanding of civilization on which *Intolerance* rests assumes that to be civilized entails looking at the errors and lessons of the past, an assumption made explicit at the start of *Intolerance* with the on-screen promise that the following "drama of comparisons" aims to show "our highest ideals."

As the instrument of his inquiry, Griffith carries on the kind of curatorial anthologizing that would become a signature gesture among the most influential literary modernists during the 1920s; hence, Griffith's intertitles include, in addition to the usual dialogue and exposition, quotations from and references to Herodotus, Wilde, Whitman, Oxford Assyriologist A. H. Sayce, the American biblical scholar James Hastings, and the French Bible illustrator J. J. Tissot, along with Longfellow and scripture and explanatory footnotes glossing "Huguenots," Hammurabi, wine in ancient Hebrew ritual, the laws of Cyrus's empire, "recently excavated cylinders of Nabonidus and Cyrus," accounts of the destruction of "a civilization of countless ages," the disappearance of a "universal written language" from "the face of the earth," and Babylonian feast customs. Its varied references and allusions and its cross-cutting segmentation make *Intolerance* a modernist "prototype" (Kawin 104), which presages the footnoted, densely allusive probing of the meaning, possibilities, and risks of civilization in *The Waste Land* five years later. Daniel Boorstin suggests this affinity in observing how Griffith "had a hard time . . . when he tried a complexly interwoven" narrative in *Intolerance* "a boldly experimental, challenging model" that—like *The Waste Land*—"has not been successfully followed, while the prototypical *Birth of a Nation* has been made again and again" (*Image* 147). Deleuze's description of Griffith's approach as "encompassing . . . epochs and civilizations" so that "the parts thrown together by parallel montage are the civilizations themselves" (131) invites such comparisons between *Intolerance* and *The Waste Land* as roughly contemporaneous moves to encompass civilization panic. As Griffith described his approach and his movie's desired effect, "events are not set forth in their historic sequence . . . but as they might flash across a mind seeking to parallel different ages" (Everson 90).

In pursuing this effect, Griffith played the auteur long before the emergence and ascendancy of auteur theory in the 1950s, when—invoking the ever-handy token of civilizing aspiration—Jean-Luc Godard conceived of "the *auteur*" as a latter-day Shakespeare. In translation, Andrew Sarris codified auteurism and pronounced "the second premise of the auteur theory" as "the distinguishable personality of the director as a criterion of value" and the "ultimate premise" of auteurism as "concerned with interior meaning" and "cinema as an art" (Kael, "Circles" 12). In promoting *Intolerance*, Griffith issued a pamphlet instructing viewers that "the entire production" resulted from "the *personal* direction of Mr. Griffith" (emphasis added) and identifying himself as more of a lone poet, as well as guardian of civilization, at the center of his production than as a director or screenwriter engaged in a necessarily collaborative endeavor. The afterlife of *Intolerance*, as William Everson describes it, also mirrored that of *The Waste Land*. Just as the poem became the benchmark for avant-garde poets pursuing what Richard Poirier has distinguished as "difficulty," *Intolerance* inspired a succeeding generation of "'intellectual' directors" and "artistic innovators" while "bewildering" mass audiences with its often "incredibly frenetic barrage of images" (Poirier 131; Everson 97). Gilbert Seldes recalled the effect of this "abrupt hail of images": "it dazzled and even hurt the spectator . . . hammered the sensibilities of the spectator . . . exactly as it was intended to do" (79).

The "innovations" pioneered by Griffith came to assume motley, often dissonant guises in Eliot's major poetry. Playing the defender of civilization throughout *The Waste Land*, a monumental curatorial and anthological project, Eliot's poetic speaker seems, at the end of this modernist touchstone, to humble himself, renouncing this lofty aspiration, along with all ambition, in the poem's famous Sanskrit finale, an injunction to "give, sympathize, and control" oneself, which reverberates more explicitly a decade or so later with the pronouncement in "East Coker" that "humility" is "the only wisdom" attainable (*Poems* 126).

Professions of humility by Hollywood auteurs posing as champions of civilization, especially by Hollywood's founding auteur, may seem even less plausible than those that issue from *the* central modernist poet, the twentieth century's "literary dictator," as Delmore Schwartz once pegged Eliot (312–13). Eliot's recurring professions of humility illustrate the extent to which even the most dictatorial arbiter of culture, the most authoritative judge of what constitutes the "civilized," depends on this rhetorical stance to establish and maintain his cultural authority. Eliot famously ratified his investment in this stance, which he assumed throughout his poetry, pronouncing in his 1920 essay "Tradition and the Individual Talent" that art shouldn't be "the expression of personality, but an escape from personality" (*Waste Land* 119). Determining whether such humility is a posture or a sustainable position depends on how warily, how skeptically, artists and performers treat their own authority, especially when claiming to represent civilization.

IV

Among Hollywood's early auteurs no one embodies this challenge more than Charlie Chaplin; no screen persona has surpassed Chaplin's in establishing and maintaining such a stance of self-effacement (Seldes 39–40). Chaplin came to embody a sensibility to which American modernists characteristically aspired and so to "support . . . the modernist enterprise" (Goldstein 47–48). A year after the publication of *The Waste Land*, Chaplin appeared in a Wallace Stevens poem, "The Comedian as Letter C," as an "aspiring clown," a model of the self-humbling "renunciation and apprenticeship" that Emerson made the *sine qua non* of the American writer's calling, a figure who "humbly served" his "grotesque apprenticeship to chance event" (Stevens 66; Emerson, *Prose* 467). Hart Crane highlighted Chaplin's "sacrificial" aesthetic (Morin 93–95) as a civilizing influence in a poem titled simply "Chaplinesque." For Crane, Chaplin's tramp persona enjoined "meek adjustments and contentment" with the "random consolations" that serve as cues to "love the world" and as a refuge from "the fury of the street" (R. Lewis 53). This self-effacing on-screen posture of the little tramp stands in stark contrast to Chaplin's reputation as a perfectionist director—as much a dictator on the set as Eliot was the "literary dictator" for a generation of American poets. A daring writer as well, Chaplin's assertiveness as an arbiter of civilization led to his tackling Western civilization's most reviled foe, Hitler, in *The Great Dictator* (1940). "A fighting star" who "doesn't want anyone else up there" (C. Roth 77), Chaplin matches the on-screen tyrant's megalomania with his own more benign megalomania. Encompassing the conflict within his own on-screen character, Chaplin plays both lead roles in the movie: a Hitler caricature and a self-abnegating Jewish barber who ends up switching places with the dictator.

Like *Intolerance* a generation earlier, *The Great Dictator* added an influential voice to an intensifying conversation over U.S. participation in a largely European global war resoundingly framed as a battle for civilization. This perspective becomes most striking in the peroration ending *The Great Dictator*. This speech amplifies Chaplin's heretofore most sustained reflection on the state of civilization in *Modern Times*, the little tramp's previous appearance, released four years earlier. This peroration has taken its place in movie history as an "interminable . . . yet too short . . . great moment in world cinema" (Bazin 110–11):

> We have developed speed but we have shut ourselves in: machinery that
> gives abundance has left us in want. Our knowledge has made us cynical,

our cleverness hard and unkind. We think too much and feel too little: More than machinery we need humanity. More than cleverness we need kindness and gentleness. Without these qualities, life will be violent and all will be lost. The airplane and the radio have brought us closer together. The very nature of these inventions cries out for the goodness in men, cries out for universal brotherhood for the unity of us all.

These broad reflections omit the new "machinery" or the modern technology closest to Chaplin: "the pre-eminent mind-machine of the modern age" (Dargis, "Folks"). The movies themselves—the film technology that Chaplin had consummately mastered and its effect in prompting audiences to "shut" down or open up, to blind us morally or illuminate our condition—served as "the technological wave" Chaplin rode to stardom and genius (Hoberman, "Like").

V

Looking back a decade later on the war that *The Great Dictator* ushered in, Elizabeth Bowen grappled with this contradiction. Bowen identified herself as a movie "fan, not a critic," approaching the movies during the 1930s as a student of movie technology or "mechanics," of movies' "epic" possibilities, their transformational promise and their implications for "civilisation" ("Why" 207, 220). From this standpoint, Bowen captured in a single image the impact Chaplin sidestepped—the effect of movies as a newly ubiquitous everyday lens.

This image appears in Bowen's wartime novel *The Heat of the Day*. Bowen ascribes a cineaste's or even a cinematographer's gaze to her narrator to gauge the realization that unfolds over the course of the narrative: the likelihood that the heroine's lover is a Nazi spy. Bowen shows the heroine's doubts surfacing during a visit to her lover's family estate. Her discovery of how little he feels at home in his family home unfolds as a movie that at once thins and heightens her perception of him:

> Reflections, cast across the lawn . . . gave the glossy thinness of celluloid to indoor shadow. Stella pressed her thumb against the edge of the table to assure herself this was a moment *she* was living through . . . she seemed to be looking at everything down a darkening telescope. Having brought the scene back again into focus by staring at window reflections in the glaze of the teapot, she dared look again at Robert . . . between his nephew and niece. Late afternoon striking into the blue of his eyes made him look like a young man in Technicolor. (114)

The detailed grasp of the very machinery of the movies that Bowen's image exhibits shows how much movies shaped public consensus during World War II. Bowen's images of celluloid and Technicolor illustrate the prevailing movie-steeped "perception of the Second [World] War" (Fussell, *Great* 222). This ubiquity of movie-minded perceptions of World War II mark a departure from public perceptions during World War I, which, by contrast, "had not caused much excitement" in Hollywood (Glyn, *Romantic* 294).

The public "perception" of World War II, in Paul Fussell's view, "takes the form of one's response to cinema." The highest grossing movie of 1941 and Hollywood's most popular Great War star vehicle—*Sergeant York*, with Gary Cooper—illustrates this response. It also illustrated the extent to which at this juncture studios were only "looking for ideas . . . about the war" (Fitzgerald, *Pat* 15). According to F. Scott Fitzgerald, when "the war had just broken out . . . every producer on the lot wanted to end their current stories with the hero going to war" and the entire industry had to accept the consensus that "everything is war now, no matter how many credits a man has" (14, 18).

As a World War II movie about World War I, *Sergeant York* exemplifies the new wartime role of Hollywood in defending civilization. Released by Warner Brothers a year after United Artists released *The Great Dictator* and apparently in anticipation of the U.S. entry into World War II two months later, *Sergeant York* moves its title character from being "first . . . in conflict with and then in step with mainstream America" as it overcame isolationist wariness and girded itself for yet another world war (Smyth 231, 234–35). By staging this transformation, *Sergeant York* demonstrated how readily "Hollywood's dominant narrative model" came both to shape and reflect "the demands of wartime moral meaning" (C. Smith; Fussell, *Wartime* 191). The plot resurrects for a new generation the previous war's media-made legend of the pacifist sniper singlehandedly defending civilization against the "Hun" onslaught. By playing York as a backwoods sharpshooter and lone hunter, Cooper also signals two conceptual challenges that the coming war would pose for writers. Writers and directors became responsible for leading moviegoers from viewing the American hero as a "hard, isolate[d], stoic killer" (Lawrence 68) to seeing him as a team-player and so would need to learn "how to adapt white hat and black hat" cowboy dramas "to the war effort" (Stead 114) and transform America's frontier, a place in need of taming and a home for the virtuous, into global civilization.

This desired conceptual transformation parallels the perceptual shift Bowen's image signals. Her evocation of the wartime transformation of

private perception into cinematic spectatorship reveals that the moviegoing public, as well as the moviemaking literati, couldn't avoid viewing
the war as a movie, even before war movies flooded screens. Her image
also calls to mind the impact of rapidly changing movie technology—at
once a product of "our" civilization and an instrument for determining
our view of this civilization—in shaping these perceptions. Encapsulat-
ing the move from basic "celluloid" (Boorstin, *Americans* 377–78, 544) to
spectacle-enhancing Technicolor, Bowen's metaphors reflect widespread
recognition that, technologically as well as culturally, movies meant Hollywood, even where there was a thriving national cinema as in wartime
England. Bowen's detailed attention to technology recalls how during the
years right before the war Technicolor became technologically paramount
with the 1939 release of *The Wizard of Oz* and *Gone with the Wind*. Within
a generation, such technology became integral to Hollywood's civilizing
mission. As Alan Nadel argues, Technicolor and lens-enhancing, visual-
field expanding successor technologies like CinemaScope established and
evinced Hollywood's "global vision," imposed "Enlightenment" in the
form of more light,[1] brighter light, and assumed the quasi-biblical authority
to proclaim "let there be light" (*Containment* 115–16, 101–2; cf. Boorstin,
Image 148).

The United States' declaration of war may have been the single most
influential catalyst of this global reach and far-reaching authority. When
the United States went to war, Hollywood, as a time-honored boast puts
it, also went to war, perhaps better prepared to defend civilization than
the government it eagerly served for the duration of the conflict. The hyperbole with which Hollywood stressed its eagerness to defend civilization
became the butt of a vivid visual joke in the following exchange in Ethan
and Joel Coen's dark 1991 satire *Barton Fink*. Set in Depression-era Hollywood, *Barton Fink* shows an earnest leftist New York playwright (loosely
modeled on Clifford Odets) in an advanced state of Hollywood-induced
dementia just as the United States enters World War II. Fink's appointment
with the studio mogul who lured him to Hollywood (compositely modeled on Jack Warner, Louis B. Mayer, and Harry Cohn) (Bramann; Grenier, "Holy"; "De Cabezas Creadoras") highlights Hollywood's support
for and exploitation of the war effort as it rallied to help save civilization.
When Fink enters the studio chief's office, his boss, wearing a berib-
boned and bemedaled officer's uniform (custom-ordered from wardrobe),
reminds Barton to address him as "Colonel Lipnik, if you don't mind,"
and proclaims his readiness to wage "all-out warfare against the Japs"—the
"little yellow bastards" who would "love to see me sit this one out."

Lipnik's boast highlights how much "the war was a godsend" for the movies, the extent to which "Pearl Harbor rescued Hollywood" (Koppes 61; M. Bernstein 176). It enabled the studios to position themselves as champions of civilization and as arbiters of what it means to be *civilized*. Though mocking such claims, over the course of their career the Coens' movies also accept this role—albeit more warily—with narratives like *O Brother Where Art Thou* and *No Country for Old Men* that mount quixotic defenses of civilized "Enlightenment" assumptions (Gerard).

Among actual wartime features, rhetoric like Lipnik's may be nowhere more earnest than in Warner Brothers' Howard Hawks feature *Air Force*. Released in 1943, the movie includes a speech by a seasoned B-17 crew chief. Suggestively if not allegorically named Sergeant *White*, he reminds a fellow noncom:

> Listen, any buck-toothed little runt can walk up behind Joe Louis and knock him cold with a baseball bat, but a clean man don't do it. Your Uncle Sammy is civilized. He says, "Look out, you sneaks, we're gonna hit above the belt and knock the daylights outta you!" (Koppes 79)

Air Force may stand out with respect to how bluntly it illustrates Hollywood's wartime commitment to upholding civilization, to exposing and discrediting Axis barbarism. Despite—or perhaps because of—its hyperbolic rhetoric, *Air Force* was representative of this broad commitment. Such hyperbole, Clayton Koppes and Gregory Black argue in *Hollywood Goes to War*, rested on the widespread view of "the war as a landmark in the revolutionary struggle for individual rights going back to Jesus Christ . . . truly a struggle between light and darkness," being fought in pursuit of total reform demanding "big-theme movies" (66, 325, 327). For Budd Schulberg, the war eventually pushed much of Hollywood beyond the initial intellectual crudity satirized in *Barton Fink*. Raising the bar with respect to Hollywood's intellectual aspirations, by 1945 world war had goaded this "insular community" to begin "a voluntary pilgrimage out into the world of real experience" and "prove that we can turn the camera around and look at ourselves" (Papers).

VI

Film historian Walter Metz describes Hollywood's overall reaction to "the impact of World War II on human civilization as the hallmark of modernity" (81) and focuses on one director in particular. "A favorite among intellectuals" (Robinson 112), Alfred Hitchcock stands out for his allegorical representations of this impact. Hitchcock's "most famous example" of "wartime allegorical abstraction," his 1944 drama *Lifeboat* (Metz 82), brings civilians and combatants, Axis and Allies, claustrophobically together to promote the view of the Allies as the champions of civilization and a particular understanding of "the civilizing process."

Norbert Elias elaborated this process the same year the European war erupted. This civilizing process entails a "decrease" in the "contrast between the situation and code and conduct of . . . upper and lower social strata" and a "reduction in the contrasts within society as within individuals" (461). Seconding Elias's account of what constitutes civilization—at least this popular egalitarian conception of it—Hitchcock and his studio defended civilization and highlighted both its fragility and durability while paying homage to, if not flattering, Hollywood's newly embattled mass audience.

Three Oscar nominations, for direction, cinematography, and adapted screenplay, bespeak *Lifeboat*'s impact and representativeness. Based on a John Steinbeck story, *Lifeboat* tempted James Agee to consider it "more a Steinbeck picture than a Hitchcock" product (72). Apparently Agee was alluding to Steinbeck's reputation as a social-problem novelist, best known at the time for such novels as *The Grapes of Wrath* and *In Dubious Battle*, intimating that historical and political anxiety—civilization panic—trump Hitchcock's renowned artfulness in *Lifeboat*. These uncertainties may reflect the need for or may have resulted from last-minute script-doctoring by yet a third Hollywood (and Broadway) legend, playwright Ben Hecht. An exemplary if occasional member of New York's Algonquin Roundtable (C. James, "Wit's"), Hecht belonged to what may be as storied a group of self-elected arbiters of civilization as the United States ever produced. The *Lifeboat* narrative similarly assembles a group to pass on what makes for civilization; in this case, the survivors of ships sunk by warring navies, pressed by despair and treachery to make an intellectual determination of who is and what is civilized.

VII

Lifeboat belongs to a popular wartime subgenre, the wartime *omnium-gatherum* narrative encompassing both the dregs and paragons of our species in order to clarify who stood with the allies for civilization. The most durable contribution remains one of the earliest examples, *Casablanca. Everybody Comes to Rick's*, its working title (taken from the unproduced stage play on which the writers based the script), stresses the alignment between the

Casablanca narrative and this *omnium-gatherum* formula. The original trailer for *Casablanca* stresses this formula by proclaiming the Moroccan port an oasis "meeting place for adventurers, fugitives, criminals, refugees," all of whom the narrative brings to Rick's café—the same kind of catchall microcosm of humanity as Hitchcock's lifeboat. Both narratives reinforce the writers'—and most of these movies' American characters'—allegiance to traditional notions of Western civilization.

Casablanca makes this argument largely through the setting of its backstory. This resonance echoes in the memorable four words "we'll always have Paris": the city that long represented the zenith of Western civilization, "civilization, ready made" (Moser 70), and "the tabernacle of everything to which the adjective *free* could be applied—free thinking and 'free love,' the Free Theater . . . free verse" (Mehring 94). The attachment of *Casablanca*'s star-crossed, war-sundered hero and heroine—Rick and Ilsa (Humphrey Bogart and Ingrid Bergman)—to the civilizational ideal that Paris represents associates them with what the allies were fighting for.

Hollywood eventually made a brittle cliché of this attachment. Vincente Minnelli and screenwriters Robert Ardrey and John Gay resuscitated the Casablanca narrative, a love triangle opposing private desire and the survival of civilization, twenty years later in *Four Horseman of the Apocalypse*. Though Minnelli also pitted Nazi occupiers against Resistance heroes who idealized Paris as the epitome of civilization, featuring Paul Henreid once again as the saintly freedom-fighting husband, the movie was greeted as "failing pretty miserably" (Alpert). This "engorged, verbose, radically overacted melodrama" hewed so much to Hollywood's clichéd Paris narrative that no moviegoer, wrote Brendan Gill in the *New Yorker*, "will be surprised that the lovers go out for a walk beside the Seine" (128). The movie's "garbled screenplay" and "fustian 'Hollywood' style" prompted Bosley Crowther to dismiss *Four Horsemen* as "vapid, sluggish, idiotic" threatening rather than championing civilization, and concluding that "the less attention paid to this picture, the better for the simple dignity of the human race" (Crowther, "*Four*").

Perhaps America's most visibly influential, anointed wartime authority on the subject of civilization and promoter of this Paris connection was the poet Archibald MacLeish, who became the Franklin D. Roosevelt administration's wartime information coordinator and image manager during same year that *Casablanca* premiered. MacLeish regarded this Paris connection as a cornerstone of the cultural homefront. In due course, MacLeish became over the course of his career civilization's de facto, perennial, and preeminent advocate (J. Bloom, *Left* 56–57). Sixty years after

World War II, Bob Dylan honored MacLeish's persisting stature as the very embodiment of civilization, describing the *eminence grise as* the "Yeats of the New World," one of "the gigantic figures," and "the man of godless sand . . . with the aura of a governor, a ruler." Having "defined the landscape of twentieth-century America" and "put everything in perspective," MacLeish "could take real people out of history . . . and deliver them right to your door" (107, 109, 110). On the basis of this impression of MacLeish, Dylan deemed meeting MacLeish when MacLeish summoned him the "*civilized* thing to do" (emphasis added).

In his 1940 manifesto *The Irresponsibles*, MacLeish characterized the Allies as fighting "for the defense of . . . civilization as men have known it for the past two thousand years" (27). Like Orwell, MacLeish equated modern totalitarianism with "the gangster outlook" (118–19), which Hollywood had made so familiar to moviegoers during the 1930s. What the Allies were fighting against MacLeish scorned as the "revolution of gangs" empowered by "a strategy and leadership brutal enough, cynical enough, cunning enough to destroy the entire authority of inherited culture" (*Irresponsible* 12, 16–17). When Paris fell to the Germans, this "authority" fell as well, in MacLeish's view. In response to this catastrophe, he proposed a museum exhibit that would expose the "totalitarian powers" as the "underworld of civilization" and highlight "its gangster politics" ("Proposal" 21). Perhaps MacLeish's most ambitious project, this collaboration with Museum of Modern Art director Alfred Barr and architecture critic Lewis Mumford to build a MOMA annex dedicated to the defense of civilization, to "clarify . . . America's 'contributions to civilization' after the fall of Paris, foundered when its patron, Abby Aldrich Rockefeller, decided that 'the whole enterprise seemed better suited to a motion picture'" (Elligott).

From this perspective the sentiment that the heroine and hero of *Casablanca* finally share, the agreement that, come what may, they'll "always have Paris," positions the elegant European Ilsa and the rough-hewn New Yorker Rick as proponents of Western civilization. The Nazis may have *occupied* Paris. But the ideological thrust of MacLeish's rhetoric and the *Casablanca* narrative insists that the Nazis will never *possess* what Paris transcendently signifies among the civilized. The script spelled out this struggle as a culture competition earlier in the movie by staging a battle of equally sanguinary war-cry anthems when Rick's Café's customers and staff, singing *La Marseillaise*, silence—drown out—a band of carousing German officers singing the *Die Wacht Am Rhein*.

The *Casablanca* narrative climaxes by clinching Rick's role as civilization's exponent. When the lovers accept separation from one another for the sake of beating the Paris-occupying Nazis, they renounce personal desire on behalf of their civilization. When Rick presses Ilsa to continue supporting her husband's anti-Nazi crusade, *Casablanca* presents "the tragic consequences" of Rick's—and all anti-fascist citizens'—commitment to the cause of civilization (May, *Big* 148–50). More broadly, Rick's famous closing homily drives home Freud's lesson that renunciation is the price of civilization: "I'm no good at being noble, but it doesn't take much to see that the problems of three little people don't amount to a hill of beans in this crazy world."

More obliquely, the main prop in *Casablanca* might also be seen as underscoring Rick's role as a champion of civilization. Rick's access to the "letters of transit" supposedly needed to leave Morocco legally, so avidly sought after by Casablanca's burgeoning refugee community, puts Rick in a position akin to that of the self-effacing artist, the position Eliot advocated and Chaplin's on-screen persona exemplified. This plot turn depends on an entirely ersatz and unhistorical plot device: these so-called letters of transit never existed in the actual history of diplomacy (Otero-Pailos). This Mc-Guffin, a civilization-affirming artifact conjured by the screenwriters, turns Rick literally into a man of letters, a phrase that recalls a largely nineteenth-century ideal singling out a heroic "few . . . not likely-to-be forgiven," whose very words champion civilization (Connolly 71; Gross 45, 76–77). Rick's letters also result in his making precisely the choice Eliot urged on the civilization-defending modern poet: eschew any "turning loose of emotion" in favor of "an escape from emotion" (*Waste Land* 119).

VIII

Daniel Fuchs's story "Triplicate," a 1979 retrospect on Hollywood's "golden" (studio) age, reflected the persistence of this aesthetic among Hollywood writers, if not among their employers. "Triplicate" features a writer-producer, who moves between Hollywood studios and the New York stage, as a paragon of artistic integrity. This retrospect reflects Fuchs's own representative position as a literary sellout whose "betrayal" made Hollywood movies intellectually richer (Schultheiss 29; Fiedler 307). Fuchs's narrator touts the paragon's "special notion about writing":

> What he was after was the intrinsic element in the image or even apart from emotion, apart from meaning . . . he dispensed with incidentals. . . . He wanted the shivery actuality, the shock of fact, the news . . . if someone tried to ask . . . ask him what he meant . . . a notion too large to explain. (91)

Fuchs's heroic producer doesn't only echo Eliot's austere brief against emotion and his influential formalist resistance to paraphrasable "meaning." Fuchs also pays homage to an even earlier modernist article of faith, Ezra Pound's 1913 advocacy of "Imagism":

> An Image is that which presents an intellectual and emotional complex in an instant of time. . . . It is the presentation of such a 'complex' which gives that sense of sudden liberation; that sense of freedom from time limits and space limits; that sense of sudden growth, which we experience in the presence of the greatest art. ("Few" 199–200)

Following World War II, this austerity and faith in the implicit waned among Hollywood's champions of civilization. Turning prophylactic, intent on imprinting on the public the apparent lessons of the war to ensure that recent history would never repeat itself, Hollywood's crusade on behalf of civilization turned toward therapeutic melodrama and histrionics. Postwar Hollywood, as Raymond Durgnat has argued, became the referee of "what is felt to be 'reasonable'" and what constitutes "good 'adjustment,'" embracing an "easy intellectual acceptance of carefully isolated aspects of Freudian theory, with a view, not to easing the demands of . . . civilization, but intensifying 'adjustment' to . . . civilization" (*Films* 152–53). Popular and acclaimed movies bore titles such as *Till the End of Time*, *Crossfire*, *Panic in the Streets*, and *Boomerang!*, each title naming a condition that organized civilization, under the aegis of Hollywood, aimed to forestall.

IX

Nevertheless, the "gangs" MacLeish fingered as the wartime enemies of civilization remain the villains in many prophylactic postwar narratives. This continuity may have been most pronounced in much of the celebrated and still controversial work of Elia Kazan, director of both *Panic in the Streets* and *Boomerang!*. As the writer-director who perhaps most earnestly and repeatedly took on the role of championing civilization, Kazan recostumes in domestic mufti the gangs MacLeish warned of in his most memorable work. Such gangs include the deceptively sophisticated Darien and uptown WASPs in Kazan's 1947 anti-bigotry fable *Gentlemen's Agreement*, the coarser gang of union racketeers in *On the Waterfront*, and the invisible gangs of TV-land spectators in his 1957 deconstruction of mass-media demagoguery, *A Face in the Crowd*.

Hollywood's postwar confidence in its civilizing mission peaked in movies slicker, less edgy, and less gritty than Kazan's durable black-and-white classics. Cold War epics, such as *The Ten Commandments*, *Ben Hur*, *Giant*, and *The King and I*, set out, like Griffith's early masterworks, to "grapple with history and its representation and . . . reinvent the past" (Nadel, *Containment* 115). With the possible exception of Stanley Kubrick's (studio-bowdlerized) *Spartacus*, such extravaganzas lacked the intellectual ambition of *Intolerance*, serving primarily to ratify "the emergence of the Pax Americana with spectacles of empire" (Mitchell 151). Nonetheless Turkish novelist Orhan Pamuk has testified to the impact of such movies, such "gems of western culture" (300), as civilization arbiters, in the tradition established by Griffith and Ince in 1916. Pamuk looked to such "big American productions" as a remedy for his own boyhood civilization panic. Despite its critical and commercial failure at home, for example, Pamuk will always cherish the Istanbul premiere of *Cleopatra* and the simple "fun" of coming "face to face with the West" and of vicariously experiencing "intimate contact with the private life of the West" (301). Thanks to the 1950s career-defining performances of the star probably most associated with this genre, as Moses and Ben Hur (the role that won him a best-actor Oscar), Charlton Heston's career persona became by the 1970s that of "a one-man surrogate for the beleaguered forces of civilization"—a "godlike" embodiment, in Pauline Kael's words, of "what makes America win" (Morgenstern, "Charlton"). In this guise, Heston emerged as a dramatic, widescreen answer to Whittaker Chambers's overwrought Cold War–defining question, "whether civilization as we know it is to be completely destroyed" (7). That Chambers's reiteration of his claim that the same question that vexed him as a Communist in 1923, whether "civilization could survive" (194), worried him as a right-wing hero in 1950 illustrates the chronic rhetorical value of civilization panic for American ideologues of every stripe.

The *Intolerance*-like narratives of Cold War sword-and-sandal epics, though, began to treat civilization as less in need of defending and more worthy of celebrating and selling as yet another irresistible product from the world's newest, most far-reaching (and first ambition-denying) empire. In 1963 John F. Kennedy's legendary trilingual "Ich bin ein Berliner" speech encapsulated this attitude. Kennedy stressed his own and his country's leadership in spreading and embodying civilization by aligning its Cold War civilizing mission with imperial Rome as his precedent. In particular, Kennedy harkened back to the legal fiction that justified rapacious conquest on the pretext of disseminating the world's first universal civilization. After identifying himself as *ein Berliner*, Kennedy proceeded with rousing pedantry to assume the role the prevailing mid-century consensus demanded of American presidents as the voice controlling "the grand narrative of Western civilization" (Khanna 62, 64). In this role Kennedy lived up to Robert Frost's boast on his behalf that, as in Rome when its empire rose and as in Great Britain when James Thomson wrote "Rule Britannia" and the force of British arms and commerce had supplanted France and Spain to "rule the waves," Kennedy had become a "new Augustus" and presided over a "new Augustan age" (Kazin 498, 500). The "Berliner" speech did so by invoking the etymological root of *civilization* (in the Latin word for "citizen"): Kennedy equated his declaration of universal *Berliner* citizenship with the recollection that "two thousand years ago the proudest boast was '*civis Romanus sum*'" (Reeves 536). This pitch for the "advance of freedom everywhere" featured besieged West Berlin, midway through the Cold War, in the role Hollywood and other cultural guardians reserved for occupied Europe a generation earlier. Like such blockbusters as *The Ten Commandments* and *Ben Hur*, Kennedy's rhetorical flourish looked to the ancient empires that Hollywood reconstructed in America's own image to legitimate the United States' position as the champion of civilization (Nadel, *Containment* 115).

Toward the end of the Cold War, a Reagan administration official joked that whenever anyone questioned the defense secretary's budget demands, he warned so often of "dire consequences" that the official kept colleagues apprised by informing them, "there goes Western civilization for the third time in the last hour" (D. Martin, "Darman"). In addition to the imperial narratives its epics promoted or explored, Hollywood also recognized this comic dimension of Cold War civilization panic. Contemporaneous with these sword-and-sandal epics, directors like Billy Wilder and Stanley Kubrick toyed with imperial claims like Kennedy's on behalf of America's civilizing mission. Most memorably, Wilder's Berlin-set *One, Two, Three* and Kubrick's *Dr. Strangelove* appealed to sophisticates by engaging the Cold War satirically and polemically, with Wilder's movie embracing and reveling in the Cold War status quo and Kubrick's savaging the doctrine of deterrence that sustained this status quo. Where *Dr. Strangelove* evokes American leadership as bewildered at best and bloodthirstily demented at worst, Wilder proclaims the triumph of the "West" in the Cold War with a plot that turns a fervent German Leninist into a bowler-topped, boutonnière-sporting Coca-Cola executive and member, via marriage to a belle named Scarlet, of Atlanta's elite. The characteristically snappy dialogue of Wilder (and longtime writing partner I. A. L. Diamond) pits a street-smart, fast-talking corporate Machiavelli—and unwitting champion of Western civilization—played by James Cagney against his buffoonish, equally venal Soviet counterparts. One of these trade commissars ends up, thanks to the Cagney character's scheming, professing a most shopworn American sentiment:

C. R. MACNAMARA: You've defected?

PERIPETCHIKOFF: Is old Russian proverb: "go west young man."

The movie's love plot, moreover, ensures that Soviet military might and its revolutionary rhetoric will prove no match for the sweet allure of both southern belles and the Coca-Cola with which their menfolk are conquering the globe.

By contrast, Paddy Chayefsky's script for Arthur Hiller's 1964 movie *The Americanization of Emily* scrupulously avoids this facile demonizing and idealizing. Chayefsky and Hiller turn familiar Cold War postures into a comic *tour de force*, in part by treating the recently concluded "good war" against the Nazis into a proxy for the newer, more morally ambiguous conflict. Set against the sacrosanct backdrop of the Normandy landings, the London blitz, and the British sacrifices at the turning-point battle of Tubrok, the narrative works as a "Shavian" inquiry into the rhetoric and imagery of heroism with dialogue that weighs the inspirational value of such rhetoric against its fatal abuse and exploitation (Crowther, "*Americanization*"). This ambition and its realization elicited praise for the movie as a consummate achievement of Hollywood intellect:

> Under Arthur Hiller's brisk direction of Mr. Chayefsky's script, which includes some remarkably good writing with some slashing irreverence, "The Americanization of Emily" comes out a spinning comedy that says more for basic pacifism than a fistful of intellectual tracts. It also is highly entertaining, and it makes a good case for pure romance. (Crowther "*Americanization*")

As in *Casablanca*, much of the intellectual work in *The Americanization of Emily* rested on a wartime romance plot as the basis for Chayefsky's exploration of the meaning of civilization as a transatlantic responsibility. As the title suggests and the casting of Julie Andrews and James Garner as romantic leads underscores, U.S. mass media had by 1964 come to ascribe this joint responsibility to the United States and the United Kingdom, partners in what diplomats and historians had come to call "the special relationship" (Cook).

Over the course of the same decade, this U.S.-UK campaign on be-half of civilization moved to prime-time television. The fledgling Public Broadcasting Service had one of its first prime time hits with a British import titled simply *Civilisation*. *Civilisation* brought to the screen a genre that became popular in print form at mid-century, with such popular titles as Will and Ariel Durant's eleven-volume book-of-the-month-club favorite *The Story of Civilization*, published intermittently throughout World War II and into the Cold War years. Max Lerner's more modestly titled *America as a Civilization* concluded in 1957 that "our civilization" (in Emerson's words) is both "the cock crowing and the morning star" (Lerner 950; Brooks, "Joe"). Stanley Kauffmann noted Hollywood's contribution to this celebratory consensus when he likened *Ben Hur* to "any church's Easter pageant" (22).

The PBS series *Civilisation* spawned a companion coffee-table tome written by the series' on-camera narrator, Kenneth Clark. Its dustjacket boasts that Clark will once and for all "distill the essence of all that is pre-cious in our heritage." Clark's TV persona as "the docent of civilization itself" (McMurtry, "Rereading") turned him into *the* public voice of civi-lization, a role Clark came to relish.

Lord Clark himself found the business of being an instant celebrity yet another source of fascination. "So many people recognize me wherever I travel and I love it," he said. "Don't have a dull moment. I'm told that real celebrities find it a bit off-putting, but I feel strongly that people want to know life and learn about happiness. And knowing a little about the history of art is a very good way of doing it."

Clark traded successfully on his reassuringly donnish bonhomie "[w]ith wit, erudition and reconciling vision" (Bohlen). Clark charmed millions by "combining a learned, patrician manner with engaging informality." As "he swept through the history of Western civilization . . . audiences were swept along with him." He opened his irresistible reaffirmation of civiliza-tion by easily answering and by gliding over, with philistine insouciance, the question that Freud, Spengler, Cullen, Bell, and scores of others ago-nized over throughout the twentieth century:

> What is Civilization? I don't know. I can't define it in abstract terms—yet.
> But I think I can recognize it when I see it and I'm looking at it now.
> (*Civilisation* 1)

The screen image during these opening reflections shows Clark gazing on Paris—not only the city that *Casablanca*'s love-crossed pair, Rick and

Ilsa, claimed as eternally theirs but also the capital that Walter Benjamin viewed as if it were a movie, experiencing Paris as a "magic-lantern show of optical illusion, rapidly changing size and blending into one another" (Buck-Morss, *Dialectics* 81).

Identifying his gaze with that of the representative civilized man, Clark describes this gaze as a function of technology, expressly print technology. The attribute of print technology that Clark singles out, however, is one most readily associated with movie technology. When Clark pictures "civilized man," he positions him "somewhere in space and time" (17). From Clark's vantage point, civilized man "consciously looks forward and back." Clark argues that the "convenience" of "being able to read and write" facilitates this perspective. Accepting Clark's own logic, then, would oblige civilization's champions to regard film and video technology, which add the ease of reversing, speeding up, and freezing film or tape, as advances in the march of civilization as monumental as print.

The waning of the Cold War and of Clark's whiggish faith in civilizational progress parallels the career narrative of *Civilisation*'s most famous—and most infamous—viewer: Richard Nixon. The consummate cold warrior, Nixon at once embodied and helped undo the prevailing whiggish consensus about civilization that Clark, the Durants, Lerner, and Hollywood had fostered. Mark Feeney's *Nixon at the Movies* documents Nixon's appreciation of Clark's series throughout his first term. Feeney speculates that *Civilisation* spoke to one of Nixon's cherished boyhood fantasies (288). As Nixon recalled "wistfully" in the last of his memoirs, *RN*, he had "two great—and still unfulfilled—ambitions . . . to direct a symphony orchestra and play organ in a cathedral" (9). Instead of realizing these typically "civilized" dreams, Nixon, who deliberately cultivated his reputation as a "cold-hearted butcher" (Dowd), led the kind of gang that MacLeish's wartime jeremiad identified with all that assailed Western civilization.

Philip Roth depicts this dubious achievement by naming his 1971 satire on the Nixon administration *Our Gang*. Roth's title shifted the screen production framing Nixon's administration from Clark's high-minded middlebrow PBS series to one of Hollywood's most durable franchises: the *Our Gang* series of theatrical shorts Hal Roach produced for MGM during the Depression. Each *Our Gang* episode typically depicted a repertory group playing neighborhood kids carrying out grandiose ideas that usually entailed tricking grown-ups or subverting their rules: rewiring (haywiring) all the pipes and wires in a modern middle-class home; organizing a mass hooky to attend a circus; staging adult-size projects like prize fights, operas, or a *Romeo and Juliet* production; devising some absurdly complicated invention with everyday bric-a-brac; or concocting an unusual financial scheme like cutting deals with the tooth fairy. Retitled *The Little Rascals*, *Our Gang* had a prosperous afterlife in TV syndication throughout the Cold War years as a nostalgic reminder of prewar Andy Hardy innocence and a precursor of such millennial TV provocations as *South Park*. In the 1990s Hollywood took to turning Cold War network comedies like *Sergeant Bilko* and *The Flintstones* into star-vehicle features. Universal released *The Little Rascals*, a tepidly reviewed family comedy, twelve weeks after the funeral of that democratically elected leader of our American gang, Richard Nixon.

Nixon's funeral capped a campaign by the surviving members of the Nixon gang that Roth lampooned to reclaim for the disgraced president the status of civilization's champion. Perhaps none did so more fulsomely than Nixon's top diplomat and in-house professor Henry Kissinger. In making this move, the Harvard-bred European turned to one of the monuments of civilization celebrated in Clark's *Civilisation*. In a revealing non-sequitur, Kissinger channeled Shakespeare's famously pensive but fatally decisive gangbuster Hamlet to burnish his boss's irremediably tainted legacy:

> When I learned the final news, by then so expected yet so hard to accept, I felt a profound void. In the words of Shakespeare, "He was a man, take him for all in all. I shall not look upon his like again." (Kissinger, "Remarks")

By the time Nixon died, the Hollywood generation ascendant following Nixon's resignation had long since discredited such anesthetizing narratives, now tainted by the legacy of what Hollywood chronicler Peter Biskind calls "the Nixon gang" (164).

X

This Nixon-era gang sensibility preoccupied influential late-century American directors such as Robert Altman, Francis Ford Coppola, and Martin Scorsese. They took on the "task," made more urgent by the shadow of Watergate and Vietnam, with which Walter Benjamin charged an earlier generation: "to brush history against the grain" (*Illuminations* 257). As a civilizing mission, this task entailed resurrecting and intensifying MacLeish's injunction to challenge the gangs in their various guises that threaten the civilized ideal we collectively claim to value. The titles of such movies sometimes speak for themselves, as with Scorsese's first post-9/11 feature, *Gangs of New York*.

Even more than titles, a director's choice of material for adaptation is likely to reflect his understanding of his gang-flouting civilizing mission. The trilogy Coppola made from Mario Puzo's *Godfather* novel and the way Coppola bemused civic-minded moviegoers by intimating parallels between the Mafia and such legal "gangs" as the U.S. Senate, the New York Police Department, and the Vatican (Browne 102; De Stefano 60–62), probably stands as the most striking example. More obliquely, Scorsese's look at moneyed Americans in his Howard Hughes biopic *The Aviator* or his 1993 adaptation of Edith Wharton's *Age of Innocence* show their heroes ganged up on, respectively, by a corporate-sponsored congressional cabal or Old New York's legendary gang of clannish, genteel snobs. A reviewer for *Rolling Stone* stressed the continuity between Wharton's narrative and Scorsese's more overtly violent gang-centered narratives, from *Mean Streets* to *The Departed*:

> Though a century apart, Scorsese and Wharton are both experts in New York's tribal warfare. Behind the elegant facade of Wharton's characters is a calculated cruelty that Scorsese's hoods could easily recognize. . . . Organized crime could take lessons in closing ranks from these reigning families, celebrated by the social arbiters. (Travers 666)

In depicting this genteel belle époque gang of New York, Scorsese recalled the gangs in Coppola's *Godfather* adaptations: gangs that rested on and legitimated the civilizing sanctions of family and tradition, at the expense of more universal civilizing aspirations.

Like Scorsese and Coppola, Altman made overt outlaw stories such as *Thieves Like Us* and represented moneyed, leisured, and genteel schemers ganging up on resisters in the postmillennial *Gosford Park* and earlier in *A Wedding*, Altman's darkly comic take on Coppola's *Godfather* milieu. Altman became the Nixon-era director *par excellence*, beginning in 1970 with *M.A.S.H.* From then on Altman repeatedly revealed the most insidious and often the most risible gangs to be those that govern America. His preoccupation with Nixon became most explicit in 1984 with *Secret Honor*, a monologue showing Nixon exposing the sinister gang, "the committee of 100," that backed him throughout his career (Keysar 326–28).

Such exposés became particularly sharp in Altman's two eponymous city movies, *Nashville* in 1975 and *Kansas City* in 1996. Like Altman's last feature, *A Prairie Home Companion*, these earlier movies expose, as essentially *gangsters*, the behind-the-scenes managers and financiers who control the entertainment industries that shape—or misshape—American civilization: popular music in particular as well as broadcasting and Hollywood in *The Player*.

Altman's most renowned movie, *Nashville*, "skewers" the chattering classes, those day-to-day arbiters of civilization: "journalists, and self-proclaimed deep thinkers" (A. Cohen). In *Essential Cinema*, Jonathan Rosenbaum recalls the timeliness of *Nashville* as Altman's critique of the civilization panic then prevalent: "After a summer full of humorless rhetoric in the American press about 'the true lessons of Watergate,' the 'failure of our civilization,'" Altman "had finally got it right" (91). Altman established his intellectual bona fides, as a counter-arbiter of civilization, by looking askance at his own milieu and medium. A party scene early in *Nashville* stages a collision between the narcissism of the narrative's fictitious country-music star and the vanity of two Hollywood stars, Elliott Gould and Julie Christie, playing themselves as surprise guests—and disruptive cosmopolitan interlopers.

With this move Altman stresses that demonstrations of what makes for civilization, as opposed to the many claims made by movies, books, and political causes to be representing and speaking for civilization, requires disowning the arbiter role—the "inside dopester" posture that Pauline Kael lambasted in her critique of auteur theory ("Circles" 20). The position Kael advocates and Altman illustrates obliges moviemakers and moviegoers alike to acknowledge complicity and perhaps even revel in the barbarism, crudity, and sanctimony being subjected to on-screen scrutiny. Hollywood makes this move as seldom as do other self-styled arbiters of civilization such as academe, legislatures, organized bohemia, and the elite institutions traditionally lumped together as "high culture."

From the standpoint of movie history, by casting Julie Christie for this *Nashville* bit part, Altman made a particularly resonant choice for probing and intervening in prevailing "failure of civilization" conversations. Four years earlier Altman had cast Christie for the lead in *McCabe and Mrs. Miller*, becoming the first American director to work with Christie. Her role as a worldly Seattle madam brought to the frontier to help establish a classy bordello built on the screen persona that she had already established on British and French screens: frankly sexual, quick-witted, and verbally agile. Her first starring (and Oscar-winning) role, in 1965 as the title character in John Schlesinger's *Darling*, "turned Christie into an international celebrity and fashion sensation" (Harris 172). Christie played the title character, a glib, sexually aggressive London model for whom being "made love to endlessly by a succession of men whom she would not have to speak to afterwards seemed" a "most acceptable fate" (Raphael, *Darling* 113–14). A

New York Times reviewer railed at "this totally corrosive film . . . sarcastic without going deep—mischievous, devastating, sometimes disgusting, and usually droll"—which shows Darling as "a selfish, ambitious, fickle wench whose tender and lovable qualities might be compared to those of a threshing-machine" (Crowther, "*Darling*"). Issuing from perhaps the most mainstream voice in movie-reviewing, Crowther's resistance illuminates the fear Schlesinger kept repeating during casting, finance negotiations, and finally during filming that "this picture will never get made" (Raphael, *Personal* 106–7).

Revisiting *Darling* a generation later, Camille Paglia also treated it as a cultural symptom. In contrast to Crowther, however, Paglia treats *Darling* as "a revelation" and contrasts it with "today's movies," which she finds characteristically "turgid and trite, with sloppy production values and buffoonish acting." For Paglia *Darling* discloses an invigorating alternative narrative and a lost opportunity, extolling especially "its extraordinary star, 'coltish, mercurial Julie Christie,' who represents 'the exhilarating burst of cultural vitality' in the 'restlessly kinetic new women' of the 1960s—completely outside the frame of feminism" ("Magical").

Frederic Raphael's script presents *Darling*'s intellectual edge more subtly than either Paglia or Crowther allows. The screenplay shows her at once representing and devouring civilization. The following exchange with Laurence Harvey, playing an even more cold-blooded consummate sexual predator, assures an end to the postwar pact that Anglophone cinema had made with *Civilization and Its Discontents* (Durgnat 152–53): When Harvey's character confronts Darling with the faintheartedness of *her* commitment to predation, she challenges him to disclose the "secret" that, she insists, he "always looks as if" he's concealing. He retorts, "There's no secret. I'm the cracker with the big bang and no motto inside" and dismissively rebukes her, "put away your Penguin Freud . . . and your sticky crystal ball. It's late"—apparently too late for Freud along with his fretfully diagnostic conception of civilization (Raphael, *Darling* 115–16).

A decade after *Darling*, in *Nashville*, Altman ratified this paradigm shift with the interplay of the subnarratives that contribute to the movie's overall kaleidoscopic effect:

- To the extent that the movie has a hero or heroine, the role goes to Lily Tomlin. She plays a boundary-crossing community-builder who signs fluently and cheerfully with her deaf children, in contrast to their father (Ned Beatty), who never bothers to learn how to sign. She also sings each Sunday, the sole white choir member,

in an African American congregation. At the same time, Altman
shows her committing adultery with pensive poise. Instead of
customary Christian or Freudian guilt, or defiant carnality like
Christie in *Darling*, Tomlin's character exhibits only disdain for her
partner, a callow charismatically predatory rock star.

- The Beatty character works as the local advance man for the
presidential candidate of the Replacement Party. This party's
very name contrasts pointedly with the names of known political
parties—Republican, Democrat, Socialist, Progressive, and so
on—because it signals no allegiance to an abstract ideal like
democracy or representative government or public ownership:
none of the historical continuity that an identification with *progress*
implies, no affiliation with legacies like Roman republicanism and
the Athenian polity, and no appeals to equalitarian Enlightenment
axioms that European intellectuals called on in articulating various
brands of socialism throughout the nineteenth century. To the
extent that civilization as a concept rests on a sense of the past
and an aspiration to sustain familiar, deep-rooted ideals into the
future, the Replacement Party's very name advertises it as the
anti-civilization party.

- *Nashville*'s climactic assassination scene turns on the transformation
of a taciturn former agriculture student (as his jacket advertises),
aspiring musician—or so he seems because he's shown always
carrying a violin case—and devoted family member, who
dutifully phones his mother on his arrival in Nashville, into a
cold-blooded, patiently disciplined assassin. By setting *Nashville*'s
climactic assassination scene at the city's second most famous tourist
destination, its centennial Parthenon replica (Stuart 258), Altman
highlighted both the claims on behalf of "Western civilization" that
mark our public discourse and the precariousness of such claims.
To underscore the fragility and deceptiveness of such tokens of
civilization as the assassin's violin case screenwriter Joan Tewksbury
insisted that "the nicest guy in the movie has to be one that pulls
the trigger" (67). These far-reaching resonances associate this
seemingly minor character—Kenny—with Periclean Athens, widely
regarded as both a font and paragon of "our" civilization, with two
of civilization's most venerable forms of cultivation—agriculture
(his jacket) and the arts (the violin he supposedly carries)—and with
its most revered institution: family. Consequently, in uncovering
Kenny's actual *métier* and his crucial plot function, Altman

underscores, at best, the frailty of civilization-as-we-know-it and, at worst, the malleability or even the nullity of those markers through which we've customarily recognized civilization-as-we-know-it. Despite mainstream Hollywood's continuing millennial commitment to championing civilization-as-we-know it, a generation ago Altman highlighted the illusoriness of this usually unconscious, nearly unanimous collective commitment.

Though Spielberg had *Munich*'s viewpoint character Golda Meir sagely philosophize about the compromises civilization must make, the *Nashville* audience had already had an opportunity to understand how civilizations cannot make—or choose not to *make*—compromises, because civilizations *are* compromises.

Notes

1. "More light" (*mehr Licht*)—reputedly the last words of one of global civilization's earliest, preeminent champions: Johann Goethe. Goethe's full request may seem even more prescient to the technologically movie-minded for whom "light is the movie camera's *raison d'etre*" (B. Wright 39) than it seems to have been a century earlier for the dying Goethe: "Open the second shutter to let more light come in here" (*Macht docht zen zweiten Fenster laden, auch auf, damit mehr licht hereikomme*).

Civilization: The Movie *Noir*

The Negro met civilization and was crushed.

—W. E. B. DUBOIS

The colonization of each other's minds is the price we pay for thought.

—MARY DOUGLAS

Shit. They act just like niggers.

—JAMES BALDWIN (NOVEL CHARACTER ON THE MOVIE *KING'S ROW*)

I

Throughout the twentieth century African American writers also grappled with, resisted, and exploited the civilization panic that marked the century from World War I to 9/11. In acknowledging and often discrediting panics that often targeted them and other ethnics "of color," these writers often looked to Hollywood for evidence of civilization panic, especially its offenses. Hollywood, however, also afforded them opportunities: rhetorical leverage for their resistance to the bigotry and reductiveness civilization panic underwrote.

Writers whose work demonstrates their own claims to being "civilized" at the same time acknowledged their collective historical role as the object of much civilization-panic-mongering and as the pretext for over a century of Europeans' and North Americans' civilizing missions.

African American novelists writing mid-century, in particular, took hold of prevailing decline narratives as a point of departure. By contrast, African American writers working at the turn of the century, who came of age before Hollywood became so predominant an arbiter of civilization, were more sanguine in exploiting the rhetoric of civilization panic and civilizing missions, finding openings to insert themselves and opportunities to establish themselves as civilization arbiters amid the decline narratives promoted by so many white literati and the "botched civilization" and "wasteland" images that became their stock-in-trade. These narratives and images, leavened from the 1920s onward with Hollywood's refractions of them, provided African American writers from W. E. B. Dubois to Amiri Baraka and Toni Morrison with what Emerson prophesied for his "American scholar": "the raw material out of which the intellect moulds her splendid products" (*Prose* 61).

In 1903, in *The Souls of Black Folk*, DuBois memorably set this agenda. DuBois pictured himself, the consummate black intellectual throughout the first half of the century, dwelling side by side on Parnassus, "across the color line," with Shakespeare and Aristotle. With this image, DuBois not only asserts his intellectual equality, but also assumes that Western civilization as nineteenth-century Europe and its offshoots knew it—what Matthew Arnold famously deemed "the best that has been known and thought"—would persist as the standard for judging cultural accomplishment (Czitrom 32). Three years earlier, in *The Marrow of Tradition*, Charles W. Chesnutt affiliated himself (or at least his omniscient narrator) with this prevailing ideal of civilization even more boldly. Assuming the role of arbiter, Chesnutt claims that membership in "the Negro race" makes one *ipso facto* "the residuary legatee of civilization" (62), proof against the epidemic civilization panic with which the century would afflict primarily white folks.

Countee Cullen crystallized these questions about the writer's and "the Negro's" relation to civilization in "Heritage" (see chapter III). Cullen's questions coincided with Hollywood's voice becoming one of the loudest in public conversations about civilization and the most powerful influence in representing race. Between 1918 and Cullen's publication of "Heritage" in *Copper Sun* in 1927, encounters between Anglo civilization and a collectively imagined African jungle primitivism became a Hollywood formula. The release during this decade of *Tarzan of the Apes*, *The Adventures of Tarzan*, *The Son of Tarzan*, and *Tarzan and the Golden Lion* served to answer for millions of moviegoing and pulp-reading Americans the question that "Heritage" repeatedly raises: "What is Africa to me?" (Torgovnick 43–46). Moreover, these Tarzan movies and Cullen's poem share much signature imagery: "goading massive jungle herds," great cats' "monarch claws," "jungle boys and girls in love . . . treading out a jungle track"—all reminders of how much "conceptions of the continent" remained "steeped in reductive romance, primitivism, and colonial sentiment" and how, in Chinua Achebe's words, writers tended to look "to Africa for" an "exoticism that demeans [its] people" (Monaghan).

These first four Tarzan features were necessarily silent pictures. Cullen, however, added a soundtrack to his printed visual jungle caricature: the songs of "wild barbaric birds," "great drums throbbing," the "savage measures" sung by dark young lovers, and the "primal measures" summoning the poet to "doff" his civilized habiliments. The archaic, stiffly "poetic" verb "doff," though, seems strikingly out of place amid all this call-of-the-wild rhetoric. This archaic verb, along with its antonym "don" and the conjunction "lest," underscores the conspicuous formality of "Heritage" as a whole and serves to highlight the conflict between the primitive and the civilized, as popularly understood. Most broadly, the conflict plays out in the incompatibility of the speaker's jungle story, with its ominous sounds and lurid sights, and the poem's highly wrought stanzaic English verse and the repeated refrain "so I lie," a confession to artificing and fabricating. These moves emphatically and implicitly claim a place in DuBois's longed-for "kingdom of culture" and declare the poem's status as a product of the most highly regarded (Anglo) civilization of the time. Cullen ends the poem, however, by relinquishing this grasp of civilization. The speaker of the poem acknowledges:

> Not yet has my heart or head
> In the least way realized
> They and I are civilized.

In reaching this conclusion "Heritage" equates being "civilized" literally with being a dead letter, part of a "book one thumbs" mindlessly: an imaginary "dark continent" constructed out of the stock images of snakes, wild cats, naked "jungle boys," and "heathen gods." Cullen frames this mindless narrative as a legacy of colonialism's "civilizing mission," popularized in Edgar Rice Burroughs's Tarzan novels as newly adopted and adapted by Hollywood.

As an early and influential promoter of Hollywood intellect, poet
Vachel Lindsay heralded this vogue with his most ambitiously conceived
work, a "wild rhapsody" titled "Congo," which Lindsay envisioned as

> equal parts (1) the death of a missionary on the Congo (2) a cannibal
> war dance (3) The Springfield, Illinois, race riots (4) The burnings alive
> of Negroes in the South (5) The camp-meetings of half-wild negroes
> (6) Bert Williams Negro Comedy Company (7) A minstrel show (8) Jo-
> seph Conrad's African sketches (9) *Uncle Tom's Cabin* (10) The Emancipa-
> tion Proclamation (11) The songs of Stephen Collins Foster (12) *The Souls
> of Black Folk* by W.E.B. DuBois—all boiled down and served to a ragtime
> tune. (Untermeyer 152)

Lindsay's seemingly contradictory mélange of progressive sympathy—
DuBois, emancipation agenda, exposés of lynching—and racist clichés—
minstrel shows, Foster songs, cannibal and half-wild Negroes—and Lindsay's
status as one of the earliest voices of Hollywood fandom evokes the cultural
climate Cullen confronts in "Heritage."

James Baldwin would come to confront this climate a generation later
in reckoning with the ascendancy of Hollywood as a predominant civiliza-
tion-arbiter and as the prime producer of "the interior life of Americans,"
particularly of America's view of "Negro bodies," as Baldwin argued in
1955 (*Notes* 50, 52). Not surprisingly, Baldwin's fiction stages and thus
implicitly asks the question "Heritage" ends with. The protagonist of
Baldwin's 1968 novel *Tell Me How Long the Train's Been Gone*, an African
American movie star, urges, some forty years after "Heritage":

> "Let's take off these clothes," I said, "and go to bed like civilized people."
> She smiled, "*Are* we civilized?" "Hell, no. But come on and take me to
> your big brass bed . . . and give me some head." (173)

Though one does so coarsely and the other stanzaically, Baldwin and Cullen
both grapple with the same questions about how others represented them
and how they might in turn represent themselves. These questions, which
challenged African American writers all century long, became increasingly
vexatious as Hollywood exerted more and more influence on drawing or
redrawing, reinforcing or blurring DuBois's color line. In his 2007 novel
Zeroville, Steve Erickson has a movie-loving mugger cite the 1981 Best
Picture Oscar winner *Raging Bull* to explain how Hollywood sustained
this cultural—racial—confusion throughout the twentieth century: "what
you got here is the confusion of white folks thinking they're civilized and
shit—arias playing overhead—while the real white *thang*, which is beating

the shit out of folks, by which I mean folks reaching down into their souls for what they really are . . . compared to what they want to be" (261).

Published during the transition from print-dominated to Hollywood-dominated mass culture, Cullen's reflections in "Heritage" on being "civilized and shit" represent the midpoint in the African American literary engagement with influential civilizing missionaries and the civilization panic these missionaries confected and exploited. A generation earlier, before Hollywood emerged as an arbiter of civilization and so became available as foil, Chesnutt's *Marrow* had similarly teased readers' "knowledge" of "the dark continent." Like Cullen's speaker in "Heritage," Chesnutt's narrator turns to stock, bookish European images of a similarly familiar, historically remote, and durably exotic desert Africa, only to turn these clichés against their promoters, by recalling how

> the Negro race was here before the Anglo-Saxon was evolved, and his thick lips and heavy lidded eyes looked out from the inscrutable face of the Sphinx across the sands of Egypt while yet the ancestors of those who now oppress him were living in caves, practicing human sacrifice, and painting themselves with woad. (62)

For the rest of the century—increasingly after the introduction of "talkies"—Hollywood persisted in purveying primitivist and exoticizing narratives and African American writers kept playing off, undermining, and complicating the clichés and material constraints that these narratives fostered.

II

Depression-era and postwar African American novelists embedded the questions about representation raised by earlier writers in the twentieth century more vividly in the conditions, "the mode of space and time" that academics and intellectuals have come to call "modernity": its boundary-defying "maelstrom of perpetual disintegration and renewal"; "the discourse and controversy" it generates "over the meaning of modernity"; and especially "its power to generate" the "'outward show,' brilliant designs, glamorous spectacles" so successfully produced by Hollywood (Berman, *Solid* 15, 33). Richard Wright's 1937 manifesto "A Blueprint for Negro Writing," for example, singled out African American writers whose "access to a wide social vision and . . . deep social consciousness" freed them to "push their claims upon civilization" while grappling with "the meaning of their being transplanted from a 'savage' to a 'civilized' culture" ("Blueprint" 38, 47). Ralph Ellison opens his 1952 classic *Invisible Man* with his narrator's banning the very word "civilization" from his lexicon (6), though he cannot do without it as part of his disparaging reflections on the "sophistication, decadence, and over-simplification" he encounters among the white revolutionaries, self-professed "scientific" modernizers, who employ him (350, 358, 418). Unlike his narrator, Ellison grew to see himself as a defeated champion of civilization. Ellison "feared that blacks" had "already opted to slide outside history to an expressionist demi-life of sometimes morbid, sometime ecstatic signs, symbols, and gestures that signaled" the collective African American "abandonment of and by civilization," argues Ellison's biographer Arnold Rampersad (quoted in Boygoda 95).

More akin to Ellison's *Invisible Man* narrator than to Ellison himself, his and Wright's younger contemporary James Baldwin looked to "the present civilization . . . the only one that matters" from a willfully alienating distance. Where Ellison saw an ideal being unfortunately "abandoned," Baldwin looked caustically upon a construct belonging exclusively to "white men" while envisioning himself as a "bastard of the West" and a "citizen" of an alienating but not alien Western civilization (*Notes* 6–7, 172–73). This cultivated alienation both from and within Western civilization figures perhaps most extravagantly at the end of Toni Morrison's first novel, *The Bluest Eye*. A thoroughly schooled, charlatan "misanthrope" (166), the neighborhood "Spiritualist and Psychic Reader," whose "business was dread" and who mock-allegorically names himself Soaphead Church, comes to embody and promote the Negrophobic, Europhile creed inherited from his Creole forebears: "Exposure to the best minds of the western world," including Christ, Shakespeare, Dante, Gibbon, and Dostoyevsky instilled in him a conviction that "all civilizations derive from the white race" (168).

Movies provided these four novelists an arena for staging, piquing, and containing both claims to civilization and critiques of civilization-panic and civilizing-mission narratives. These narratives found sponsors both among guardians of elite culture and purveyors of mass entertainment. Consequently, these writers promoted resistance to both elite cultural authority and to the allure of the movies as an alternative to this authority. Targeting them jointly as equally corrosive and playing these sources of cultural authority off against each other provided Wright, Ellison, Morrison, Baldwin, and playwright Amiri Baraka a set of artistic opportunities unavailable to pre-Hollywood African American writers. Tensions in the novelists' narratives, between narrators and characters, or, in Baraka's work, between cultural authorities and cultural suitors, also help flesh out the theoretical argument Manthia Diawara made in 1988 about failures, and the consequent imperative, to account for "the experience of black spectators" at the movies and about how African American moviegoers "may circumvent" or "resist the . . . Hollywood narrative" and especially its "racial representations" (*Film Theory* 892).

In Wright's critically and commercially successful first novel, *Native Son* (1940), these tensions emerge early in the narrative with the title character reacting to the movies. Wright shows a group of young men, neighborhood friends from Chicago's Black Belt, prompted by their contact with a movie "screen" that "flashed with the rhythm of moving shadows" to try on alternative but unattainable identities by "playing 'white,'" mimicking the "manners of white folks" (18). When protagonist Bigger Thomas tries playing a general he commands his buddies to "attack the enemy's . . . flank"; one friend asks, "What's a 'flank'?" to which Bigger replies that he doesn't know but he "heard it in the movies" (18). Actually attending a movie, however, shrouds these young men in darkness, a cover for ritual group masturbation, piqued by fantasies of sexual prowess—the power of eliciting groans of pleasure from their absent girlfriends. The feature they had been waiting for while each enjoyed "polishing my nightstick" (30) illustrates the gap between the empowering identities they fantasized about and the everyday roles demanded of them in the light, outside the theater.

An online synopsis of *Trader Horn*, the feature Wright chose to show his protagonist Bigger Thomas and his friends watching, reverberates caustically with the novel's title. *Trader Horn* features a great-white hunter on safari, though the online imdb.com blurb for the movie signals the extent to which "natives" and presumably "native sons" invariably played leading roles in such familiar civilization-panic narratives. *Trader Horn* at once exploits and questions the very narratives Bigger Thomas and his friends get to consume while having had no hand in producing them:

> While on safari in an unexplored area of Africa, Trader Horn and Peru find missionary Edith Trent killed by natives. They decide to carry on her quest for her lost daughter Nina. They find her as the queen of a particularly savage tribe, and try to bring her back to civilization.

As Bigger watches *Trader Horn* the screen shows naked Africans "whirling in wild dances" to the roll of tom-toms punctuated by "images" in Bigger's "mind" of fashionable "white men and women" laughing, talking, dancing, and drinking (37).

Intelligentsia Café, Sunset Boulevard. Courtesy of L.A. Filtered, spaffy.wordpress.com/.

The Savage Eye (1960). Courtesy of Kingsley-International Pictures.

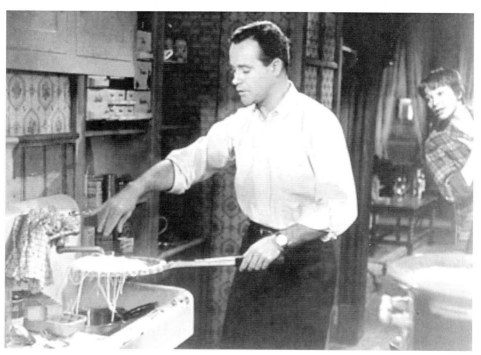

The Apartment *(1960). Printed with the permission of MGM Studios.*

Night of the Hunter *(1955). Printed with the permission of MGM Studios.*

Love and Death *(1975). Printed with the permission of MGM Studios.*

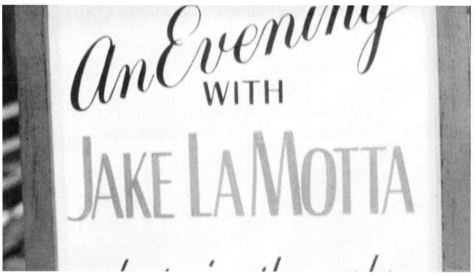

Raging Bull (*1980*). *Printed with the permission of MGM Studios.*

Raging Bull (*1980*). *Printed with the permission of MGM Studios.*

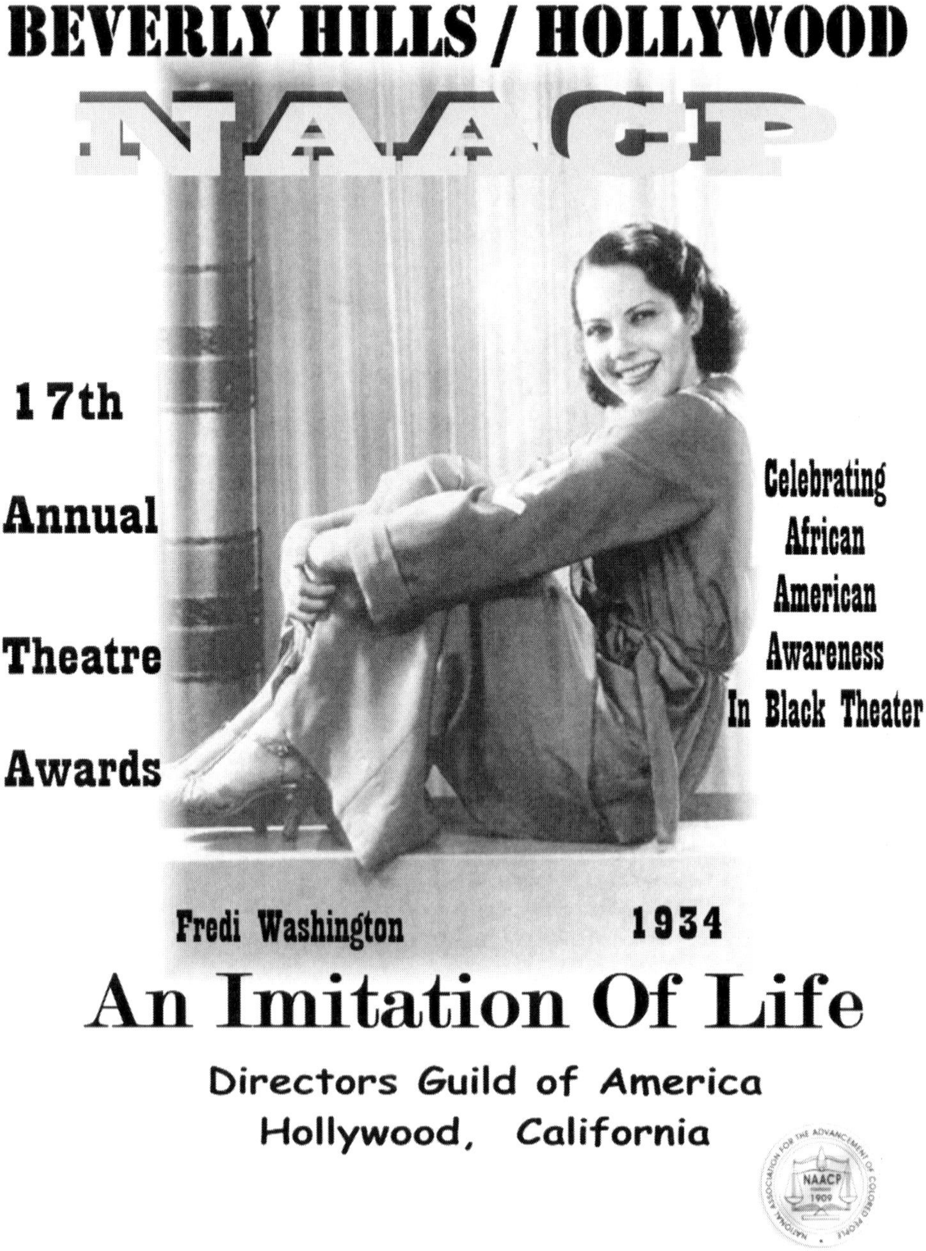

BEVERLY HILLS / HOLLYWOOD
NAACP

17th

Annual

Theatre

Awards

Celebrating
African
American
Awareness
In Black Theater

Fredi Washington   1934

An Imitation Of Life

Directors Guild of America
Hollywood, California

Beverly Hills/Hollywood NAACP.

THE SIDNEY POET HEROICAL

AMIRI BARAKA

Amiri Baraka. Reprinted by permission of SLL/Sterling Lord Literistic, Inc. © Amiri Baraka.

Annie Hall *(1977)*. *Printed with the permission of MGM Studios.*

Annie Hall *(1977)*. *Printed with the permission of MGM Studios.*

Annie Hall (1977). Printed with the permission of MGM Studios.

Annie Hall (1977). Printed with the permission of MGM Studios.

Like Cullen, Wright counterpoints a familiar primitivist Africa with an understanding of what's popularly taken to be civilized. This 1933 MGM release is an adaptation of Ethelreda Lewis's 1927 (as-told-to) "autobiography" of a "talkative old adventurer" (2:61) from Lancashire named Aloysius Horn. Twenty years later in Billy Wilder's *Stalag 17*, a passing wisecrack addressed to the black-market conniver played by William Holden—"Come on, Trader Horn, let's hear it. What'd you give the krauts for that egg?"—illustrates Horn's sustained mass-cult appeal between the world wars.

Trader Horn recounts its narrator's African exploits and his "relations with civilization, 'so-called' as he puts it" (McFee 11). Filmed partly on location in both the Nile and Congo basins and touted consequently for its documentary verisimilitude, this movie aimed expressly to answer Cullen's question, "What is Africa?" A trailer for *Trader Horn* promises and boasts that the movie "reveals the long hidden secrets of the dark continent." The screenplay establishes Horn's authority to address Cullen's question through his familiarity with local languages and wild fauna, his rapport with and deference to his native "gun bearer," and the love and appreciation of Africa he repeatedly expresses: "Aye, you needn't think there isn't beauty to be found in Africa—beauty and terror." Such sage pronouncements punctuate both the movie's safari and rescue narratives. At climactic moments Horn declares "that's Africa," adding such truisms as "when you're not eatin' someone you're trying to keep someone from eating you" or (after a rhino charge) "one dead man, two dead beasts, and no one the better." When Wright describes Bigger reacting to the movie, he edits out Horn's mediating commentary. For instance, "the roll of tom-toms" that *Native Son* registers seems to counter Horn's view of the drums as a reflection of the local Africans' sophistication and not simply the inarticulate "throbbing" Cullen evoked. Civilized in conception while seeming "primitive" to Europeans, the tom-toms function, in Horn's view, like "a telegraph" that strikes European ears as "a sound that'll crawl up your spine and down to your gizzard."

With this move Wright dismisses Cullen's images both of Africa and "the West" (which figures metonymically in "Heritage" as the Villon sonnet Cullen quotes, *Ou Sont les Neiges d'Antan*) as a "book" or print text. Wright instead shows Bigger's imaginary geography as mapped by movies, Hollywood-made images (Perez 156–57). As the images become fully amenable to the demands of "his own mind," Bigger's consciousness seamlessly segues between equally stock, pat scenes and erases conventionally invidious differences between black and white, between "darkest Africa" and café society, and between one Hollywood cliché and another.

> [T]he screen flashed with the rhythm of moving shadows. . . . He looked at *Trader Horn* unfold and saw pictures of naked black men and women whirling in wild dances and heard drums beating and then the scene gradually changed and was replaced by images in his own mind of white men and women dressed in black and white clothes, laughing, talking, dancing, and drinking. (36)

Five years later, Wright's autobiographical narrative *Black Boy* registered more discursively both the transformative promise and the corrupting limitations of attachment to the movies. As in *Native Son*, the conception of the movies in this autobiography includes the movies as a milieu—a cultural climate or what sociologists call a habitus—as well as a stock of on-screen images and narratives. Wright even attributes his escape from unbearably oppressive circumstances to slightly more open conditions, his departure from Mississippi and the "peasant" fate (35, 284) that he knows awaits him if he stays in the South, to his brief job at a movie theater as a ticket-taker (202–5). The graft and petty criminal opportunities the job affords Wright enable him to pay his way to Memphis, a crucial urban way-station on his journey north to Chicago. Chicago brings gradual enlightenment. In *Black Boy* Wright turns the same movies that stirred Bigger Thomas's disruptive, self-destroying longings and prompted Bigger to "lose himself" in *Native Son* (278; Perez 157) into the raw material of "consciousness":

> Slowly I began to forge in the depths of my mind a mechanism that repressed all the dreams and desires that the Chicago streets, the newspapers, the movies were evoking in me. I was going through a second childhood; a new sense of the limit of the possible was being born in me. What could I dream of that had the barest possibility of coming true? I could think of nothing. And, slowly, it was upon exactly that nothingness that my mind began to dwell, that constant sense of wanting without having, of being hated without reason. A dim notion of what life meant to a Negro in America was coming to consciousness in me. (*Black* 267)

In addition to turning repeatedly to the "movies" in these narratives, Wright also stands out among mid-century African American novelists as particularly gripped by the interwar contention over the meaning of civilization and culture and even by the protracted contest many intellectuals saw framing the world wars: the twentieth century's ideologically explosive conflict between *zivilisation* and *kultur* (Benhabib 11–12). *Black Boy*, which Wright completed during World War II, keeps revisiting while cumulatively broadening this contest.

Worrying early in *Black Boy* about having "never been allowed to catch the full spirit of Western civilization" (37), Wright goes on to recollect the epiphany he experienced after moving to the Dixie metropolis of Memphis, the realization that "I was living in a culture and not a civilization" (196). Wright recalls later extrapolating from this epiphany that "wherever my eyes turned they saw stricken black faces trying vainly to cope with a civilization they did not understand" and sets out to confront, if not "solve . . . the deeper problem of American civilization" (263, 298).

III

James Baldwin, writing a decade later, looked to a particular movie for such an "understanding . . . of American civilization." In reviewing Otto Preminger's *Carmen Jones*, Baldwin argued that unwittingly, as "a series of images" rather through "dialogue" and plot, *Carmen Jones* made its mark through "the questions it leaves in the mind" about "the interior life of Americans" (*Notes* 50, 53). Baldwin made this remark in the course of panning rather than praising *Carmen Jones*, viewing this 1954 adaptation of the Bizet opera and Mérimée novel, more as a symptom of rather than a response to "the deeper problem" Wright had targeted. Baldwin characterized this problem by belittling himself as a "bastard interloper" in a "civilization" created by and for "white men" and as at once cursed and endowed with a "heritage" he "could not hope possibly to use" (6–7).

As Baldwin's oeuvre indicates, though, he *did* use various legacies of "Western" and American civilization, to the point of recreating one of his own traumas in the heart of European civilization as a movie. His arrest as recounted in "Equal in Paris" prompted him to equate his initial administrative processing in the French penal system and the architecture of his prison with sequences recalled from "movies I have seen" (148). Despite his initial impression of incarceration as movie-like, Baldwin goes on to identify parts of prison life that "the movies fail to give any idea of" (152). As with Bigger Thomas, though blessed with the self-reflectiveness Bigger lacked, Baldwin finds movies setting his mind in motion, providing images with which he at once envisions his condition and distorts or constricts his understanding of his condition.

Baldwin's 1957 story "Sonny's Blues" stresses these failures, preempting the possibility and blunting the promise that movies might prove illuminating. Early in "Sonny's Blues," the narrator presents himself an agent or at least a voice of civilization. This Harlem high school algebra teacher, a self-appointed if questionably effective paterfamilias, contemplates his students' and his own coming of age, envisioning them, as Wright did in the dark, at the movies:

> These boys, now, were living as we'd been living then, they were growing up with a rush and their heads bumped abruptly against the low ceiling of their actual possibilities. They were filled with rage. All they really knew were two darknesses, the darkness of their lives, which was now closing in on them, and the darkness of the movies, which had blinded them to that other darkness, and in which they now, vindictively, dreamed, at once more together than they were at any other time, and more alone. (*Going* 104)

Dispelling darkness, the darkness Baldwin links to the darkness moviegoers necessarily inhabit, signals metaphorically a shared ideological commitment among African American writers of Baldwin's generation—the generation that effectively integrated American letters—to grapple with the power of movies.

IV

Ralph Ellison demonstrated this commitment most broadly in the prologue of his National Book Award–winning 1952 novel, *Invisible Man*.

> My hole is warm and full of light. Yes, *full* of light. I doubt if there is a brighter spot in all New York than this hole of mine, and I do not exclude Broadway. Or the Empire State Building on a photographer's dream night. But that is taking advantage of you. Those two spots are among the darkest of our whole civilization—pardon me, our whole *culture* (an important distinction, I've heard)—which may sound like a hoax, or a contradiction, but that (by contradiction, I mean) is how the world moves: Not like an arrow, but a boomerang. (6)

Anxiety over the meaning of "civilization"—over the very appropriateness of the word—and over the technological (photographic) representation of "our whole civilization" or "culture" converge in the consciousness of Ellison's narrator. An instance of what Elizabeth Yukins called Ellison's "keen interest in the relation between visual perception and politics" (1249), this postcard skyscraper image presents civilization itself as a mediated, filmed illusion. What this illusion veils Ellison's narrator comes to recognize much later in the novel. In this sequence the narrator peers at a barroom poster of a young woman advertising beer and sees there an image of a "cold-steel civilization" (271). With this phrase, one more literally applicable to the skyscraper cited in the novel's prologue, Ellison equates the way modern technology shapes the built environment with the way it shapes gazing and the desires it prompts. In concocting his dazzling "photographer's dream" out of darkness, Ellison's prologue sheds light on the contested meanings of civilization and culture and broadens Baldwin's understanding of movies as "literally, a series of images" to a concept of civilization itself. *Invisible Man* repeatedly contests the meaning of civilization and highlights the role of race—or color—as well as sex and social status in this discursive struggle over who gets to determine the criteria for being civilized.

First Ellison shows his narrator's Garveyite antagonist Ras exposing civilization as most Americans, especially educated African Americans, understood it. Though built with "black blood," civilizations inevitably get represented by the "blahsted lies in some bloody books written by the white man" (375–76)—like the "book" Cullen's speaker "thumbs" in "Heritage," for example. Later Ellison shows his narrator fretting over the prospect of having been corrupted by the decadent "over-civilization" (418) he comes to associate with white affluence, particularly the "primitivist" erotic fantasies about African Americans such affluence often sponsors. Such passages in *Invisible Man* cumulatively anticipate the narrator's later realization that a civilization or culture rests largely on the way it presents itself, on its image or the "face" it shows the world. This realization comes to Ellison's invisible man as he recalls a lecture on James Joyce he heard in college (a "Negro college" like the one Ellison himself attended). The lecturer, he recalls, insisted that "Stephen Daedalus's problem . . . was not actually one of creating the uncreated conscience of his race" (as Joyce wrote), "but of creating the *uncreated features of his face*" (354). With the creation of such a face, the narrator's professor prophesied, "we will have created a culture."

In the apocalyptic climax of *Invisible Man*, a *Walpurgisnacht* of ominously shifting chiaroscuro, the movies displace Joyce as the cultural given—the raw materials with which the "uncreated features" of the coming culture will be forged. The movies join jazz and all the many literary and historical references and allusions through which Ellison refracts his narrator's experience (Nadel, *Invisible* xii, 32, 53–56). Attacked and rescued in front of "a movie house," the invisible man finds himself "in the dark," whereupon he flees into a crowd "all wearing dark glasses" like his own. This dark-glasses "fad," which the invisible man previously "had considered an empty imitation of Hollywood," suddenly becomes "flooded with personal significance" (482). With this "signifying" (Gates 105, 111, 121), the act of imitating America's countless Hollywood wannabes mutates from group vanity to a significant personal—aesthetic or ideological—choice. Ellison's narrator registers this change in perspective, rapidly and montage-like, only to have his new insight immediately displaced as he finds his "personal significance" overshadowed and "muted" by "the garish signs of movie houses" (484).

This movie-house perspective moves to the foreground in Ellison's unfinished, posthumously released novel *Juneteenth*. Like the professor's culture-forging imperative in *Invisible Man*, instructions about vision and image issue forth in this novel too, from a wise elder, a preacher named Daddy Hickman. Hickman, who serves as the variously named, racially mobile protagonist's mentor and guardian angel, reflects on the experience of going to the movies, where moviegoers are likely to find "the light of darkness" and to learn that "it's not so much a matter of where you are as what you see" (221). For both mentors images take precedence in changing the world, in transforming both the self and the self's enveloping culture or civilization. Both mentors challenge the perennial wisdom reflected in proverbs that warn against judging books by their covers or that preface the phrase "skin deep" with the adverb "only."

Cinematically and for members of a modern mass audience, the "face" of the "created culture"—or civilization—prophesied in *Invisible Man* shows up on screen as a close-up or an extreme close-up in *Juneteenth* as the narrator evokes this sensation of belonging to this audience and of watching culture being created on screen. Bliss (a.k.a Sunraider and "Mr. Movie Man"), the novel's protean protagonist, recalls finding civilization in its entirety on the flat 2-D screen surface the first time he went to the movies, where he could "watch . . . the flickery scenes . . . unreeling inside my eye just as daddy Hickman could make people relive the action of the Word. . . . I could feel myself drawn into the world . . . shared so intensely . . . I felt that I had actually taken part not only in the seeing but in the very actions unfolding in the depths of the wall . . . in a darkness I'd never known . . . a whole world uncoiling through an eye of glass" (63).

To the degree that the Bible, "the Word," has presumably helped preserve and disseminate what we call Western civilization and to the extent that we regard a civilization as a social body, movies appear in this passage to represent the most forceful instrument of civilization. This sequence continues to show Bliss finding in the movies an elaborate revelation of "meanness transcendent" in the "one overwhelming face" that appears on screen as he

> sat dizzy with the vastness of the action and the scale of the characters and the dimensions of the emotions and responses . . . mouths so broad and cavernous that they seemed to yawn well-hole wide and threaten to gulp the whole audience into their traps of hilarious maliciousness . . . made concrete through the pantomime of conflict. (234)

"Meanness," "maliciousness," and "conflict" recall and elaborate the steely "coldness" Ellison ascribed to civilization itself in *Invisible Man* and the threat of violence on which civilization, in Freud's account, rests. The power of technology that *Invisible Man* associates with electricity, photography, subways, and skyscrapers, Ellison links to the movies in *Juneteenth*. When Ellison depicts a movie as "wavery . . . smokelike . . . light," which looks "more real than flesh or stone," he suggests a rough emblematic equivalence between the illuminated skyscraper as a "photographer's dream" in *Invisible Man* and the movies in *Juneteenth* as luciferous artifices that heighten and promise to transform perception.

Early in *Juneteenth* Ellison shows Bliss, a director repeatedly referred to as Mr. Movie Man, musing on this transformative power, "watching the rushes" on his moviola and wondering, "why these images and what was their power" (85). "Flying Home," an early story by Ellison, provided one answer to this question by showing its supposedly educated, sophisticated hero, a Tuskegee flight cadet named Todd, subjected to this power. At the start of story, as his plane crashes, Todd's first visual impression reflects not any immediate sensation but rather the "jagged scenes, swiftly unfolding as in a movie trailer" that "reeled through his mind" (*Flying* 147). Todd's rescuer, a local Alabama "peasant" sardonically named Jefferson, sets out to persuade the cadet to "know his place" instead of wanting "to fly way up there in the air" (153). Jefferson spins an autobiographical tall tale about how he died and went to heaven where he got to fly with angel wings, though the heavenly authorities subjected his flight to Jim Crow restrictions "'cause us colored folks had to wear a special kin' a harness when we flew" (158).

This seeming piece of "peasant" folklore recalls, allusively and ironically, a more recent, modern source than "folk" typically suggests. This source, *The Green Pastures* a 1936 Warner Brothers feature, was popular enough to open at the new Radio City Music Hall. Ellison had, more-

over, attended a stage version of *The Green Pastures* while an undergraduate at Tuskegee Institute (Rampersad 58). Thanks to its rhetoric and its
authorship *The Green Pastures* came to stage and screen as unimpeachably
well-intentioned and "progressive" and "as good a religious play as one
is likely to get from a practiced New York writer" (Greene, *Film* 122).
Written and codirected by the avowedly leftist playwright Marc Connelly, it reflected the "Popular Front" attitudes prevalent among intellectuals, artists, and their publics in 1936. Nevertheless, even a favorable
review praised *The Green Pastures* in terms likely to pique wariness in
African American audiences, even some "resistance" (Diawara). *Times*
reviewer Bosley Crowther enthused about this "naïve, ludicrous, sublime
and heartbreaking masterpiece of American folk drama." With its "simple and gratifying theology," *Green Pastures* exudes a "nostalgic feeling"
in part by showing a winged black actor (Oscar Polk) playing the angel
Gabriel in "robes of monumental descending folds." Heaven appears as a
cluster of "luxurious overstuffed clouds in mid-empyrean that the angels
fish from," with a single flaw, which God readily remedies. Like the
daunting skies in "Flying Home," heaven has "a lot of firmament . . . too
much firmament," as God—like Ellison's Todd—learns. Earth, which
frames the narrative about biblically recounted heavenly interventions,
appears in *Green Pastures* as "a peaceful, churchgoing Negro community"
in "a little back-country church house" and its congregation of "pious
townsfolk going along to meeting." At a considerable distance from the
African American conditions that Ellison and probably even Connelly
knew, Graham Greene found *The Green Pastures* "patronizing, quaint"
and "sentimental," such that it made him "uneasy" with its "humor" and
prompted him to "wonder whether the Negro mind is quite so material"
(*Film* 122). Not surprisingly, therefore, from a writer with Ellison's famously wary sensibility, resistance took the form of "signifying." Arnold
Rampersad's account of Ellison's sparse movie criticism indicates that he
"harbored no illusions about Hollywood's . . . treatment of blacks" (247)
while Ellison's familiarity with Connelly's work makes it likely that the
"signifying" in "Flying Home"—the angel trope—is in part a response
to *Green Pastures*, a measure of how "stuck in a plantation attitude" Hollywood remained, in Ellison's view, throughout its first talkie decade
(Crafton 410).

A generation later, *Juneteenth* would serve to elaborate Ellison's indictment of Hollywood's heavenly charms. The "camera" Bliss wields,
"instead of taking in a scene" passively, "becomes catalytically aggressive"
and "seemed to focus forth" his "own point of view," empowering him

to feel that his "images" are "blasting . . . the world" (265–66). Recalling the structure of the Greek tragedies customarily grouped among Western civilization's foundational texts (just as "Flying Home" recalled Icarus), Ellison shows Bliss's first moviegoing experience, his response to the "spill of light" with which movie cameras frame images: "*Far shot to medium, to close: poiema, pathema, mathema.*" The third Greek term in Ellison's sequence, *mathema*, the term matched with the close-up, can translate from classical Greek as knowledge or perception. Greek tragedy, especially the trilogies of Aeschylus and Sophocles, often enacted the civilizing process—our species' progression away from accepting internecine killing, blood feuds, and human sacrifices—as moving toward the codifying of knowledge, even wisdom, in the form of laws and institutions. With a plot that transforms Bliss from a moviemaker to a U.S. senator felled by hubris and with his characteristically allusive, erudite sequencing, Ellison intimates the connection in *Juneteenth* between the knowledge the close-up provides and the moment one becomes or at least recognizes what it means to be *civilized*.

Bliss's post-showbiz career as the white supremacist Senator Sunraider calls into question the value and effectiveness of the cinematic civilizing equated with Bliss's coming of age and of the lessons he learned as a young man in his first adult career as a moviemaker. The incompleteness of Ellison's narrative and the very multiplicity of identities Ellison attributed to Bliss over the course of the novel leaves this question open. Toni Morrison's 1970 novel *The Bluest Eye*, in contrast, emphatically and darkly answers this question by at once recognizing and discrediting the civilizing power of movies.

V

The villains in *The Bluest Eye* never appear in the foreground, in the narrative proper. Nevertheless, they haunt the characters in flashbacks and reflections. They also exert their influence from movie screens, their names resound in the casual remarks of grownups, and their faces even peer out from studio-licensed, star-promoting merchandise like dolls and milk mugs. Morrison echoes Baldwin's derision two years earlier in *Tell Me How Long the Train's Been Gone* of Ann Sheridan and Ronald Reagan in *King's Row* (196–99). A prime example, Parker Tyler protests, of how Hollywood has ritually "snubbed reality," *King's Row* affirms Hollywood's all-too-typical "look the other way" aversion to cruelty and "sadism" (164), which Morrison savages in *The Bluest Eye*.

In *The Bluest Eye* Morrison's Hollywood-bashing ratchets up Baldwin's earlier critiques in his essays, in "Sonny's Blues," and in *Tell Me How Long the Train's Been Gone*. Morrison scourges such Hollywood immortals as Shirley Temple and Claudette Colbert, as well as the now-obscure faded star Jane Withers, because of the extent to which several characters in the novels—girls and women—self-corrosively identify with them. Frequent explanatory interruptions of the narrative that afford various characters, including the first-person narrator, opportunities to take ideological positions and enunciate their principles spotlight these villains. Though they can hardly be held accountable for Hollywood's ideological and mass-psychological impact, Morrison identifies these vilified stars' Hollywood movies with the always-looming civilization panic and audience-belittling civilizing-mission narratives that Hollywood has long sponsored.

Morrison's narrator, speaking as a child, establishes herself early on in the narrative as a visceral film critic and intuitive cultural commentator. With her countercultural observations, she resists the supposedly universal appeal of Shirley Temple. Franklin Delano Roosevelt affirmed this appeal and Temple's role in maintaining domestic hegemony by reassuring Americans that "as long as we have Shirley Temple, we'll be all right" (Kehr, "Shirley"). Temple's popularity peaked in the first talkie decade when Hollywood's "plantation attitude" still prevailed (Crafton 410). Here Morrison's narrator challenges the assumptions on which the child star's appeal rested. Directing her "unsullied hatred" at a "blue and white Shirley Temple cup" and the cup's "silhouette" of the child star's "dimpled face," the narrator reacts to two older girls' "loving conversation about how cu-ute" the star is:

> I couldn't join them in their adoration because I hated Shirley . . . because she had danced with Bojangles, who was *my* friend, *my* uncle, *my* daddy, and . . . ought to have been soft-shoeing it and chuckling with me. Instead he was enjoying . . . a lovely dance with one of those little girls whose socks never slid down under their heels. (19)

Morrison shows this young observer feeling loath to voice such sentiments. Her precociously sophisticated understanding of how Shirley Temple's "popularity" "rests on a coquetry quite as mature as Miss Colbert's and on an oddly precocious body as voluptuous in gray flannel trousers as Miss Dietrich's" (Greene, *Film* 92), of the typical Temple script as covertly depicting adult-sponsored child torture (Morin 140), and of the actress herself as "a bossy brat who faked her way forward" so much so that "if you met a kid like that in real life, you'd want to smack her" (Basinger 7) mirrors the brutal child abuse that *The Bluest Eyes* probes. Morrison shows her narrator displacing her just, if unutterable, antagonism toward Temple and what she embodies with the "puzzling" and "incomprehensible" announcement that "I like Jane Withers." A child-star contemporary of Shirley Temple's, completely eclipsed by the time *The Bluest Eye* was published in 1970, Withers was groomed by Twentieth-Century Fox in an effort to clone Temple and thus reduce her financial leverage in contract negotiations (Basinger 290). Looking back on this moment from an adult perspective, Morrison's narrator records her realization that she can't beat Hollywood. She accepts the cultural imperative to relinquish her "frightening . . . hatred for all the Shirley Temples of the world" and concedes that "the development of her psyche" through adolescence and into adulthood "would allow"—actually require—her "to love Shirley Temple" (190).

Hollywood's inexorable victory and this narrator's surrender to the idolatry that Hollywood demands on behalf of its stars functions as a partial explanation for the incurable damage—parental abuse and incestuous rape—suffered by the protagonist, the narrator's schoolmate Pecola Breedlove. The very name Pecola, the narrator notes, comes from Universal's early talkie *Imitation of Life* (67). Released in 1934 and remade in the 1950s by Douglas Sirk, the plot features a light-skinned black girl who repudiates her heroically self-sacrificing mother. Starring Claudette Colbert, Louise Beavers, and Fredi Washington, the 1934 version that Morrison alludes to has come to be regarded as "perhaps the most powerful Hollywood film about race until the civil rights movement of the 1950s," a "protest against a system as unjust as it is deeply ingrained" (Kehr, "Shadows"). The rhetorical thrust of Morrison's allusion stresses nevertheless how, in naming her daughter after this character, Pecola's mother (mis)cast her to pass for white—to the play the part Fredi Washington played in 1934. Without Pecola's requisite lack of pigmentation, however, this homage to Hollywood has the effect of bemusing and outcasting Pecola, precluding her from ever belonging—anywhere.

This corrosive relationship between Pecola's mother and the movies becomes the focal point of Morrison's rhetorical agenda in *The Bluest Eye*. The narrator's observations about this relationship prompt broader reflections on some of Western civilization's basic assumptions, on "ideas" throughout "the history of human thought," that Hollywood sustains. Morrison follows the simple observation that Pecola's mother Polly "went to the movies" with an account of how these movies affected her. This account recalls the metaphoric movie-house darkness that enclosed the young men Wright and Baldwin depicted in *Native Son* and "Sonny's

Blues": "In the dark her memory was refreshed, and she succumbed to her earlier dreams." Back home after the movie, Polly decides to "fix" her "hair up like" she'd seen Jean Harlow's (122). Looking back as an adult on Polly's Hollywood-inspired behavior, Morrison's narrator makes a sweeping pronouncement about the baleful effects of Hollywood and about Hollywood's place in the development of civilization:

> Along with the idea of romantic love, she was introduced to another—physical beauty. Probably the most destructive ideas in the history of human thought. Both originated in envy, thrived in insecurity, and ended with disillusion. . . . She was never able, after her education in the movies, to look at a face and not assign it some category in the scale of absolute beauty, and the scale was one she had absorbed in full from the silver screen. (122)

By stressing the harm it causes, Morrison places Hollywood in the chronological continuum encapsulated in phrases like "the history of ideas" or "Western civilization."

Plot and character in *The Bluest Eye* extend the exploitation value of these "destructive ideas" beyond Hollywood—beyond the stars, producers, and financiers who profit directly from the movies—and beyond Pecola and her mother. These ideas reach into the narrator's home and neighborhood. Morrison first embodies this reach in the character of the neighborhood child molester. A boarder in her parents' house, he exploits this "most destructive idea" in order to ingratiate himself to the narrator and her sister, with the reiterated greeting: "Hello there. Greta Garbo. Hello there, Ginger Rogers" (16).

A decade later the penumbra of the white Hollywood star would persist in shadowing Morrison's heroine in *Tar Baby*. Its heroine, a fashion model with a Sorbonne education, couldn't differ more from the marginal proletarians in *The Bluest Eye*. Nevertheless, as she begins her vacation in a "tranquil" Caribbean Eden, on a plantation where "there is no fear," she wakes up "rigid and frightened" from a Hollywood dream, of "Norma Shearer's and Mae West's and Jeanette McDonald's" hats (*Sula/Song/Tar* 45).

Though scathing, Morrison's critique of Hollywood in *The Bluest Eye* diverges from most such mass-cult-bashing jeremiads, which claim customarily to speak from the vantage point of high or elite culture. Morrison disavows this facile vantage point with a sadistically self-discrediting—child-abusing and dog-killing—representative of elite Western civilization. Named Soaphead Church, his attitudes and actions align the corrosive effects of the silver screen with those that come from "exposure to the best minds of the western world" (167). These supposedly civilizing influences underlie his promises to turn Pecola's eyes blue so that she'll come to resemble the Hollywood stars she and her mother idolize and emulate. Resonantly and mordantly naming this deceiver Soaphead Church, Morrison associates him with the civilized virtues of sanctity, intellect, and hygiene. Accordingly she introduces him as a proud heir to and aficionado of "the civilized thing" and an adherent of the hypothesis popularized by early twentieth-century race-science. This "science" (cited by Tom Buchanan in *The Great Gatsby*) legitimated civilization panic and civilizing missions by "proving" that "all civilizations derive from the white race" (*Bluest* 168; see chapter III).

Cumulatively, Morrison's sweeping indictment surpasses earlier critiques of Hollywood as a sponsor of prevailing conceptions of civilization and as a powerful regulator of what constitutes civilization. Morrison, moreover, doubles this critique by positioning Hollywood as part of intellectual history—a source of "ideas in the history of human thought" and a provider of powerful "education" (122). Like *Native Son*, Ellison's novels, and "Sonny's Blues," *The Bluest Eye* challenges the complacencies of civilization's established champions by drawing on the dark/light imagery associated with moviegoing and moviemaking. Showing how Polly, like Bigger, got "educated" in "civilization" at the movies and became persuaded that she found the light in the dark, Morrison inverts the Enlightenment faith in civilization as progress and the belief that civilization will eventually enable everyone to *see the light* and so become part of a more just and more humane future:

> The onliest time I be happy seem like was when I was at the picture show. . . . They'd cut off the lights and everyting be black. Then the screen would light up . . . them pictures gave ma a lot of pleasure, but it made coming home hard. . . . There I was five month pregnant trying to look Jean Harlow, and a front tooth gone [from candy bite]. (123)

Targeting both mass and elite culture—Harlow and the literary canon that Soaphead Church had mastered—Morrison's indictment doesn't simply raise the questions her predecessors had raised about how effectively and honestly Hollywood, along with the traditional "great books" canons, has performed or deformed their supposed civilizing mission. Morrison discredits all such arbitration, all moves to claim the authority to determine what constitutes "the civilized thing."

VI

Discrediting such claims even more starkly, Amiri Baraka's 1964 play *Dutchman* fuses the authority of Western civilization and the meretricious eros of Hollywood in a single figure. This play has only two named characters. Clay, a bookish, college-age African American man, ends up sharing a subway seat with a twentyish blonde named Lula (a.k.a. Lena and Tallulah). Baraka shows Lula as intent on seducing Clay throughout most of the play, only to show her fatally stabbing him in the end.

Baraka ensured that readers and playgoers would see Lula as Western civilization incarnate. With stage directions calling for her to carry a bag of apples (5, 8 11, 14, 18, 23, 28), which she offers Clay, Baraka aligned her with Eve, the book of Genesis, and the Abrahamic creation narrative. The title of the play, moreover, recalls Richard Wagner, his 1843 opera *Der Fliegende Hollander* (*The Flying Dutchman*), and his consummately multimedia, all-encompassing aesthetic *Gesamtkunstwerk*. The *Flying Dutchman* libretto recounts the misadventures of a ship's captain doomed never to reach port until redeemed by love. As in *Romeo and Juliet*, the lovers in the opera end up killing themselves as result of being left in the dark. Baraka expressly adds this *Romeo and Juliet* connection with Lula's reference to her walkup as "Juliet's tomb" (26). Thus she—and Baraka—could claim (in DuBois's phrase) to sit with Shakespeare. Baraka has Lula clinch her role as the voice of cultural authority when she repeatedly pronounces Clay "the black Baudelaire" (19–20), a vocation Baraka shows Clay readily embracing.

Baraka also shows Lula representing Hollywood. She identifies herself, albeit inconsistently, as an actress. To Clay, the scenarios with which Lula regales him "sound great. Like movies" (*Dutchman* 28). Baraka's career-long preoccupation with Hollywood's products dates back to his Newark childhood. In a 1982 interview Baraka revealed that "radio and movies" exerted "the biggest influence on" him ("Revolution" 87). This fascination embraced the extremes of vilification and full-fledged complicity.

This attraction-repulsion stance toward Hollywood constitutes one of the few obvious parallels between Baraka's and Baldwin's roughly simultaneous careers. After Baldwin skewered Hollywood in his 1955 essay on Otto Preminger's *Carmen Jones*, he elaborated this critique in 1968, four years after Baraka premiered *Dutchman*, in *Tell Me How Long the Train's Been Gone*. This first-person narrative charts the career of an African American star of stage (primarily) and screen. "One of the biggest stars we have," he must continuously reflect on and react to his unwanted representative status as the token *Negro* star. Because "no Negro's ever made it that big," this status "must mean a lot to" him and his "people," insists a reporter who questions him about his career plans (275). The novel stresses its hero's stage career, delaying even mentioning his "first movie" for nearly four hundred pages. Nevertheless, the novel's opening shows the hero preferring to view himself cinematically: "not on stage but on screen" in a "long close-up" shot.

At about the same time as *Tell Me How Long the Train's Been Gone* was published, Baldwin found himself "settling down in Hollywood" and "staying at the plush Beverly Hills Hotel" to begin work for Columbia Pictures. His project was a screenplay adaptation of Alex Haley's ghost-written *Autobiography of Malcolm X* (Weatherby 328). Later issued in book form as *One Day When I Was Lost*, Baldwin's script never made it to the screen. (Working from a new script of his own, Spike Lee released an adaptation of Haley's book in 1992 that starred Denzel Washington.)

Like *Tell Me How Long the Train's Been Gone*, Baraka's 1969 play *The Sidney Poet Heroical* (unstaged until 1973) also grapples with the then recent phenomenon of the African American crossover movie star. When Baraka self-published the play text in 1979 the cover contained only a single word beside the title and the playwright's name. Curved arc-like over a light-skinned African American sporting an executive hairdo and wearing a suit made of U.S. paper currency appears the name "HOLLYWOOD" in capital letters. Unlike Baldwin, Baraka eschews fictionalizing his protagonist. Expressly reviling Hollywood's star integrators, Baraka aims squarely—some might say slanderously—at Sidney Poitier. Nonetheless, in this 1969 play Baraka has anticipated the "immense historical significance" Poitier would come to assume (Ryfle).

The cover-illustration caricature of Poitier overstates long-standing consensus views of the contradictions that Poitier's career and screen presence incarnate. With Poitier, Richard Dyer observed a generation ago, "the consummate ease of his manners comes up against the backlog of images of black men as raging authenticities" (*Heavenly* 12). Retrospectives on the "revolutionary" 1967–1968 movie season recall how Poitier, at the height of his career at the end of the 1960s, emerged as "Hollywood's all-purpose answer to America's race problem" (A. O. Scott, "Two"), "the noble Negro who shows up the evils of prejudice" (W. Smith).

Early in *The Sidney Poet Heroical*, Baraka presents his Poitier caricature as a "dreadfully talented brown man." Disappearing into the flickering light of "movie marquees," Sidney is poised to become "the most important star in the whole solar system" (11). Over the course of the play,

Baraka goes on to cast hero-poet Sidney as a twentieth-century Faust who sells his soul to a white agent who turns out in the end to have been the "real star" (76).

Replaying the Faust legend as he replayed the *Flying Dutchman* myth in *Dutchman*, Baraka draws again on the Western canon. He also "sits with Shakespeare" (or at least with Goethe and Marlowe) in accordance with DuBois's indelible aspirational image of cultural arrival. Baraka ends up, though, turning this canon-immersion into a parodic cure for "civilization panic" and the missionary impulse it typically prompts and justifies. One scene plays off Poitier's 1967 star turn in Stanley Kramer's *Guess Who's Coming to Dinner* as "a superachiever, potential Nobel laureate a regular Albert Schweitzer" (Harris, 188, 373), one of two roles that year that led theater owners to vote Poitier "America's biggest box office star" (424). The scene has the Spencer Tracy "father of the bride" character challenging his daughter's black suitor—Poitier in the movie and Sidney in the play—with a "light-weight test" of his mastery of "the law of civilization and decay" (36). Recognizing such names as Shakespeare, Beckett, Kafka, and Stravinsky, Sidney "comes through with flying colorlessness" (35).

The play ends happily. "Through in Hollywood," Sidney has "quit that movie star bullshit" (86) and been rescued from despair by a character named Leader. Echoing a favorite precursor of Baraka's, Dante (as the title of his 1965 novel, *The System of Dante's Hell*, indicates), Leader assures Sidney that after "disappearing out the end" (86)—like Dante returning to the his living world at the end of *Inferno*—he can now "reappear in the real world." Leader urges Sidney, "Don't quit making movies." A chorus seconds Leader, chanting, "we need movies," inspiring Sidney to establish his "own studio" (92). Acerbic as it is, Baraka's take on Poitier's career was part of a broader consensus, which, Mark Harris recounts, prompted Poitier to start winding down his movie career (425). Despite its box-office success, *Guess* met with critical opprobrium that disparaged the story as "a minstrel" spectacle. Reviewers found it at once "lumbering . . . timid and neutral" *and* provocative, bound to "insult its audience," black and white alike (373–74).

A generation after savaging Hollywood at such lengths in *Sidney Poet Heroical*, Baraka, like Sidney, apparently found a home in the movies, ironically at the heart of the reviled studio system. A featured player, Baraka played Rastaman the Griot in Warren Beatty's 1998 Twentieth-Century Fox release *Bulworth*.

Reflecting this complex, if not conflicted relationship with Hollywood, *Dutchman* shows Clay as similarly and also ambivalently star-conscious as he comes to identify Lula as a Hollywood star at the end of the play. Among the three names she bears during the play, her last name is part of Clay's climactic tirade. He calls her "Tallulah Bankhead" (34), naming her after the flamboyantly impulsive and unabashedly promiscuous 1930s and 1940s star. "An exhibitionist and alcoholic" (Douglas 49), Bankhead not surprisingly became a favorite among Hollywood gossip merchants. Her "Rabelaisian" persona mordantly counterpoints the till-death-do-us-part fidelity of Shakespeare's and Wagner's heroines with whom Baraka also aligns Lula. Like Jean Harlow, whom Morrison singles out as a paragon of unattainable Hollywood beauty, Bankhead made her blondness central to her persona. Truman Capote reports that Bankhead once attended a pool party where her hostess offered to lend her a bathing suit, which Bankhead refused because she "just wanted to prove that" she "was a natural ash blonde" (Douglas 48).

In the twilight of her movie career, Bankhead assumed the role of what we now would call a public intellectual in a cover story she wrote for *Ebony* magazine in 1952. This article honors Louis Armstrong (who figured as tutelary genius in *Invisible Man* the very same year) and opens with Bankhead assuming the role of a defender of civilization. Taking a stand against all "the chaos prevailing in the world," she appeals in an Arnoldian voice to "the best human qualities by which people should conduct their lives"; like a Romantic sage, she invokes "transcendent genius," and, like an Enlightenment *philosophe*, she stresses the importance of "illuminating the mysteries of human existence." Bolstering her credentials as a voice of both civilization and Hollywood, Bankhead equates Armstrong with other legendary geniuses: Mozart, Chaplin, Shakespeare, Nijinsky, Joe Louis, Babe Ruth, Caruso, Einstein, and so on. Following DuBois's famous trope, she securely positions Armstrong "across the color line" in "the kingdom of culture."

Though a granddaughter of the Confederacy born into Alabama's leading political clan at the height of Jim Crow, Bankhead gingerly alludes to the bigotry with which much of the public was likely to regard Armstrong, dismissing as "uninitiated" listeners who regard the trumpeter as "nothing more than a stereotyped clown." Since *Ebony*'s target readership consisted of African Americans, Bankhead's purporting to "initiate" these readers as jazz aficionados and to provide the "social or cultural context" needed "to appreciate" Armstrong's art might seem presumptuous—not only in hindsight, but might have in 1952 as well.

In *Dutchman* Baraka targets such presumptuousness early in the play, by showing Lula making several seemingly accurate guesses—"picking things out of the air"—about Clay's background and his friends—"well-known types"—and even his name:

> I bet your name is . . . one of those hopeless colored names . . . it's got to be Williams. You're too pretentious to be a Jackson or Johnson. (15)

However honorably intentioned, Bankhead's *Ebony* article reflects how much she shares in the thinking with which Baraka shows Lula culturally colonizing Clay. This treatment of colonization may help explain the animus toward Bankhead reflected in Clay's name choice when he rechristens Lula Tallulah and proceeds to single her out as the embodiment of murderous whiteness and of the unassailably unified elite and mass-culture complex that Baraka and Morrison both savage. While Morrison's narrative highlighted how Hollywood and a reverence for Western civilization paralleled one another in their corrosive effects, Baraka's fusing of these two institutional sources of cultural authority showed their power to shape identity and aspiration—their power, in Lula's phrase, "to control the world" by lying (9)—as even more alluring, irresistible, and lethal.

Baraka shows Clay in his climactic rant, his failed rhetorical resistance to this "control," moving between and mastering the extremes of civilization panic narratives: murderous savagery and civilizing "Western rationalism" (36). In place of the courtly Armstrong whom Bankhead extols—like her a Hollywood player in his own right in such movies as *Café Society* and *Hello Dolly*—Clay offers up the "unruly" and famously appetitive Bessie Smith and the aesthetically contumacious Charlie Parker, both fatal victims of their own failures to sublimate or perhaps simply to accommodate. As Lula embodies the movies and the voice of civilization, acting decisively and brutally on its behalf, Clay's various reactions to her—submitting, engaging, resisting, joking, ranting, lusting, and dying—come to represent the range of stratagems for bidding to enter DuBois's "kingdom of culture" (109). The kingdom has grown since DuBois's 1903 exhortation and has since come to encompass Shirley Temple and Tallulah Bankhead as much as DuBois's "unwincing" Shakespeare and Voltaire. While recording this expansion, Baraka also offers a warning about how such bids to join this "kingdom" are likely to be received.

Unseen Melodies/Reel Time

Language retains the umbilical, binds one to messy sources; film severs it.

—FREDERIC RAPHAEL

[T]he trouble with you innerleckchuls. You don't never have nothing to show for what you're saying.

—FLANNERY O'CONNOR

Clouds so swift an' rain fallin' in / Gonna see a movie called Gunga Din.

—DYLAN

I

Hollywood persists in grappling with the same intellectual challenge that has stymied artists, theorists, and spectators for much of recorded history (Trimpi 2). This challenge dates back at least two millennia to the formulation in his *Ars Poetica* by the Roman poet Horace of a fundamental classical aesthetical principle, *ut pictura poesis*: a view that poems can do what pictures do and pictures, still as well as moving, can do what poems do. Easier said than done, as Hollywood's perennial moves to act on this principle continue to reveal.

One 2006 release, an adaptation of a classic novel probably more discussed than read or watched, helps explain the challenge of bringing poetic "pictures" to the screen. In covering Michael Winterbottom's adaptation of Laurence Sterne's 1767 novel *Tristram Shandy*, the press couldn't resist characterizing Sterne's novel as "unfilmable" (Rodrick; Foden; Mc-Grath). Frequent use of this adjective, "unfilmable," tends to enforce an informal but apparently extensively policed border between filmability and unfilmability. This border implicitly but decisively limits the range of Hollywood intellect. It checks aspirations of moviemakers, screenwriters and directors in particular, to do intellectual work comparable to intellectual work in print.

More of a journalistic expedient than a reference to some inherent characteristic of the movies, a declaration of *unfilmabilty* frees reviewers, financiers, and studio deciders from intellectual heavy lifting. It shelters them safely inside a shared, reflex consensus: an intellectual "comfort zone." These entrenched, universally and tacitly accepted assumptions about the filmability of a limited range of texts have resulted in the peremptory exclusion of other texts, thereby domesticating Hollywood intellect. This *unfilmability* evasion of verbal density flies in the face of a bluntly articulated point in lines Billy Wilder wrote for Charles Boyer's character in 1941 in *Hold Back the Dawn*. He declares that, like movies themselves, "I've always been full of words."

A look back at pre-Hollywood moviemaking reveals the strait-jacketing consequences and the arbitrariness of such notions of filmability. In Thomas Leitch's account, the earliest commercial movies were more likely than their Hollywood successors to draw on poetry as source material—to adapt poems such as Browning's "Pippa Passes" and Poe's "The Bells" for the screen (27). A Hollywood consensus has, by contrast, come invariably to prefer narrative to scrutinizing and playing with language. *Tristram Shandy*, for example, stands out as a vivid instance of pyrotechnically language-centered, plot-belittling fiction. Far more than in most "classic" fiction, Sterne made language rather than *story* the focal point of his unfilmable novel.

Anyone who tried would quickly be overwhelmed by counting the novels, short stories, plays, and biographies adapted for the screen at least since Griffith adapted Thomas Dixon's *The Klansman* in *Birth of a Nation* in 1915 or since Sarah Bernhardt played Hamlet on screen in 1900 or Queen Elizabeth in 1912. Michael Atkinson has explained this genre-source imbalance in describing "movies" primarily as "constructs of impressions and sensations," which render "cinema's essence more lyric poetry than novelistic narrative," even though the latter has invariably proven "easier to sell" ("Anna" 5–6). Consequently, discussions of Hollywood's literary dimension usually follow a well-worn track. Focus on adaptations of fiction and plays and on the adapters—especially during Hollywood's big studio era, when the "majors'" payrolls included novelists such as Faulkner and Fitzgerald and playwrights such as Ben Hecht and Clifford Odets.

By the end of the twentieth century these encounters had become legendary enough to become movie fodder themselves. The plot of Ethan and Joel Coen's comic 1991 Grand Guignol *Barton Fink* turns, for example, on the binge-drinking friendship and romantic rivalry between a fictional but recognizable Odets knockoff (Schultheiss 36–37) and a more *outré* Faulkner caricature. This pairing of playwright and novelist reflects how much we take for granted that Hollywood literary adaptations draw on plays and narrative. For generations authorities on Hollywood have been reinforcing this consensus, with Gilbert Seldes, in the 1920s, prescribing "Victorian novels" as the ideal source for screen adaptations (56). In 2008 self-proclaimed scriptwriters' champion David Kipen singled out novellas as the basis for the best movies (25–26). Bruce Wagner, himself a novelist, stresses the appeal of reportage as movie material. His 2003 novel *Still Holding* shows a director in search of a new movie project, as he "flipped through the paper . . . always looking through articles in the *Times* for movie ideas. Maybe there was something to develop that he could direct" (15). Wagner's image of a director at work taps into a durable legacy. Howard Koch recalls how his *Casablanca* cowriters, Julius and Philip Epstein, began their Hollywood careers with "ideas . . . garnered from newspapers and . . . periodicals, which they constructed into screenplays" (Koch 248). Lary May has argued that by the Depression the news had become the basis for mass entertainment as well for intellectual consensus. May cites Will Rogers's disingenuous disclaimer, "all I know is what I read in the papers," as showbiz wisdom (*Big* 25).

What tends to get lost in all these efforts to make movies out of narrative and to draw on literary classics is poetry (notwithstanding Vachel Lindsay's vision of and D. W. Griffith's stabs at wedding movies and poetry). This apparent incompatibility of movies and poetry prompted Italian playwright Luigi Pirandello, in the 1920s, to advocate that the movies' divorce themselves not just from poetry but from "the literary" in general:

> In order that characters born of a poet's fancy might speak, literature gave birth to theater. But film does not need to call upon theater. I have shown, and I think unquestionably, that cinema will never "arrive" by setting out on a literary road, if indeed it does not succeed in annihilating itself. Cinema must liberate itself from literature in order to find its own form of expression and accomplish its own true revolution. It should leave narrative

> to romance and leave drama to the theater. Literature is not film's proper
> element. Its proper element is music. (221)

Closer to Hollywood and Vine, veteran writer-director Ben Maddow, whose credits include *Intruder in the Dust* and *Asphalt Jungle*, recalled a career in which he set out "to achieve a new form of cinema, the 'cine-poem,' in which a continuous voice would serve as a 'sort of ground-bass to the images on screen'" (Hagan), only to discover that, when working in movies, "being a poet wasn't of any use" (Maddow 171). His sense of failure notwithstanding, Maddow's one late-career venture as a co-director, *The Savage Eye*, belies this seeming renunciation. Along with an anonymous man-in-the-street cast of thousands, the two-character, black-and-white documentary-embedded work of fiction, which visually recalls Agnes Varda's *Cleo from 5–7* (1962) and Diziga Vertov's *Man with a Movie Camera* (1929), has only two *named* characters. "The poet," a disembodied voiceover played by Gary Merrill, assumes the burden of conveying "the agony of comprehension," chronicling lives comprised of "masturbations by proxy," and revealing "eternity as a toy." In pursuit of such wisdom the poet guides, bullies, consoles, and interrogates Judith (Barbara Baxley), a newly divorced young woman, tracking her all around Los Angeles through unwonted solitude. Judith serves variously as the poet's therapeutic charge, his prompt for philosophical reflections, and his muse. A mixed review in the *Times* caviling about the "clouding" effect of Merrill's "overabundantly lush, consciously poetic narration" (Weiler) illustrates that, for all its "uselessness," Maddow never fully abandoned his calling as a poet in Hollywood.

Not surprisingly, the uselessness of poetry in Hollywood, as well its irresistibility, has become a commonplace of movie history. In 1937 Graham Greene insisted that movies become "poetic in the broadest sense" ("Subjects" 61) finding few movies attaining this "goal of getting closer to the poetic and yet commercially viable possibilities" of movies in which "a sense stays in the mind of an unsophisticated mind fumbling on the edge of simple and popular poetry" (63–64). In 1969, Robert Richardson contrasted the "countless novels and plays" with the "few poems" that "have been done into films" (15). Thirty years later Timothy Corrigan noted how, "of all the different literary genres that film has drawn on and influenced," poetry has proven "the most elusive," citing only three examples to come out of Hollywood since Griffith set up shop (15). Even the rare movies that are expressly adapted from poems favor narrative over the nuances of voice and style that supposedly distinguish poems from other kinds of writing. For example, in reviewing Hollywood's first talkie release of a movie based on Edgar Allan Poe's often-adapted schoolbook standard "The Raven," the *New York Times*'s Frank Nugent treated Poe's poem only as "plot material" best left to the "pulpies."

Successive Hollywood adaptations of Alfred Tennyson's tragic or at least melodramatic poem *Enoch Arden* illustrate this evolution away from poetry. D. W. Griffith's 1911 adaptation maintained the temporal rhythms of Tennyson's original and the fatalistic melancholy at the end of it (Blum 83–84; Leitch 44–46; Corrigan 20). Griffith's effort anticipates sporadic efforts over the course of the century to claim movies as primarily a poetic art (L. Marcus 171–72, 175, 282). After Griffith, few directors chose "to apply to" movies the "principles of the modern revolutions in poetry" (Farber 97). The advent of "talking pictures" ironically nurtured this deficit with a "sedulous realism . . . anchored in" the "rotting aesthetic" of nineteenth-century narrative (98).

Talkie-era adaptations of *Enoch Arden* so eviscerated the poet laureate's rhetoric and sensibility that *Enoch Arden* ended up in its most durable incarnation as comedy, first as a Cary Grant/Irene Dunne screwball classic, *My Favorite Wife*, and then as a Doris Day vehicle titled *Move Over Darling* (Crowther, "*Favorite*"). Noting that Lewis Carroll's seven-quatrain "Jabberwocky" "inspired" Terry Gilliam's 1977 movie of the same title, Vincent Canby's review stressed instead Gilliam's narrative spoofing "of everything from *Jaws* through *Ivanhoe*" as central to Gilliam's conception ("Jabberwocky"). A generation later another reviewer, evaluating Gilliam's career, characterized him primarily as a "teller of fantastic tales," never mentioning his poetic bent (Gillespie).

Among the most acclaimed poem-based Hollywood hits, one still regarded as "sheer poetry" ("TV"), George Stevens's *Gunga Din* stands out as the first—and long-belated—swashbuckling, tongue-in-cheek "romp" of the sound era (Everson 145). Stevens, a "purist" whose work spanned most "of the history of the American movie business," earned a "reputation as a consummate, versatile" studio "craftsman . . . with a gift for bringing out greatness in actors" and consistently made "pictures with guts and meaning" (Erickson 89; Harris 150–51, 112). Stevens explicitly aligned himself with Hollywood intellect in 1942. In *The Talk of the Town*, Cary Grant seized an exchange between a pedantic Harvard legal theorist played by Ronald Coleman and a fugitive anarchist played by Grant as an opportunity for showing "schools of thought in action."

As a proponent of Hollywood intellect, Stevens kept poetry *as a literary practice* in the foreground of *Gunga Din* by showing Rudyard Kipling as an on-screen character. Played by Reginald Sheffield, Kipling appears on screen, briefly. (Christopher Plummer reprised this role twenty-six years later in *The Man Who Would Be King*.) *Gunga Din*'s final scene shows Kipling actually writing the poem that the preceding narrative inspired, hastily scribbling impromptu what the audience never sees but probably had already heard or read: the forty-two dialect couplets leading up to the indelible closing line, "you're a better man than I am, Gunga Din." Kipling then hands the sheet to the regimental commander to read as a eulogy to the eponymous *bhisti* hero. This on-screen appearance served, in a phrase W. H. Auden wrote during the same year as the movie's release, to "pardon Kipling for his views" (50). This appearance of Kipling on screen prompted *Times* reviewer B. Crisler to take an interest in the "poet in the credit lines," in "the collaboration of the late Mr. Kipling, who wrote for the cinema without knowing it," and in the ways in which *Gunga Din* begins and ends with "the sheer poetry of cinematic motion." Crisler's patronizing judgment that Kipling writes cinematically "without knowing it" overlooks his 1904 story "Mrs. Bathurst," the plot of which turns on going to the movies, and stands in contrast to the current view that Kipling was presciently attuned to the power and appeal of movies and pitched his style accordingly (Kipling 375–93; J. James).

Moving beyond these particulars of Kipling's own accomplishments, Crisler concludes, with *Gunga Din* as his prime example, that "the movies at their best really appear to have more in common with the poets [*sic*] than with plain, straightforward, rationally documented prose." Despite his enthusiasm for poetry itself and for this production's particular cinematic poetry, Crisler has nothing to say about Kipling's poem. Instead he devotes most of his review to his admiration for the movie's typically Hollywood virtues.

Thanks to these virtues, *Gunga Din* has stood the proverbial test of time among 1939's *annus mirabilis* hits (along with *The Wizard of Oz*, *Gone with the Wind*, *Dark Victory*, *Stagecoach*, and *Mr. Smith Goes to Washington*) (Basinger 466) as an epic spectacle rather than as a much-quoted piece of inspirational Victorian verse. The movie has maintained its appeal as a slapstick screwball romp thanks to performances by Cary Grant, Sam Jaffe (in the title role), Victor McLaglen, and a cow elephant named Annie; a stock marriage-plot romance between the bankably photogenic Douglas Fairbanks Jr. and Joan Fontaine; and a western in which pith helmets and turbans replace Stetsons and feathers. As a young movie-besotted Oxonian, T. S. Eliot mused about such a genre fusion nearly a generation before the advent of talkies. Plotting his own "great ten-reel cinema drama," Eliot observed that "you simply have to have either a red Indian or an East Indian . . . exactly alike . . . distinguished from each other" because one "wears feathers and a very old silk hat . . . while" the other "wears a turban and polo boots" (*Letters* 62, 71). Stevens's poem-based 1939 spectacular superlatively met the mandarin modernist's criteria for a successfully popular movie. Emphasizing this success of *Gunga Din* as a genre hit, Crisler singled out the screenwriters' plotting, the deft handling of a well-worn Hollywood "genre," and the movie's artfully crafted violence: the "original story by Ben Hecht and Charles MacArthur" (and an uncredited William Faulkner) Crisler found "quite unlike other predecessors in the same genre . . . taut with suspense and enriched in the fighting scenes with beautifully timed, almost epigrammatic bits of 'business' and a swinging gusto." This "timing" elicits a Keats allusion from Crisler, who enthuses that with this "business" Stevens "makes of every roundhouse blow a thing of beauty."

Screen adaptations of Kipling's fiction, including John Ford's direction of Shirley Temple in *Wee Willie Winkie*, Disney's two versions of Kipling's jungle tales, MGM's Cold War–shadowed, Technicolor, on-location version of *Kim* (Radio City Music Hall's Christmas feature in 1950), and John Huston's 1975 Oscar-nominated adaptation of *The Man Who Would Be King*, far outnumber poem adaptations. Thirty years after the release of *Gunga Din* British moviemaker Lindsay Anderson made an exception to this unwritten rule. Like Stevens, Hecht, and MacArthur, Anderson turned to Kipling's poetry as the point of departure for his memorably ambitious *If . . .*, winner of the 1969 Palme d'Or at Cannes. Indian-born like Kipling himself, Anderson rebelled against having Kipling thrust upon him "as one of our three great poetic geniuses" (after Shakespeare and Tennyson)—against "If" in particular and more generally Kipling's "nauseating sentiments, and vulgar, blatant, superficial versification." Shipboard as an intelligence trainee during World War II, Anderson told the ship's captain that he "did not like Kipling and mentioned with disfavor his jingoistic imperialism" (Sutton 6–7). While thus talking back, ironically and angrily, to Kipling's much-memorized schoolbook lesson on manhood, "If" (*If . . .*), Anderson did more than mock Kipling's no longer fashionable sentiment and his quasi-biblical sententiousness (Orwell 121–22). He also meets Kipling's plainspokenness with a formal complexity modeled on Jean-Luc Godard's recent cinematic innovations (Canby, "*If . . .* Begins"). Anderson conceived *his If . . .* explicitly in opposition to Kipling's, as revenge for having been "forced," as a schoolboy, "to endure Kipling's poem."

Because Anderson leavens the influence of the French avant-garde with the kinds of youth-culture energies that Hollywood exploited in such movies as *Wild in the Streets* and *Easy Rider*, *If . . .* works both as an intellectually challenging film and as a viscerally gripping movie. Anderson refracted Kipling's inspirational rhetorical and aspirational lessons through two cultural movements that chronologically bookended this 1968 release. The rage motivating Anderson's English public school protagonist looked back to the "angry young men" movement. Sparked by John Osborne's hit play *Look Back in Anger*, this work "hectored Britain and took its temperature" throughout the 1950s (Lahr 61). The desires and fantasies Anderson evoked—most vividly the scene showing Mick (Malcolm McDowell) dream of carrying out a machine-gun massacre by "spraying down bullets" during a chapel assembly (Sutton 80)—highlight Anderson's challenge to Kipling's "excessive reliance on administration and authority" (Trilling 65–66). Such scenes also presaged the "anarchy in the UK" program of English punk rockers prevalent in the 1970s. Whatever his anti-establishment animus and Godard-derived ambitions, Anderson ended up endorsing in *If . . .* the very Hollywood conventions Anderson committed himself to flouting by refusing to "pander to 'American' taste" (Sutton 103). Overriding this animus and recalling Godard's own homage to Hollywood, to such movies as *Westbound* and *Whirlpool*, in *Breathless*, Anderson opened *If . . .* by honoring his own favorite Hollywood classics, *Meet Me in St. Louis* and *They Were Expendable*, and acknowledging his debt to the "American [Hollywood] money" Paramount provided to make the movie (Sutton 46–47), and perhaps to his "idol John Ford" (Catsoulis). In a similar contradiction, though Anderson avoided engaging Kipling the poet, *If . . .* ended up honoring Kipling the story-writer. Though Anderson took his title from his aversion to "If," his concept for *If . . .* as a whole, to provide "a peculiarly English . . . romantically passionate" critique of "the corrupt, the ugly, the old and the foolish," entailed "a radical updating of Kipling's 1899 story-sequence *Stalky and Co.*, in which prankish rebels are groomed to police the Empire" and to embrace the "callousness, arrogance, and brutality" this work demands ("*If*"; Trilling 65).

Favoring the "romantically passionate" against their enemies also aligns the avant-garde Anderson with a durable Hollywood consensus, since the Romantic sensibility inherited from English Romantic poets has long held sway in Hollywood. Nowadays screenwriter and Hollywood's "frankest, funniest explainer" William Goldman (Kipen 108) looks to English Romantic poets to help buoy Hollywood intellect. "[William] Wordsworth has many lessons for us," Goldman advised would-be scriptwriters, because "what screenwriters want to do" is what Wordsworth did (*Lie* 197–98). Goldman's appeal to Wordsworth won't surprise anyone familiar with recent histories of the arts. Romanticism, with its axiomatic valuation of expression, creativity, inspiration, and originality, has functioned normatively and implicitly as our measure of aesthetic worth for over two centuries now, so effectively that Romantic standards have often "hoodwinked" readers and audiences by exploiting our insatiable and "naïve" appetite for authenticity. Goldman, however, resists this snare by recognizing English Romanticism's most compelling corrective to Romantic "rhetoric," "polemic," and "propaganda" (Fussell, *Johnson* 64–68). Thus Goldman quipped summarily in what has become his most famous pronouncement about Hollywood that "nobody knows anything" (*Adventures* 39). This pronouncement concisely updates what John Keats, even more memorably, described as "negative capability": the capacity to be "in uncertainties . . . and doubts without any irritable reaching after fact and reason."

Notwithstanding Goldman's poetry-minded legacy-grabbing, most of Hollywood's poetry recognitions have been fleeting and perfunctorily allusive, as titles or as character markers rather than conceptually embedded or compositionally integral. Title allusions in popular releases include *Chariots of Fire* (William Blake's prophetic book *Jerusalem*), *Splendor in the Grass* (Wordsworth's "Immortality Ode"), *Paths of Glory* (Thomas Gray's "Elegy in a Country Churchyard"), *Now Voyager* (Walt Whitman's "Now Finale to the Shore" via Olive Higgins Prouty's novel), *No Country for Old Men* (Yeats's "Sailing to Byzantium" via Cormac McCarthy's novel), and *The Eternal Sunshine of the Spotless Mind*.

The Eternal Sunshine of the Spotless Mind director Michel Gondry and his cowriter Charlie Kaufman took their title from "Eloisa to Abelard," a dramatic monologue by Alexander Pope. Pope, who seldom worked in this form, adapted this monologue from Ovid's Latin poetic sequence *The Heroides*, which Ovid composed during the reign of Augustus. These dramatic monologues channel the voices of abandoned women—mythological figures such as Penelope, Medea, and Ariadne. Pope updated Ovid's work in 1717 by adding the historical and sensationalist account of doomed Parisian lovers, a famed twelfth-century scholar and his precocious maiden protégé. Though Pope's didactic, strictly formal verse may seem an unusual choice for Hollywood's sentiment-selling dream factory and especially for the writer who wrote *Confessions of a Dangerous Mind* and *Being John Malkovich*, Kaufman and Gondry's rhetorical agenda in *Eternal Sunshine* challenges a pervasive modern hope (a virtue Pope questioned in his immortal maxim in his "Essay on Man" that "hope springs eternal").

Just as the lovers whom Pope renders repudiate, by agonizing example, the redemptive promises of passion and learning, Gondry and Kaufman debunk our contemporary faith that therapy and technology can bring peace of mind. Their narrative asks the same harsh rhetorical question Pope asked in 1717. Gondry and Kaufman give Pope's title lines to their bemused, bewitched, and besotted Eloisa character. Played by Kirsten Dunst, she inaccurately renames the lines' source "Pope Alexander" while accurately and aptly quoting Pope's words.

> How happy is the blameless vestal's lot!
> The world forgetting, by the world forgot.
> Eternal sunshine of the spotless mind!

Though decidedly not a virgin, despite her character's Christian name (Mary), Dunst's character becomes a failed "vestal" over the course of the narrative. As an office assistant and keeper of secrets that she doesn't even know she's keeping for most of the story, she plays the traduced guardian of an altar dedicated, literally and figuratively, to an old flame. Until she discovers his multiple betrayals, Mary works for and worships, as a genius mentor, Dr. Mierzwiak (Tom Wilkinson). This revered healer and clandestine sexual predator promises, with his patented high-tech therapy, to cleanse his patients' minds of the misbegotten loves that haunt them and to purge all their passion-engendered distress and despair. Mary joins the line of betrayed women stretching back through Pope to Ovid on discovering that Mierzwiak had seduced and possessed her before turning her into his sorcerer's apprentice.

In contrast to Pope, who garnered a rare Hollywood acknowledgment in *Eternal Sunshine*, the homegrown Whitman has long been a perennial Hollywood favorite, dating back at least as far as 1915. In *Intolerance* Griffith cited "Out of the Cradle Endlessly Rocking" in a screen title as well as lines from Longfellow's *New England Tragedies*. One of Hollywood's most versatile and durable characters actors, Rip Torn did a star turn as Whitman in an otherwise forgettable indie 1990 biopic about a pioneering Canadian alienist titled *Beautiful Dreamers*. The injunction "now voyager depart!" from Whitman's "Now to the Final Shore" reverberates both as the title of a 1942 classic Bette Davis weepie and throughout Richard Kwietniowski's *Love and Death on Long Island*.

In *Love and Death on Long Island* the eloquence of Whitman's phrase and the elegance of the character who embodies literary tradition leverages the plot into a comically critical homage to literariness *and* Hollywood. Poetry and the aura ascribed to these lines pique the interest of and begin to refine intellectually a beefcake movie star played by the heartthrob TV star Jason Priestly. This heterosexual star of a series of movies reminiscent of the popular *Porky's* and its sequels comes to value the affections, without embracing the desire, of an aging, reclusive, London man-of-letters. Casting John Hurt in the role, Kwietniowski modeled him, as the title suggests, on Thomas Mann's Aschenbach in *Death in Venice*. This latter-day Aschenbach masks his lecherous designs so well that his pose, that of an impartial intellectual inquiring into Hollywood's artistic practices, becomes just as credible by the end of the narrative as were his carnal motives from the outset.

Kwietniowski highlights and finally reconciles these motives by showing the Londoner repeatedly picturing the neo-Aschenbach's would-be disciple as the supine figure in Henry Wallis's Victorian painting *The Death of Chatterton*. Parodic repetitions of this image signal an allegiance to poetic bygones (like Chatterton's fraudulent "medieval" originals and Wallis's rendering of him as martyred by the disclosure of his deception). Forgiving all in the name of art, including his hero's duplicitous motives and his lust-object's resistance to the "higher artistic" calling Hurt's character embodies, Kwietniowski seems to countenance fraudulent misrepresentation (like Chatterton's, like the movie's hero's, and like *Porky's'* distortion of adolescent angst) as long as all's well that ends well.

Kaufman, Gondry, and Kwietniowski stand out because they steeped both narrative and imagery in *Eternal Sunshine* and *Love and Death*, respectively, in the poems their movies draw on. More typically, Hollywood nods cursorily to poetic tradition. Such acknowledgments can serve to flag a protagonist's heretofore unrecognized depth or to signal her transformation. The volume of Emily Dickinson poems, a present from her new boyfriend, on the Ashley Judd character's nightstand in Victor Nunez's eponymous 1994 coming-of-age narrative *Ruby in Paradise*, serves as a token of the "soul work" Ruby undertakes (E. Levy 172; Waites 433). In the 1989 Robin Williams hit *The Dead Poets Society*, director Peter Weir and screenwriter Tom Schulman demonstrate this Hollywood tendency on a grand scale. Studding the script with aural cameos by Whitman, Byron, Frost, Shakespeare, and Tennyson, as well as such literary also-rans as Abraham Cowley and Vachel Lindsay, these references and quotations help stress the immeasurable intellectual riches that the counterculture Mr. Keating, played by Williams, bears. Thanks to these gifts, in the space of a (128-minute) school year, a hoard of *Playboy*-besotted preppy rowdies flourishes, becoming a coterie of autonomous, sensitive adults.

Harold Ramis and his cowriters satirized such facile poetry appro-
priations in *Animal House* by naming the artsy women's college whither
put-upon Delta Brothers make their "road trip" in search of female com-
panionship Emily Dickinson College. Clint Eastwood's Oscar-winning
Million Dollar Baby, by contrast, illustrates the fecklessness with which
Hollywood typically honors poems and poets. Repeated reminders surface throughout the movie that the hero, a genius boxing coach played
by Eastwood himself, reads Yeats's poetry avidly. But *Million Dollar Baby*
ends up entirely discrediting this homage to the poet and to "Romantic
Ireland" (Yeats 107) that inspires him when Eastwood's character informs
his protégé that he has been translating Yeats from the "Irish," a language
Yeats never learned to speak, let alone write in.

The last season of the cable-TV phenomenon *The Sopranos* serves as
a revealing contrast to Eastwood's misappropriation of Yeats. During his
aborted matriculation at Rutgers the title family's twentyish son A.J. at-
tends a lecture on Yeats's "The Second Coming." A lecturer reads and
explains the poem on-screen. This scene's very detail—including the text
of the poem, the instructor's gloss, A.J.'s facial response during the lecture, and the aftermath of this exposure—underscores the extent to which
Yeats represents the sum of A.J.'s academic experience. The closing lines
of "The Second Coming," in particular, become a recurring part of A.J.'s
thinking and conversation throughout the rest of the season. The series'
writers introduced this interest not in simply dropping literary names but
in probing literary value during an earlier season. A.J.'s sister's exposure in
a class at Columbia to *Billy Budd*, and Leslie Fiedler's reading of it, became
the stimulus for a dinner party argument with her mother over changing
assumptions about homosexuality and the impact of such changes on everyday conversation.

The literary canon in each instance becomes a catalyst in the series'
ongoing family psychodrama and a cue to view *The Sopranos* as part of a
more complicated tradition and denser conversation than Hollywood's
worn Mafia-movie clichés encompass. As Geoffrey O'Brien argues, "the
appropriately apocalyptic literary reference point" in the last season "was
Yeats's 'The Second Coming'" because "A.J.'s absorption in it led [A.J.'s
mother] Carmela to protest, in a desperate attempt to restore a lost equi-
librium." In a humbling challenge to literary critics, English teachers, and
promoters of Hollywood intellect alike, she asks, "What kind of poem
is that to teach college students?" ("Northern" 20), calling into question
not only the aptness of Yeats in the classroom but the effect of poetry
on-screen as well.

II

The Sopranos highlights the extent to which Hollywood welcomes poetry without agreeing about or even knowing what to do with it. Easy explanations of this quandary run to broad assertions about the nature of the medium and the sociology and psychology of mass audiences. This discrepancy between Hollywood's professedly poetic soul and its obstinately prosaic perennial preferences, however, might also reflect common assumptions about the relationship of various arts to one another. Throughout the nineteenth century major thinkers preoccupied themselves with deciding exactly what constitutes "art" and how to rank the various recognized arts. Among the most influential rankers, Walter Pater established as axiomatic the principle that art inevitably aspires to the liberated and unmediated, nonpareil "condition of music." Midway through the twentieth century, poet-critic Delmore Schwartz revised this aspiration and its implicit relegation of poetry to a lesser rank when he characterized his own status, as a "language" artist, as that of "a second violinist":

> Every modern poet would like to be direct, lucid, and immediately intelligible . . . one of the most fantastic misconceptions of modern literature and modern art in general is the widespread delusion that the modern artist does not want and would not like a vast popular audience, if this were possible without sacrifice of some necessary quality in his work. But it is often not possible. And every modern poet would also like to be successful, popular, famous, rich, cheered on Broadway, *sought by Hollywood.* . . . The renunciation of popularity does not arise from any poet's desire to punish himself and deprive himself of these glorious prizes and delectable rewards. The basic cause is a consciousness of the powers and possibilities of language, a consciousness which cannot be discarded with any more ease than one can regain one's innocence. (28—emphasis added)

Writing with apparent but unsurprisingly uncanny foreknowledge of this quandary, the challenge and temptation with which "Hollywood" confronted twentieth-century poets, Emily Dickinson both grappled with and imaginatively "solved" the problem Schwartz identified. Laura Marcus has warned against speculatively discovering "cinematic vision before the invention" of movie technology (20); nonetheless echoes in Dickinson's poems of the poetic self-fashioning Schwartz ponders plausibly position Dickinson among such alleged cinema precursors as Dickens, Zola, Tolstoy, and Degas whom Marcus herself cites (19).

In this role Dickinson maintains her characteristic poetic persona: always and proudly an anachronism; ever-attuned to the imminence of "renunciation" (#745), which Schwartz describes, and to the "temptation" (#792) that "auctions of mind" (#709) held for writers; and ever eager to "dwell in" the kind of "possibility" (#657) of fulfilling the "Hollywood" allure that piques Schwartz's conjecture. In her foreknowledge of the movies, Dickinson evokes what it would be like to experience the poet's movie. She voices an otherwordly longing for "pictures no man drew"—like movies—that drew "people like the moth" and left them "almost contented" (#374). In a later poem, she looks to an audience that found itself:

> *Departed* to the judgment,
> A mighty afternoon;
> Great clouds like ushers leaning,
> Creation looking on.
>
> The flesh surrendered, cancelled
> The bodiless begun;
> Two worlds, like audiences, disperse
> And leave the soul alone. (#524)

Though Dickinson died in 1886, just as the inventions that came to constitute movie technology began to emerge, "Departed to the judgment" embraces the power of the disembodied image and the paradox of solitary mass-audience membership that the movies made commonplace. Likewise, she anticipated the projector beam, "the light beam interrupting the darkness of the theater" (Weideman 112), known only by the dust in its path as a "slant of light" (#258), and the power of this beam, its "evanescence" notwithstanding (#1463). By means of a "revolving wheel"—or reel—such beams would, soon after Dickinson's death, start to bring instantaneously to the "minds of" moviegoers what once seemed immensely remote: movies made "the mail from Tunis an easy morning's ride."

Some thirty years have passed since Adrienne Rich elaborated this freeing, movie-made state of mind that Dickinson could only, though vividly, imagine. In this elaboration, "Images for Godard," Rich locates and reflects on the "poet at the movies." The preposition in Rich's flat-out statement that "the poet is at the movies" (49) positions the poet in the audience, *at* the movies, in her workplace. This view reinforces the consensus against treating poets as movie*makers*. It implicitly resists valuing the poet's language as figuring significantly *in* the movies and in their production because Rich seems to limit the poet's role "at the movies" to the passivity of a spectator.

The 1993 publication by a London publisher, with an eminent literary pedigree, of an anthology titled *The Faber Book of Movie Verse* seconds this constraint since nearly every selection favors the spectators' experience, most notably selections by American poets known for their interest in the movies: Vachel Lindsay (French, *Faber* 33), Theodore Roethke (125), Karl Shapiro (126), and Frank O'Hara (104). Laurence Goldstein's title allusion to Rich in his consistently illuminating and nuanced study of such poets, *The American Poet at the Movies*, also seconds Rich's acceptance of spectatorship as the norm in characterizing the place of poets in relation to the movies. Rich also decisively severs "the poet" she envisions from Hollywood in her choice of the particular movie—or film, more precisely—for focused meditation. As the title "Images for Godard" announces, Rich confines her reflection on movie images to work by the polemically anti-Hollywood French auteur Jean-Luc Godard, who spurred half a century ago the now-perennial vogue of affecting to be "fed up as we all now are with contemporary Hollywood" (Bray). The novelist John Edgar Weideman recently registered Godard's perceived distance from "Hollywood. Ha-ha" from the point of view of an American "homeboy." Weideman showed his narrative alter-ego, struck by how much "critics . . . love Mr. Godard" who hides "behind his shades . . . whether he'[s] laughing with them or at them" and whose "movies [*sic*] are kind of a pain in the ass to make sense of" (106, 111).

Despite the narrow range of Godard "images" that Rich cited, she has at least peered beyond what's on the screen to the impact of these images on the spectator, valuing onscreen images as catalysts to "change" and as stimuli to "free" the spectator-poet's "mind." Writing nearly forty years later, film historian David Thomson singled out this understanding of movies as transformative poetry as their superlative value, when he declared that "there isn't a sight in the movies as momentous as shots of a face as its mind changing" (*Whole* 86). What differentiates the ways in which Thomson and Rich each cherish mind-changing and consciousness expansion, though, lies in where they look for such change, with Rich turning away from Hollywood and Thomson turning toward it.

III

Over the past seven decades, the "Hollywood novel" has often positioned poets between being *in* the movies and being *at* the movies, by showing them as screenwriters. Since the subgenre came of age in the early 1940s, American and British novelists have been playing out this tension, between spectating and contributing, with Hollywood's allegedly inhospitable climate for poetry and poets as its backdrop.

Widely regarded as the consummate "Hollywood novel," *What Makes Sammy Run* by Budd Schulberg goes so far as to represent Hollywood as a destination where poets end up only to find—like Othello—that their "occupation's gone." Early in the narrative (51–53), as a Hollywood newcomer, Schulberg's narrator receives an invitation to dine with a literary friend from college, who now describes himself as the "Poet Laureate of Hollywood." As an underclassman at Wesleyan, the narrator had idolized his friend as "a romantic figure," his "ideal of what a great poet should look like." Triple-named (*comme il faut*) and unimpeachably pedigreed, Henry Powell Turner had won a Pulitzer Prize for his "book-length poem on the history of New England which he read to the Literary Society while he was still in college." A decade or so later, Turner has ensconced himself in "the largest example of the worst kind of architecture I have ever seen, Hollywood Moorish." This symptom of Turner's aesthetic degeneration augurs Turner's overall decline: "a few strands left of the old youthful fellow . . . already well on his way to the state of drooling intoxication," which "he managed to achieve with monotonous regularity." As the evening wore on, Turner "recited some of his lyrical poetry," then "mocked his own poems with dirty lyrics composed extemporaneously, 'which,' he laughingly informed me three or four times, 'I have seen fit to create in line of my duties as Hollywood's poet laureate.'" The evening ends with Turner's "eloquent resolutions to return to New England and His Muse, 'as soon as I finish the McDonald-Eddy script I have to do.'" When Schulberg's narrator reflects on this reunion, he realizes that what he "had taken merely for boredom or disgust came into sharper focus." As if he had been observing Turner from "ringside seats for great personal tragedies," he leaves Turner's mansion "stunned by the horror and sense of mental nausea."

Where Schulberg found cautionary tragedy in the plight of the poet-gone-Hollywood, English novelist Evelyn Waugh, soon after arriving in Hollywood in 1947, rendered the poet's encounter with Hollywood as what would come to be called black comedy a generation later. Waugh found a place that not only "ain't got time for tragedies" but that, to Waugh's surprise, also embraced him as "representing the intellectual elite of MGM" (*Loved* 121; "Very" 361). Waugh's English contemporary Christopher Isherwood nominally stretched the boundaries of Hollywood—and Hollywood fiction—by finding his own Hollywood in London. Isherwood's depiction of wartime English commercial moviemaking illustrates Pauline Kael's reminder that Hollywood novels don't require a Hollywood setting (D. Martin, "Virtel"). James Farrell's review of Isherwood's 1945 novel *Prater Violet* describes the novel's British studio head, whom Isherwood shows "at work on a melodrama about a flower-seller marrying an Austrian prince" that "could have been made in Hollywood," as "hardly distinguishable from any corresponding Hollywood mogul" (128, 131, 132).

Though he set it in London and based it on his experience adapting Ernest Lothar's novel *Little Friend* for its 1934 UK release, Isherwood wrote *Prater Violet* soon after settling in Hollywood, which he regarded sanguinely, predicting a future in which most of "Hollywood's films will be entertainment fit for adults" and writers "of talent will come to the movie colony not as overpaid secretaries . . . but as responsible artists" ("Wake Up" 366). In the meantime *Prater Violet* skewered the London's movie industry Hollywood-like indifference to poetry. The protagonist and narrator is a novice dialogue-writer, a "declassed intellectual type," named "Mr. Isherwood" (Hitchens 307). He works for, while learning from, Bergmann, a legendary, "gargantuan" Austrian director. A new refugee from the Nazis, Bergmann becomes for Mr. Isherwood a "Virgil who will guide me," even though Isherwood starts his movie job with the literati's commonplace snobbery:

> this was movie work, hack work . . . essentially false, cheap, vulgar . . . beneath me. I ought never to have become involved in it, under the influence of Bergmann's dangerous charm, and for the sake of the almost incredible twenty pounds a week. . . . I was betraying my art. No wonder it was so difficult.

But on further reflection about movie-writing, "hack" proves too facile, too trite a dismissal of scriptwriting. Isherwood's account of his "wrestl[ing] with words and meanings"—Eliot's definition of what poets do alone (*Poems* 126)—consequently ends up highlighting the resemblance of poets' efforts to the work screenwriters do, collaboratively, "haggling over each word" (Stead 127). Confessing his snobbery and deciding that nothing's vulgar about a screenwriter's work (making "people talk"), the narrator takes as models for screenwriting Shakespeare and Tolstoy because they knew how people talk. The narrator's boss immediately discards his novice screenwriting efforts and then rhapsodizes about the movies as symphonies and philosophizes about why artful screenwriting, which requires differentiating "poems" and "prostitution," is "not so easy" (34)—actually impossible for him as he confesses his own inability to write movies, with the excuse that "inventing" an "idiotic story" for the screen is "prostitution . . . a woman's business" (35–36).

As agilely as Isherwood shows his hero moving from the poetry associated with the *Kultur* he left behind in Vienna to the "prostitution" of modern moviemaking—to "prose" from "possibility," thus reversing Emily Dickinson's formulation—Evelyn Waugh elaborately enmeshes *his* poet-come-to-Hollywood in the natives' extravagant snares and macabre follies. Waugh's 1948 novel *The Loved One* opens with the arrival of his hero-foil, Englishman Dennis Barlow, in an eccentric-filled Hollywood wasteland. Hailed as "the hope of English poetry" (13) and acclaimed in London for his wartime writing, Barlow comes to Hollywood from a milieu circumscribed by "great" poems. Waugh describes his and Barlow's England as a "dying world" where "quotation is the national vice" and "no one would think of making an after dinner speech without the help of poetry." He has come to California aiming to get the poet unequivocally *into the movies*—to "help write the life of Shelley for the films" (23, 139). The "ancient and comfortless shore" to which Barlow ultimately returns Waugh describes as "an older" and "earlier civilization with sharper needs," a home where Barlow had "sought the intangible . . . hidden graces" (164, 54). Nevertheless, comfortable but graceless Hollywood and its environs is where Barlow ends up courting his muse: a mortuary cosmetician named Aimee. Bedeviled by "the tongue" and the "unpoetic air of Los Angeles," Barlow ends up "squandering [his] affections on [this] girl." He turns a blind eye to Aimee's ignorance "of the commonest treasures of literature" on realizing that "the English poets were uncertain guides in the labyrinth of California courtship" (160, 139).

Barlow's courtship fails, definitively, thanks to Aimee's macabre suicide. After quitting screenwriting Barlow finds more congenial work in a memorial park that serves as the final resting place for Hollywood's cosseted, "beloved" house pets. This change of career plans positions Barlow to transform his desire for Aimee into the "intangible," poetic transcendence he initially "sought," so that his "beloved" (literally her corpse) ends up in "heat so intense that"—like poetry traditionally conceived, as in Dante's *fuoco gli affina*, or "refining fire"—it leaves "all inessentials . . . volatilized" (43). With this incineration of "all inessentials" Waugh frees Barlow to return to his "dying" but gracious and "poetic" Old World home.

Some fifty years after Waugh staged Barlow's cold-blooded flight from an apparently poetry-resistant Hollywood, Rick Moody recovered and reinstated the poetic as Hollywood's legitimate concern. His novel *The Diviners* bridges the chasm between "unpoetic" Hollywood and the inherently poetic depth of "earlier civilizations" (37) with which Waugh aligned Barlow. Moody melds the poetry of Hollywood and the sensibility of the superlatively venerable "Indus river civilization . . . the millennia of accomplishments on the part of Vedic Aryan civilization." These geographically and chronologically divergent perspectives converge in the consciousness of Ranjeet, an immigrant chauffeur enamored of American movies. As he passes into the West through "the stone towers, east and west," supporting the Brooklyn Bridge, and heads toward 42nd Street, where "the whole of Western civilization rises up" to resist him, Ranjeet overhears his passenger, a harried producer, ask a cell phone interlocutor "about the new project," about "how the fuck" she's "supposed the get one of these movies made" (42, 39). This kvetching stirs Ranjeet to reverie. It casts

> the spell of that perfect word, that pair of syllables that changes everything. *Movies*. It is a word as perfect as the two perfect etymological American exports: *okay* and *Coca-Cola*. The word *movies* may have its origin in Sanskrit, *movati*, in which one *pushes* or *shoves;* movies, culturally speaking, involve a fair amount of pushing and shoving. It is a global romance, a word of American promise as is no other, a word that summons the glittering prizes offered by this land of opportunity, the word *movies*. He knows about movies . . . films of bodybuilders, about teen sex comedies. He knows about sequels . . . animated cartoons with violent passages. (39–40)

The very word *movies* transports Ranjeet to a mind-made Hollywood that so closely resembles an insider's Hollywood that simply by speaking to his fare Rajeet effortlessly goes Hollywood. As a result of the enthusiasm and savvy he exhibits, Ranjeet becomes his passenger's assistant and (aptly) her guru as she struggles to "develop" her vexing project.

This project resembles the most venerable kind of poetry: epic. This envisioned epic will "tell a story that reaches out to every population," trace humanity's struggle for water since prehistory, and "confront thirst on a historical basis" (248–49). Moving this project through development, Moody's comic plotting meets the demands for financing this epic with the introduction of a charismatic Mormon entrepreneur whose perspective reinforces the prospect of endowing even the mass media's most commercially prosaic current image of itself as "content provider" with poetic possibility. Moody's visionary financier reasons, expansively and nostalgically, that

> [v]enture capitalists used to think like poets. They were dreamers, they were renegades. And now it's starting to look like those doors are going to be closed for a long while. And that's why I'd like to make a leap into

content, you know, because content is forever. The world always needs the artists and dreamers. I appreciate the energy on the content end of the Internet story. You know, out West, back when everyone was a rancher or working the fields, there were the stars to navigate from. Men would be out in the fields with the livestock, looking up at the stars. And that was their entertainment. Stars and a campfire crackling in the desert. There are no stars here in the city, except the poets and dreamers and actors and filmmakers, the content providers, so that's where I want to concentrate my attention. (169)

Moody's comic paean to content-providing imparts a challenging insight. These poetic sentiments about "entertainment" and the simple "perfection" of single words that Moody shows Ranjeet associating with *movies* point to a broader understanding of the Hollywood writer's calling and call attention to a persisting if *sotto voce* strain of Hollywood intellect.

Despite the predominance of narrative, Hollywood has maintained an intellectual tradition of making movies poetic. Such efforts have aimed beyond perfunctorily mentioning poems and lines from poems; beyond the formulaic inclusion of poetic characters; and beyond the "Aristotelian" strait-jacketing Gerald Bruns has ascribed to a "premium on narrative, with its corresponding bracketing or erasing of language" (105–6). Such aspirations have contributed to what has long distinguished Hollywood movies as "recognizably American": "how their screenwriters made them sound" (Kipen 46–47). Pauline Kael has even argued that *only* movies that value language, "movies with good fast, energetic talk," deserve a continuously profitable afterlife on TV ("Movies" 497).

IV

Moody pinpoints where content-providers striving to make their scripts poetic in the most traditional sense have often looked. Hollywood has always looked to "earlier civilizations," however much the results may have proven intractably modern and "recognizably American" (see chapter III). Studios often thwarted and deformed such efforts, as in the notorious case of Stanley Kubrick's 1960 adaptation of Howard Fast's anti-imperialist novel *Spartacus*.

Such deformations aside, during the era of the studio system, production executives were more hospitable to screenwriters' poetic aspirations when their projects looked to earlier civilizations and could be sold as "epic." The signature literary genre among literate ancient civilizations, "epic" became in modern Hollywood a term-of-art for hyping such star-studded, big-budget historical narratives as *King of Kings*, *The Ten Commandments*, *Quo Vadis*, and *Ben Hur* (both remakes of silent epics adapted from novels popular around 1900).

Over several decades the obvious appeal of the very word epic reflects a durable aspiration among Hollywood studios to do the intellectual work C. Wright Mills described as sustaining "the organized memory of mankind" as part of its "cultural apparatus" (*Causes* 124), as well as to function as a glib promotional ploy. At the peak of studio-system domination, any picture a studio could "book into Grauman's Chinese theater" could qualify as an epic, the Depression-era poet-content provider Joseph Moncure March recalls ("Young" 33).

V

Now barely remembered, March was an exemplary poet-content provider who troubled himself only spottily about the art-commerce conflicts (Hunter 269) rendered in Hollywood novels—from *What Makes Sammy Run* and *The Day of the Locust* to Mailer's *Deer Park* and Didion's *Play It As It Lays*. With this attitude, March prospered, briefly, in Hollywood at the peak of big studio dominance. March's better known, epic-obsessed English contemporary John Collier arrived in Hollywood around the same time and prospered there far longer than March did. These writers represent a counternarrative that challenges the elitist disdain toward "the industry" reflected in most Hollywood novels, in Ben Maddow's conclusion about the uselessness of poetry in Hollywood, and in the high-modernist scorn for the entire enterprise of "kinema" as inevitably prosaic and anti-poetic that Ezra Pound voiced in 1917 in his lament about the overall deterioration of civilization in "Hugh Selwyn Mauberly."

John Collier quit school in his teens and with his father's blessing and modest financial backing set out to become a poet (Hoyle xvi; Milne 104). Collier ended up instead making his mark as a screenwriter and novelist, best known for his short fiction and his first novel, *His Monkey Wife* (1930). In one story he set in Hollywood, "Pictures in the Fire," Collier signaled the persistence of his poetic calling. Collier named the story's narrator, shown "blazing" his way to becoming "the hottest writer in town," "Mr. Rhythm." Collier's concern with the role of intellect in Hollywood surfaces later in "Pictures in the Fire" in an exchange with a would-be "film star" signed to play a "modernized" Juliet with "a Cleopatra touch," who enthuses, "I'm not going to be an ordinary actress, Mr. Rhythm. I'm going to be intellectual" (*Reader* 237, 245, 243, 241).

Late in his career Collier ambitiously revisited his poetic calling, and affirmed his intellectual aspirations, by adapting English literature's most monumental epic for the big screen. Collier embraced the canonic English poet whom the movie-averse Pound couldn't keep from repeatedly calumniating. Debunking Milton's legacy as *the* epic poet in English— emperor of words in English and "all-around house intellectual" of the Puritan Revolution (Lerer 149; Rosen 74)—Pound made much of his loathing "donkey-eared Milton" for his allegedly "gross and utter stupidity and obtuseness" (*ABC* 103) and trashed his legacy of "driveling imbecility" (*Essays* 72).

In looking to Milton for "content," Collier was following in another modernist pioneer's footsteps, one as image-conscious as his contemporary Pound and arguably more influential.

The Soviet director and film theorist Sergei Eisenstein introduced Milton as a proto-Modernist because of the model for emulation he provides. It may seem surprising to link these two disparate revolutionaries, but even the traditionally formalist poet Richard Wilbur treats Milton's "pre-Edison" epic poetry as "genuinely cinematic" (224). Jonathan Rosen's observation that Milton's "enduring relevance" rests in part on how he "confuses the very notion of old and new" (76) calls to mind some essential features of movies as a medium that makes temporal fluidity itself an ordinary experience with its flashbacks, flashforwards, wipes, dissolves, and so on (L. Marcus 43; North 135), and that has come to exploit formulaically both past and future with its most popular narrative genres. While westerns and sword-and-sandal epics continuously remake the past, futuristic interstellar combat and technological fantasies have made *Star Wars* and *Star Trek* durably popular and profitable franchises.

Collier's long-incubating, published but never-produced screenplay for *Paradise Lost* reflects this understanding of these affinities between movies and Milton. It seems especially to elaborate Eisenstein's praise for Miltonic's epic as "a first-rate school for 'the study of montage and audio visual relationships'" and for the preparation of "a shooting script" (58). In contrast to Eisentstein's homage to Milton as an unwitting fellow-traveler cineaste, Pound's repulsion toward Milton seems to parallel his aversion to infant kinema.

In addition to Eisenstein, early Hollywood's most influential moviemaker, D. W. Griffith, also singled out Milton as singularly cinematic among English poets. Where Pound, along with T. S. Eliot, "had no use for Milton" (Goldstein 62), Eisenstein and Griffith revived Milton's legacy in such montage-intensive epics as *Alexander Nevsky* and *Intolerance*. Milton's place in Hollywood extended beyond Griffith's pioneering aesthetics. In Gore Vidal's account, Milton also provided the master allegory for the accommodation of many "Parnassian writers" to Hollywood and for literary Hollywood's "tendency to play Lucifer": "'Better to reign in hell than to serve in heaven' was more than once quoted—well, paraphrased—at the Writer's Table" in studio commissaries ("Who" 573).

Collier aimed to sustain this legacy and to give both Milton and his devil their due with his own version of the "shooting script" Eisenstein had envisioned as ideally cinematic. When Collier realized he had little hope of seeing this work produced, his publisher, the prestigious Alfred A. Knopf, published it in 1973 as a stand-alone poem. The published text proved, as John Updike fretted in his *New Yorker* review, "technically implausible" in its "specification of *trompe-le-oeil* effects" and offered "no clue as to what possessed" Collier to publish it (Milne 108). A few years later Collier described what possessed him: "a faith that the 'thrilling story' and 'theme of *Paradise Lost*'" are "singularly suited to attract a wide audience and especially the young."

In an exhibit celebrating Milton's quadracentennial the New York Public Library underscored this appeal and the difficulty Collier faced in setting out to attract "the young" to Milton: "For the Movies, John Collier adapted *Paradise Lost* into a serious screenplay not long before Milton drew sophomoric ridicule in *National Lampoon's Animal House*" thanks to Donald Sutherland's playing the burned-out Professor Jennings, who concedes mid-lecture ("Milton"):

> Now, what can we say of John Milton's *Paradise Lost*? It's a long poem, written a long time ago, and I'm sure a lot of you have difficulty understanding exactly what Milton was trying to say. Certainly we know that he was trying to describe the struggle between good and evil, right? Okay. The most intriguing character, as we all know from our reading, was . . . Satan. Now was Milton trying to tell us that being bad was more fun than being good? [no response] OK, don't write this down, but I find Milton probably as boring as you find Milton. Mrs. Milton found him boring too. He's a little bit long-winded, he doesn't translate very well into our generation, and his jokes are terrible. [Bell rings, students rise to leave] But that doesn't relieve you of your responsibility for this material. Now I'm waiting for reports from some of you. . . . Listen, I'm not joking. This is my job!

In contrast to Professor Jenning's despair, Collier's confidence that the 1970s were ripe for a Hollywood Milton seems to have rested on, as

Collier recalled, getting "promises." These promises included an advance from a producer and rumors that "Fellini had agreed to do it" (at least a plausible hope in the wake of Fellini's 1969 adaptation of the far more historically and linguistically distant and more outré classic, Petronius's *Satyricon*) "in which event United Artists were [*sic*] willing to do it" (Milne 108). In the event, "none" of the Hollywood players and financiers he was counting on "were willing to go out on a limb for" Collier or Milton.

Instead of relegating *Paradise Lost* to spending eternity in proverbial "development hell," Knopf published Collier's *Paradise Lost* with an explanatory subtitle, "screenplay for cinema of the mind," which accentuated Collier's impulse to appeal to intellect—to the so-called life of the *mind*. Collier rationalized resigning himself to publish *Paradise Lost* rather than persist in trying to get it produced by invoking literary tradition, pointing out that "print" is "after all the medium of epic itself" (*Paradise* vii).

Praised as an "old fashioned" formalist disposed to "bow to tradition," Collier reportedly "believed in the durability, relevance, majesty, and civilizing effect of Great Literature" (*Fancies* ix) (as Waugh's canon-worshiping Barlow might have). Collier titled his short stories with such allusive phrases as "season of mists" (Keats) and "green thoughts" (Marvel). Collier, however, excepted the movies from this reverence for the canon, observing that

> a screenwriter of my sort pays no reverence to the original, nor feels he owes any, even to the most august original. All his duty is to what he hopes, in vain, will appear on screen. (*Paradise* vii)

This disclaimer notwithstanding, Collier never abdicated his affiliation with the British literary canon, not only as an adapter of Milton's epic but as a professed "disciple of Joyce," the master of the encyclopedic, twentieth-century mock-epic (Hoyle xv). Collier made a point of aligning his poetic aspirations with his work as a Hollywood scriptwriter. This work includes such movies as *I Am a Camera*, adapted from Isherwood's account of his interwar Berlin adventures, George Cukor's adaptation of Compton MacKenzie's *Sylvia Scarlet*, and John Huston's version of C. S. Forester's *The African Queen* (for which Collier received no screen credit even though he initiated the project) (Milne 107). His writing credits also include episodes of such popular television series as *The Twilight Zone* and *Alfred Hitchcock Presents*. Collier's successes and talents in screenwriting seem to be what prompted grudging praise in Updike's otherwise disparaging review of the *Paradise Lost* screenplay. Updike conceded

Collier's effectiveness in encouraging contemporary readers to recognize how much of the "virtues of psychological tenderness and lively sensuality . . . Milton possessed."

Such praise, along with Collier's choice of a subtitle for *Paradise Lost*, reflects the extent to which he considered the screenplay a work of intellect as well as a work of poetry. He envisioned his *Paradise Lost* screenplay in particular as an engagement with the conceptual and philosophical questions Milton's poem prompts as well as its sensory, aesthetic dimension, which Updike highlighted. This aspiration took hold well before Collier's screenwriting career and his move to Hollywood.

As an apprentice man-of-letters in the United Kingdom, Collier made his bid to become what came to be called a public intellectual, to join in and help shape the civic conversation about social and cultural conditions in interwar England. In *Just the Other Day*, a British version of Frederick Lewis Allen's classic of reportage and commentary *Only Yesterday*, Collier's and cowriter Iain Lang's "pointed and vigorous comments" "reminded" readers of developments "most of us would perhaps like to forget," an unsigned *Spectator* review observed. A reviewer for the *Times Literary Supplement* praised Collier and his cowriter because "they have been very careful in ascertaining the truth about public events that have often been misrepresented" and because "their passing judgments on social, literary, and artistic movements are free from many of the follies of contemporary prejudice" (Scott-Thomas).

Associating Collier with perhaps modernity's most influential founding intellectual, a *Herald Tribune* reviewer compared Collier's work to *Candide* (Barry). Some forty years later Tom Milne's retrospect on Collier's career elaborated this Enlightenment connection. Milne claimed that Collier's early style succeeded in "combining the manner of Sterne with that of Diderot" (107). When Wyndham Lewis reviewed Collier's third novel, a broad comedy of manners titled (with a nod to *King Lear*) *Defy the Foul Fiend*, he cited an even more venerable precursor. Lewis characterized *Defy the Foul Fiend* as a reworking of *Don Quixote* ("Demos"). With its "wrong side of the blanket" hero, a priapic wastrel beguiled by "revolutionary notions" (28, 382), Collier stages what Lewis describes as a "Homeric political debate" as a result of which the novel's "idiot" hero has "all his proletarian illusions ground to the dust."

Accordingly Collier's introduction to the *Paradise Lost* screenplay focuses on the dissonance between Milton's archaic "orthodox" ideas and "those commonly held today" (viii), the explosive rhetorical "impact" of Satan's "utterances" (viii), and Milton's sifting of "explanations" in order to reach "a more likely and a more tolerable one" (x). Collier also set out to explore contradictions with which *Paradise Lost* confronted its readers, in particular the irresolvable "monstrous inconsistency" that the pious have traditionally explained away as *felix culpa* but that Collier characterized as a "thicket of lesser contradictions where I find myself comfortably at home" (xi). Most ambitiously, Collier strove to stage familiar but perennially recalcitrant ideological conflicts, most notably tensions between promoting the "status quo and" agitating for "change" (xii).

Even Collier's character descriptions home in on traits such as "intellectual curiosity" (Beelzebub) and skepticism (Eve) (41, 70). Associating the former trait with the quandary perhaps most vexing to mid-century intellectuals (most influentially Hannah Arendt), Collier ascribes to Satan's lieutenant a "look of intellectual detachment common to those who advise the murderers of mankind." Then Beelzebub and Lucifer listen avidly to "the piercing shriek of the napalmed child . . . the muted dirge of the hundreds marching to the gas chamber at Buchenwald[1] . . . the desperate clamor of the multitudes blinded on the outskirts of Hiroshima" (41).

Collier's Eve, by contrast, appears as a more unformed yet also more promising avatar of intellect. Since "Satan has lent her his unlimited powers of vision" (86), Collier shows Eve (as if on-screen), according to her body language, as an intellectual-in-waiting: "Standing with her hand on her hip," "less a reverent listener than an eavesdropper . . . free to indulge in a private opinion, and to express it . . . with a skeptical look" (70). This detailed rendering of her demeanor introduces Eve as humanity's first intellectual and, drawn as she is to "discovery and perdition" (P. Bayard 42), a distinctly modern one. Collier's characterization of Eve reflects what Martin Jay, reviewing the screenplay for the *New Republic*, described as her intellectual primacy in the Fall narrative: as the intellectually dominant member of the first couple and even as Satan's "superior" because of the clarity of "vision" that Collier ascribes to her and because she "never begins to delude herself" ("Praise"). Collier's Eve consequently "discovers and eventually learns to celebrate human incompleteness and imperfection and, above all the labyrinthine dynamism of her own mind."

The fall itself, in Collier's account of the first couple's morning-after colloquy, turns them into doubters and epistemologists. Reacting to Eve's claim to "know the names of things" and to "know the difference," Adam retorts, "How can you know?" (112). Collier signals Eve's transformation into a doubter by beginning her next speech with adverbial hesitation and ellipses: "Perhaps. . . ." Even though Jay regards Collier's Eve as intellectually superior to his Satan, Jay nevertheless looked upon

Collier's Satan as a representative figure, as the arch 1960s intellectual: "as a guerilla leader and speculative philosopher." Taking sides in the perennial controversy about Satan's appeal and legitimacy, which Dryden, Blake, and Shelley have kept alive over the past three centuries, Jay and (in Jay's view) Collier adopt the "sympathy for the devil" stance then prevalent (Berman, "Faust" 500, 504; Gordon 232; Lee and Shalin 256; Bromell 127; Friedlander 118).

The appeal of *Paradise Lost* as movie material, which Collier recognized, persists, even though 1960s "sympathy for the devil" posturing may have long ago gone the way of granny glasses and bell bottoms. A 2006 report in the British press, for example, noted a persistent interest in adapting Milton's epic for the screen: "A couple of versions of *Paradise Lost*" have been biding their time "in development hell—where else?" (Foden). In 2007, reflecting the persistence of this aspiration and the challenge, Time Warner's New Line studio cinema "failed" more spectacularly and extravagantly than Collier could have conceived—"at a cost of $180 million" in its effort to bring Milton's epic to the screen with its adaptation of Philip Pullman's novel *The Golden Compass* (Gee).

VI

The prescience of his intellectual aspirations notwithstanding, Collier's voice barely registered among those of several other mid-century Hollywood writers eager to show and tell moviegoers "all about Eve." "All fine and kick-ass . . . all versions of the same fox or as William Demarest puts it down in . . . *The Lady Eve*, 'Positively the same dame,'" enthuses a cinephile in Steve Erickson's 2007 homage to movie-love, *Zeroville* (47, 118). Embracing "the artful Eve . . . practiced in double dealing," "the beguiling but potentially treacherous . . . devious schemer," and film noir's "deadly, seductive dames who trouble our assumptions about the survival of innocence," such classics as Joseph Manckiewicz's *All About Eve* and Nunnally Johnson's *The Three Faces of Eve*, along with Preston Sturges's *The Lady Eve* and Collier's "screenplay for the mind," all illustrate Hollywood's fascination with the countless faces of Eve (DiBattista 301, 305).

VII

Collier's American contemporary Joseph Moncure March also took an interest in Eve. In contrast to Collier's stress on Eve as a modern reasoner and inquirer, March evoked Eve as a corrupting "tart" or as a temptress "built to drive men mad" (*Wild* 167, 38) in his two long narrative poems adapted for the big screen, *The Wild Party* and *The Set-Up*. As one of the few American poets to have his work—*two* poems—become Hollywood adaptations, March became even more versatile than Collier as a poet-content provider.

Successively a protégé of Robert Frost in New England and of Howard Hughes in Hollywood, the triple-named March also offers a more resilient real-life avatar of Schulberg's fictional self-defeated Hollywood poet Henry Powell Turner. Like the Schulberg character, March came to Hollywood with an elite East Coast pedigree (as the nephew of Army Chief of Staff Peyton Conway March and grandson of the eminent classicist Francis March). Like Schulberg's and Waugh's fictional Hollywood poets, March showed early poetic promise as the senior-class poet at both Lawrenceville and Amherst. As an Amherst English major, under Frost's tutelage, March recalls absorbing his mentor's "dim view of 'poetic' phraseology, and pretentious purple passages," and becoming, like Frost, "fascinated by the English language as it's spoken" and "the cadences of everyday speech," which "he didn't like to see fancied up" (*Wild* 38).

This tutelage later stood March in good stead. He spent the 1920s—his twenties—in Manhattan as an aspiring man-of-letters. The revolt against literary gentility with its vogue for slumming, the kind of flouting of social boundaries associated with the Harlem Renaissance and its "mongrelizing" impact, was in full swing (Doulgas). March mastered and took full advantage of this climate. His early work prompted the literary editor of the *Chicago Evening Post*, Llwellyn Jones, to hail March as "a poet who is here to stay" while in 1929 a *Times* reviewer greeted a collection of March's poems by declaring March "a writer of great originality" (Cavanaugh).

Like Collier's, March's father staked him to his first writing project soon after Harold Ross fired March from the *New Yorker*. March had served as Ross's first managing editor (known as "Jesus" to colleagues) and inaugurated the magazine's opening "Talk of the Town" feature, after earning his "Lost Generation" *bona fides* as a Great War combat veteran (*Wild* 6, 10; Cavanaugh). Unlike Schulberg's success-despoiled Turner, March's devotion to his poetic calling bore a saving, self-suspecting ironic taint, a self-deprecating distance, illustrated by his recollection of his star turn as "an idiot" delivering the class ode at his Amherst graduation and his description of his "drifting" through "boredom" as a Village bohemian in the early 1920s (*Wild* 15, 35). Out of his Jazz Age escapades issued March's first acclaimed and provocative narrative poem, *The Wild Party*. Despite a threat from municipal vice-suppression authorities in New York and blessed with the requisite banned-in-Boston imprimatur, Pascal Covici published it in 1926 with illustrations by Reginald Marsh and a foreword by Louis Untermeyer (March, *Wild* 46–49). While its retrograde form might have reassured censorious traditionalists, its graphic language and lurid story overshadowed the couplets and the stanzaic form: *The Wild Party* recounts, in tetrameter couplets, a "roaring twenties" Manhattan bacchanalia—an orgy—that leads to murder.

While its form and story may seem dated, *The Wild Party* enjoyed several rebirths at century's end. James Ivory and Ismail Merchant, the duo renowned for bringing to the screen classics by Henry James, E. M. Forster, Jean Rhys, and V. S. Naipaul, released its adaptation of *The Wild Party* in 1974. The Pulitzer Prize–winning *New Yorker* cartoonist Art Spiegelman reissued and reillustrated *The Wild Party* in 1995 as a graphic novel. In explaining his decision to resuscitate March's work, Spiegelman groups March with Hemingway, Chandler, Fitzgerald, and jazz in shaping the 1920s sensibility (Blume). *The Wild Party* also became the basis for two different musicals, on and Off-Broadway, in the same year.

March had no hand in adapting either of his poems for stage or screen. After RKO bought the rights to film his second popular narrative poem, *The Set Up*, March recalls, "I was out in Hollywood . . . and tried to get work on the screenplay, but they didn't want me around" (*Wild* 58). Like many novelists (L. Bayard, D. Smith), March then repudiated the studio's ideological evisceration of his work. Nonetheless this 1949 release has remained a classic in the *film noir* genre: "a sizzling melodrama . . . brought to vivid throbbing life" by Robert Wise's "shrewd direction" and Art Cohn's "understanding, colloquial dialogue" (Pryor). Starring Robert Ryan as a ring veteran resisting mob control of the fight game, *The Set Up* does its ideological and intellectual work in the way boxing screenplays—Schulberg's *On the Waterfront* and *The Harder They Fall*, Paul Schrader and Mardik Martin's *Raging Bull*—often do. Boxing becomes an allegory for the struggling honest artist beleaguered by corrupting working conditions.

The Hollywood version of *The Set Up* didn't do the cultural work March ascribed to his poem. March had set out to grapple with "race prejudice" by depicting "the treatment a Negro receives when he runs afoul of the white establishment" (*Wild* 54). Consequently, the RKO release left March "really disgusted to find that the hero of the picture was no longer a Negro fighter: they had turned him into a white man. . . . The whole point of the narrative had been tossed out the window" (*Wild* 58). Rather than warping by omission, the posthumously released adaptation of *The Set Up*, in contrast, warped March's poem by addition. The Merchant-Ivory version featured an *a-clef* Fatty Arbuckle character and changed the venue from Manhattan vaudeville to up-market Hollywood. Even Walter Marks, who wrote both the screenplay and the music, conceded that the movie "was the kind of thing we were glad to have done, although it wasn't everything we hoped it would be" (Cavanaugh).

March had much more impact as a screenwriter and a journalist after his precocious star turn as a *Wunderkind* Village poet and man-of-letters-about-town faded. During the 1930s March worked on some twenty movies as a contract writer for MGM, Republic, RKO, Paramount, and Howard Hughes's shortlived Caddo Productions. At Caddo, the apparently versatile March worked briefly as a production executive, serving as Hughes's second-in-command. March's most memorable work for Hughes entailed converting Hughes's still legendary (Miltonically titled) aerial combat epic *Hell's Angels* from a silent movie to a talkie and writing Jean Harlow's most memorable line. With this one perennially provocative question, March turned Harlow into Mae West's most formidable rival in Hollywood's witty trollop niche: "Would you be shocked if I put on something more comfortable?" (March, "Young").

Soon before quitting Hollywood, March collaborated on his most intellectually ambitious script, *Three Faces West*. Starring John Wayne and Charles Coburn, *Three Faces West* addresses the most pressing concerns of the 1930s: the Depression and the rise of totalitarianism. The story links the fortunes of a Viennese medical professor and his refined daughter fleeing the Anschluss and joining a band of North Dakota farmers. Also refugees, these farmers are forced to flee chronic drought in their Dust Bowl town. Not surprisingly *Three Faces West* invited comparisons with Nunnally Johnson's adaptation of Steinbeck's bestselling novel *Grapes of Wrath* for John Ford. A *New York Times* reviewer, making this comparison, dismissed the work of March and his cowriters as a "glib . . . fairy-tale version of *Grapes of Wrath*" (Strauss). The reviewer objected to the narrative and particularly the dialogue as "uneven" and *too* intellectual, "sometimes turning a dramatic situation into prolix discussion." Despite these "good intentions" and evident intellectual aspirations, *Three Faces West*, in this reviewer's estimate, exhibited—like many caricatured intellectuals—"insufficient stamina."

Back in New York, March looked to Hollywood from his new perch at the *New York Times Magazine*. As a feature writer March became the magazine's in-house expert on "the basic patterns of Hollywood behavior," on the offices "where clichés fly through the cigar smoke, taking on a spurious and beguiling glitter that makes them seem new," on "the political intrigue of the lot," and on the mysteries of studio office furniture ("One"

29). In this role March raised the vexing question—"the crux of the whole matter" in Hollywood studios: "How fast can a picture be made—and still be good?" Like many writers who cycled through the big studios between the world wars, March leavened his reportage with intellectual disdain for his former employers, for their pandering to the "twenty million people who want to keep Hitler off their minds" while "keeping up the Horatio Alger myth," and with condescension toward his former writing colleagues whose "average level of creative effort" proved, in March's view, "fairly low" ("Star-Gazing" 29).

In the 1970s, March elaborated on and complicated his understanding of the "creative effort" of screenwriting during his Hollywood decade. In this later recollection, March more generously overlooked what differentiated him, as a poet, from the countless novelists and playwrights the studios were "bringing . . . out from the east by the carload" to usher in the "new Era of Sound" ("Young" 30). As part of these "carloads," March identified himself with the movement heralded in 1932 by the *New York Times*, which announced that with producers newly pressed to provide "lyrical sentences and coherent plots," the movies "had gone literary" (Giovacchini 17). March's railroad metaphor ("carloads") also calls to mind his recognition from the outset that his literary vocation—his way of "thinking about myself as a writer"—would always be conditioned by technology. While delivering the class ode at his Amherst graduation, March "had no sooner started when a locomotive . . . let out a blast that" repeatedly "drowned me out" prompting March to realize as he "read on grimly" that "I was no match for the locomotive" (*Wild* 15).

March's first assignment in Hollywood, writing dialogue for the high-tech combat-aviation spectacle *Hell's Angels*, came after several months of "doing nothing" at MGM, and prompted March to wonder whether he was involved in producing "art or an Assembly-line Product" (Young 30, 9). After leaving Hollywood, March wrote exclusively about technology and its producers. March made less of a career change than snobbish purists might imagine since, as Richard Poirier once observed, poetry is "a form of technology" just as technology provides opportunities for "self-articulation" (128, 123).

March's first career in technology occurred during World War II. March's stint as a sheet-metal cutter and fitter in a Connecticut shipyard resulted in a rhapsody titled "Shipyard Symphony," which ran in the *New York Times Magazine* midway through the war. In the 1950s, March wrote rhyming scripts for films such as *Design for Dreaming* and *A Touch of Magic* (Cavanaugh). These celebrations of the "magic of the present" were produced and distributed annually by General Motors and its Whirlpool affiliate as part of their campaigns to unveil new car and appliance models. Even in these meretricious dance-and-music extravaganzas, March didn't fully relinquish long dormant intellectual and poetic aspirations. The very titles of two of these extended commercials both recall and anticipate ac- claimed movies by some of Hollywood's most sophisticated star directors and writers: Orson Welles's *A Touch of Evil* (his last major Hollywood movie) and *Design for Living*. This 1933 adaptation by Ernest Lubitsch and Ben Hecht of a Noel Coward comedy caught the censorious attention of Hollywood's newly empowered Hays Office. March looked to another outré literary voice, Lord Byron, by smuggling the following allusion into *A Touch of Magic*:

> She walks in beauty like the night.
> She rides in Buicks like a bird in flight.

These commercials and March's career trajectory illustrate, if nothing else, March's resistance to hard-and-fast distinctions between serving "culture" and serving industry, between producing poetry and "providing content," between working as a *literary* writer and as a screenwriter, between writ- ing movies and writing "copy." His unique[2] career narrative, from hav- ing "trudged along" in the snow as Frost's peripatetic protégé (*Wild* 118) before paying his dues under the palms as Hughes's aide-de-camp, reflect his rare conception of the literary career as at once mercantile, even mer- cenary, *and*, at the same time, requiring a sense of transcendent aspiration. March realized while working for Hughes that he wasn't an original or a genius but was "like most writers" and as such "quick to theorize about human behavior" ("Young" 50). In contrast to legendary high Modern- ists, such as William Carlos Williams, who described poetry as what "men die miserably every day for lack of what is found there" (318), or Pound, for whom poems are "news that stays news" (*Pisan*, Cantos xxix), March conceded that "there's really nothing very useful about a poem": it "won't put food in your stomach" or provide "solace in times of catastrophe and disaster," as March recalls learning as an infantryman in World War I (*Wild* 19–21). As a teenager on the western front, March appears to have antici- pated Auden's more dourly phrased conclusion twenty years later, in eu- logizing Yeats, that poetry makes nothing happen. Consequently, March conceived of *The Set Up* as having an "effect as unpoetic as an aluminum jockstrap" (arguably itself a poetic image). At odds with the "standards by which lyric poetry is judged," March nevertheless conceded that what he wrote has something "in common with its lovely sister, Poetry: balanced cadences . . . the mysterious magic of incantation," which "at the risk of sounding pretentious," March chose to "call . . . the Beauty of Form" (*Wild* 54–55).

March's education, as he recounted it in his sixties, not only defies genre, but also flouts and blurs recognized, hierarchic institutional boundaries. His 1968 memoir *A Certain Wildness* singled out the three schools he attended. In addition to Lawrenceville and Amherst, March attended one last "school": "my school for storytelling was the cinema" (39). March's career as a content-provider and his lifelong "education" as a poet rested on the unresolved "contradictions between" movies "as merchandise" and movies "as art" ("Young" 9). Viewing these contradictions as "central to the American motion picture" as cultural practice and as a commercial product, March highlights the aspirations of Hollywood intellect, explicitly in such reflections, and implicitly in the very course of his career. Both show what differentiates the "socially idealistic and less highbrow" Hollywood *intelligenti* (Nabokov 277) committed to appealing to the "wider public" (Elshtain) from intellectuals as customarily pictured (see chapter I).

These characteristics converge in the unusual biographical facts that make March's career so remarkable, particuarly his apprenticeships to Frost and Hughes. Looking back on this career, March gave intellect pride of place by singling out Frost as "the most important influence in my literary life," an influence March later judged "permanently embedded in my character" (*Wild* 16–17, 38). March became a Hollywood insider overnight thanks to Hughes's patronage and March reminisced about Hughes more extensively and more critically than about Frost, perhaps in part because Hughes betrayed March when he tried to dissolve their employment contract. Thanks to Hughes's earlier sponsorship, though, March had by then become important enough to get Hollywood powerhouse David O. Selznick to represent him in settling the debt ("Young" 51).

This simple monetary debt contrasts with March's more crucial vocational debt to Hughes, beginning with *Hell's Angels*. When released, this movie's ambition and expense not only elicited unprecedented hype as "the most extraordinary output ever to emerge from a motion picture studio" with even the trades assuring skeptics that "superlatives . . . ordinarily extravagant may be justly used in describing this picture, particularly the sequence made in the air" (Crafton 350). Some seventy years later Martin Scorsese revisited *Hell's Angels* in *The Aviator*. The

Oscar-winning biopic about Hughes treated this legendary moviemaking project at length.

Working for Hughes also afforded March opportunities to collaborate with director James Whale as well as with the novice actress Jean Harlow. March's most memorable lesson resulted from observing Whale's interaction with Harlow: Whale became so exasperated by her "stilted wooden" delivery that he groused, "I can't tell you how to become a woman" (March, "Young" 20). Harlow's evolution into Hollywood's quintessential blonde bombshell furnished March with a lasting lesson. Decades later he still marveled at how, in a two-word phrase, a studio publicist turned this "girl who had nothing" except her "ash blond" hair into America's first "platinum blonde" (March, "Young" 20; Morin 138). Both Whale and Harlow became such legends in their own right that, like Hughes, they were eventually subjects of biopics. The BBC released *Gods and Monsters*, about Whale, in 1998 and two releases, both titled *Harlow*, came out of Hollywood in 1965.

VIII

Students of poetry and movies finding themselves hard-pressed to see Hughes and Frost sharing common ground will find it in pairing Frost's embrace of "extravagance" with Hughes's reputation for it in his careers in oil, movies, and aviation as a "visionary" (Courtwright). In 1930, Frost voiced his faith in extravagance, preaching counter to common sense that "a penny saved is a mean thing" and a "penny spent is . . . a big thing" (447). Frost could have had Hughes in mind when he rejoiced, "What an *extravagant* universe it is. And the most extravagant thing in it . . . is man— the most wasteful, spending thing in it—in all his luxuriance." Likewise, Alfred Hitchcock insisted that movies must "always deal in exaggerations . . . to put new words into the screen's visual language" (11).

After Hughes's extravagantly budgeted transformation of the silent *Hell's Angels* into a talkie, noteworthy mostly for its expensively and dangerously choreographed biplane stunt-flying (Courtwright), Hughes went on to develop in the 1940s an extravagantly laughable—gargantuan and quixotic—seaplane made out of birch-wood. (These trees, as Frost depicted them in "Birches," will, once down, "never right themselves," though they invariably spur the aspiration to "get away from earth awhile.")

The public and the press derisively turned Hughes's aeronautical fiasco into a metaphor by naming it "the Spruce Goose." The phrase's pointed dendrological inaccuracy, changing the hardwood birch that Hughes actually used into the less dense coniferous "spruce" in order to make the rhyme work, illustrates another of Frost's lessons. Frost taught that "Education by Poetry" works when readers learn how to "ride" metaphor and then "watch" metaphor "breaking down":

> All metaphor breaks down somewhere. That is the beauty of it. It is touch and go with the metaphor, and until you have lived with it long enough you don't know when it is going. You don't know how much you can get out of it and when it will cease to yield (335).

The opposition between the material inaccuracy of the phrase "spruce goose" and the catchiness of its rhyme show both "how much" Hughes's mockers got out of it and how little information or insight the phrase ultimately yielded. "Watch" and "touch" also serve as reminders that poems engage more than one sense at a time. So do movies, as Hughes implicitly stressed by insisting on transforming the silent *Hell's Angels* into a talkie.

IX

Memorable exchanges in the movies since the release of the first talkies have become as poetic as *Hell's Angels* but more subtly so. Such exchanges have come to highlight both this interplay of senses and to demonstrate the way metaphor reaches the breaking point Frost noted. Such impasses include being outwitted into silence or incredulity, the awe of facing death, or merely the strain of describing it. Dialogue and gestures in such poetic movie passages all convey a figurative afterimage or a relevant but only implicit narrative as they propel a movie's plot and sustain its overt main narrative.

- In *To Have and To Have Not*, Howard Hawks's wartime adaptation of a Hemingway novel, Lauren Bacall instructs the gunrunner played by costar Humphrey Bogart to "put [his] lips together and blow" in order to whistle. Bacall's tour de force in this scene conveys the power of wit to stun masculine cockiness into silence and makes one of the most memorable contributions the to broad discourse-transforming impact of Hollywood as our primary source of poetry: "Political figures, who used to quote poetry, now quote famous movie lines such as Bacall's" (Safire) or, as so memorably quoted by Ronald Reagan, Clint Eastwood's challenge to "make my day." Bacall and Hawks achieved this poetic effect because her performance "displaced virtually all other dramatic concerns" (Schatz 424). Phrasing, timing, and camera focus on the actor's lips eclipsed narrative so much that *To Have and Have Not* garnered rare praise as pleasurably plotless, atmosphere-centered, and "Nabokovian" in its verbal pyrotechnics (Agee 121; Thomson, "Howard Hawks" 616).

- "Plastics" is the notoriously glib life counsel Dustin Hoffman receives as Mike Nichols and Buck Henry's "graduate" in this eponymous 1967 release. This single noun—the "one-word" career advice from a family friend—reaches beyond the actual on-screen utterance. "Plastics" conjures up visually and tactilely an entire counterculture's conception of American adulthood circa 1967, as empty and exhausted, and succinctly intimates the life narrative satirized with this "one word," its contemporary connotations, and the story that follows.
- The visual cue, a dead fish in butcher's paper, at once counters and intensifies the famous metaphoric euphemism uttered in *The Godfather* by Sal Tessio (Abe Vigoda): "Luca Brasi sleeps with the fishes." When image and utterance are paired, a colleague's murder becomes at once sad, acceptable, and necessary. Business as usual, an act of nature, and a mysterious sea change concealed in fathomless depths, death becomes only a natural state of rest and the deceased little more than a decomposing "lower" animal meant to serve, like the butcher who provides the message paper, human appetite—a creature who now rests where, according the laws of nature, he belongs.[3]

Few Hollywood releases demonstrate the poetic possibilities of the movies, both narratively and metaphorically, as much as Alfred Hitchcock's and Ernest Lehman's *North by Northwest*. As it morphs generically from thriller into romance, *North by Northwest* turns into one of the most traditional kinds of poems, "pastoral"—as defined by William Empson and subsequently applied to the movies by Frederic Raphael as the litmus test for "the most successful films" (*Personal* 137). Hitchcock's *tempus fugit* timing and Lehman's suspenseful plotting make "pastoral" a particularly apt way to characterize the poetics of *North by Northwest*, dependent as it is on train and bus schedules, on UN meeting dates and times. *North by Northwest* illustrates Raphael's take on the "pastoral" genre of movie poems, even more so than his favored prime example, David Lean's *Brief Encounter*.

Among the forms of pastoral he catalogued, Empson included works which cover a limited span of time . . . all "romances" in which the lovers celebrate (and lament) their passion within a tight schedule. This kind of thing has elements of both contest (trial) and sporting event. It is played, to the last second, in the knowledge that the whistle will go. The return to "reality" signals the end of the eclogue. Film often makes use of this artificial limit in order to lend pathos to the improbable. (127)

The last, abrupt image-segue in *North by Northwest* at once compounds and mocks this "pathos" of the "improbable." This sequence's metaphoric work becomes famously vivid as a lovers' dialogue yielding to a silent image, part of a series of images that produce this movie's metaphoric closure. With these images, Hitchcock challenges one of Hollywood's most hackneyed metaphors: "cliffhanger." This phrase, well worn by publicists and reviewers to describe suspenseful narratives, becomes part of the way in which, throughout *North by Northwest*, Hitchock weds Lehman's espionage narrative to a metaphoric pattern of "elaborate verticality" (Pomerance, *Eye* 22–23). Not surprisingly for a director "all of [whose] films are metaphorical" (66), Hitchcock rides this metaphor, as Frost urges, until it breaks down. Literally and graphically, the movie's denouement turns—or tropes—cliffhanging from a narrative incident into a dream-memory, from wide-angle action to an erotically charged romance in close-up. This "concluding twist," a "manipulation of our knowledge" (Bordwell and Thompson, 393) of narrative conventions and genres, produces what Empson singles out as the fundamental poetic ambiguity: "A sort of ambiguity in not knowing which" reasons, explanations, or narratives "to hold most clearly in mind . . . covers almost everything of literary importance" (3).

Empson's influence as a critic and as *the* authority on ambiguity had its greatest impact during the Cold War, when ambiguity as a poetic device became, in the view of Hungarian novelist Peter Nadas, *the* primary device for "outsmarting" and "triumphing" over state-policing (Kimmelman), over the kind of surveillance and intimidation the hero and heroine of *North by Northest* defy and overcome. This threat shadows and motivates the Cary Grant character, Roger Thornhill, throughout *North by Northwest* and climaxes at the end in a shot of Thornhill's (assisted) rescue of the cliffhanging heroine (yet another Hollywood Eve), Eve Kendall.

Played by Eva Marie Saint, Kendall dangles off Mount Rushmore while holding precariously to a sheer drop. As she dangles, a Soviet agent played by Martin Landau tries to kill the pair. Suddenly this shot fades to close-ups

of the couple in pajamas in a Pullman compartment. When Thornhill pulls his bride (his third) to the top bunk, just as he appeared to be pulling her to safety over the cliff an instant ago, the pair describes what they're doing as "silly" and "sentimental," as opposed to heroic and suspenseful. Hitchcock follows this intimate, self-deprecatorily comic exchange by cutting to an image of their train hurtling into a mountain tunnel. With this image, "an obscene pun" long a cue for lewd smirks and knowing eyebrow lifts (R. Allen 30; Pomerance, *Eye* 57), the narrative literally enters one genre (romantic comedy) and exits another (espionage thriller) and turns from the *tempus fugit* classical tradition to the *carpe diem* tradition. Rather than simply making a single-genre thriller, Hitchcock manages to "exploit suspense in order to foster" responses "counter to the" narrative "resolution ostensibly desired" in such movies and turns the idiom of the thriller into a playfully perverse challenge and so manipulates our customary moral and emotional responses (R. Allen 39).

This poetic turn beyond genre works metaphorically as well as narratively. The closing image sequence in *North by Northwest* signals both openings (sexual and narrative) and the closure, lifelong monogamy, that typically resolves such romance plots. A metaphor so overdetermined affords moviegoers opportunities to feel "at home in the metaphor" (Frost 332). Yet the metaphor also breaks down, along with genre continuity, because of the contradictoriness of the images' metaphoric meanings. This contrariness raises such open-ended, ambiguity-sustaining questions as: Should we, in Empson's phrase, "hold most clearly in mind" the unseen but impending coupling as the beginning of a beautiful, lifelong partnership or as more of the celebrated Cary Grant fecklessness to which Hollywood has accustomed moviegoers (D. Thomson, "Cary Grant" 610) or as yet another impulsive *misalliance* for the alimony-burdened Thornhill? The pairing of danger-on-the-cliff and the comfort hailed in the popular song "Autumn in Vermont" as "the thrill of first nighting," followed by the unsettling reminder that Eve has just become a third "Mrs. Thornhill," underscores the understanding that "we never . . . say what we mean"— not Hitchcock, not the movie's characters, and especially not the typical Cary Grant character, who embodies the "living and disturbing ambiguity" Frost so cherished (613). The information the narrative has provided about Thornhill's earlier marriages, moreover, reinforces the plot's pastoral frame. Pastoral, in Raphael's elaboration of Empson's account of pastoral, characteristically "blinks at the facts," the facts in this case of Thornhill's apparent marital incompetence (*Personal* 127).

The Cold War conditions that bring Mr. and Mrs. Thornhill together reflect Raphael's observation that pastoral can frame "sexual episodes but also social" ones and illustrate another lesson Frost associates with "education by poetry" and by metaphor in particular: the effect and implications of metaphor extend beyond private meditation and self-expression to the public realm, to matters of "national belief," because metaphors "throw" our shared experience "into shape and order" (340, 336). Hughes's legendary career illustrates this imperative and the tensions it produces. It also highlights how metaphors in the public arena compete with one another and then break down.

One of the most recounted chapters in the Howard Hughes saga provides an actual, historical ("ripped from the headlines") illustration of metaphoric breakdown. Two derisive metaphors for Hughes's birch seaplane emerged from the controversy it stirred. Less famous than "Spruce Goose," "Flying Lumberyard" came out of the Capitol, introduced by Senator Owen Brewster of Maine, who sought to thwart Hughes's other notoriously extravagant—albeit more successful—initiative: challenging Pan Am airline's monopoly over intercontinental air travel with his fledgling airline, TWA. Though less public—less controversial and less spectacular—than Hughes's extravagant aeronautical technological folly and his high-stakes corporate warfare, the goal of making movies out of poems seems, over the course of Hollywood history and as a reflection of the aspirations characteristic of Hollywood intellect, no less extravagant than what Frost called for and what Hughes's career, at least as popularly perceived, embodied. Hughes's ambitions, like some of the achievements of directors such as Hitchcock, Gondry, Maddow, Nichols, Altman, Hawks, and Coppola, among others, may reflect a vision of movies as promising more room for metaphoric elaboration and conceptual play than even the most lasting poems on the page.

Notes

1. A lapse of accuracy since Buchenwald, primarily a concentration camp rather than a death camp, had no "gas chambers."

2. *Unique*, an adjective I eschew and forbid students from using, may apply here.

3. The more prosaic version in Mario Puzo's novel *The Godfather* ended up on "the cutting room floor": "The fish means that Luca Brasi is sleeping on the bottom of the ocean. It's an old Sicilian message" (Jones 94).

POV Pandora VI

I'm curious, that's my profession.

—SUSAN SONTAG

I

Amid abundant discussions of Hollywood-made stereotypes or archetypes, one type of stock character sometimes gets short shrift or even lost in the crowd of cowboys, mobsters, swashbucklers, wily Eves, hard-boiled gumshoes, fast-talking dames, rubes, and slickers: *inquirers* and *researchers*. Such characters embody the defining trait of intellectuals, who, in C. Wright Mills's estimate, "must reason and investigate" (*Causes* 125). A recurring type in Hollywood movies since the advent of talkies, this inquirer figure has undergone many permutations and assumed many guises.

Though easily overlooked, inquirer-protagonists resemble heroes in the two most "successful" American movie genres, gangster stories and westerns (Warshow 135). They all focus on the "man who walks alone" (Canby, "*Wild*" 399). Typically, these solitary figures draw on their "wisdom" and "ambiguous skills" as they "aggressively" promote some widely misunderstood or unappreciated "rational enterprise."

Consider, for example, Edward G. Robinson's acting repertoire and the scripts the studios offered him once he became an established star. Robinson made his name early in the talkie era with his tough guy persona, especially playing gangsters. By 1940 *Little Caesar*, *Outside the Law*, and *The Last Gangster* had made Robinson a marquee draw.

While becoming typecast as a tough guy, though, Robinson was also playing dissident inquirers, especially over a two-movie span as an eponymous "doctor." As the hero in 1940 of the biopic *Dr. Ehrlich's Magic Bullet*, Robinson's character risked public opprobrium by developing a microbicide to cure victims publicly perceived as promiscuous degenerates of syphilis. Two years earlier *The Amazing Dr. Clitterhouse*'s obsessive curiosity about criminal minds turned this dogged inquirer into an accomplice rather than an observer of criminals in a narrative that shows the title character at work on a study tentatively titled "crime and research," with which he aims to "solve the terrible problem of crime"—the very "problem" that had already made Robinson a star. Robinson's role in *Clitterhouse* melds his early starmaking gangster roles with his later inquirer roles and so enacts Pierre Bayard's understanding of modern culture itself as a "site of discovery and perdition" (42).

These roles suggest, moreover, the comparative ease of discussing Robinson's performances according to conventional hero–villain distinctions instead of viewing them with the complexities of inquiry and research in the foreground. Describing a Soviet physicist entangled in the Red Army's victory at Stalingrad, Russian novelist Vaseily Grossman explained these complications, the challenge of recognizing intellectual heroism as readily as we recognize similar heroism in westerns, crime, and war dramas:

> We often make fun of intellectuals for their doubts, their split personalities, their Hamlet-like indecisiveness. When I was young, I despised that side of myself. Now, though, I've changed my mind: humanity owes many great books and great discoveries to people who were indecisive and full of doubts; they have achieved as much as simpletons who never hesitate. And when it comes to the crunch, they too are prepared to go to the stake; they stand as firm under fire as the people who are always strong-willed and resolute. (748)

From this perspective, repeatedly affirmed by Hollywood, cowboys, gangsters, and scientists—at least as characters—ultimately face the same "crunch" and the same risk of "going to the stake," though the motives and narrative circumstances that drive inquirers "to the stake" may be more intellectually complex than those that impel more familiar kinds of heroes, villains, and martyrs. Across genres and decades such heroes share a brand of contrarian curiosity. As defined by Michel Foucault, in opposition to the conscientious student's eagerness to learn and please, this heroic curiosity does "not . . . seek to assimilate what it is proper for one to know, but that which enables one to get free of oneself" (*Use* 8).

Though inquirer-protagonists appear in many movie genres, Depression-era screwball comedy probably did the most to establish researchers as stock figures.

- *My Man Godfrey*: William Powell as a millionaire amateur sociologist doing field work, going undercover as a butler to probe the plight of the Depression-displaced homeless.
- *The Lady Eve*: Henry Fonda as a herpetologist, an Adam who knows his serpents but, unschooled in the pitfalls of eros, falls prey to a wily seductress.
- *Sullivan's Travels*: Joel McCrea as an A-list screenwriter-director, another amateur sociologist, going undercover as a hobo to probe the plight of Depression-displaced transients.
- *Bringing Up Baby*: Cary Grant as a paleontologist mistaken for a zoologist.
- *Ball of Fire*: featuring Barbara Stanwyck as a streetwise chorus girl who teaches colloquialisms to a houseful of pedantic encyclopedists.
- *My Favorite Wife*: about an anthropologist who comes between long-separated spouses.

The plots and acting styles in such screwball comedies typically turn a male researcher from a bumbling foil or a would-be impartial observer into a romantic hero—a triumphant suitor *malgre lui*.

The screwball decade was also "a period of 'respectable' film biographies" (Greene, *Film* 2), featuring several popular Hollywood biopics, including hagiographies of some of history's most revered researchers: "young Tom Edison," Louis Pasteur, Alexander Graham Bell, and Paul Ehrlich. Though this genre persisted after these peak years, Hollywood has more intermittently worked this biopic formula to depict the drama of inquiry or discovery during the latter part of the twentieth century. Universal released both *A Beautiful Mind*, the story of mathematics Nobel laureate John Nash, which won the 2001 Oscar for best picture, and, nearly forty years earlier, John Huston's *Freud*, which stirred controversy by ranking its title character with Copernicus and Darwin and with a *noir*-ish expressionism unusual in Hollywood movies of the era. With its "intellectual plot" (crafted in part by an uncredited Jean-Paul Sartre), *Freud* traced "a bold and momentous quest for knowledge" and depicted enough "exciting confrontations of individuals and ideas to generate heat," *Times* reviewer Bosley Crowther enthused. This effect reflects Huston's (quasi-psychoanlytic) aim as a moviemaker to prompt moviegoers to find themselves "not so much looking at a scene but" by "exploring inside" scenes (May, *Big* 238).

The impact and professed aim of *Freud* reflects not only a commitment to stirring curiosity. It also highlights the "tension" elaborated in Barbara Benedict's recent history of curiosity. Since the Enlightenment, Benedict argues, curiosity has "signified a transcendental value" because of its "power to make the aberrant valuable . . . to usurp meanings, co-opt categories, and overturn conventions" (4). As a narrative impetus, curiosity typically prompts the Promethean conflict these biopics stage: "the contest" between "individual and public truth" (253). Writing at about the same time Hollywood became ascendant, Walter Lippmann characterized this impetus as a reaction to the recognition that mediating institutions surround us with "a moralized and codified version of the facts" (125). With suggestively photographic or cinematographic hints of framing and lighting, Lippmann went on to argue that these "versions" determine—or at least regulate—"*what facts we shall see* and in what *light* we shall see them" (emphasis added).

John Ford's last classic offers an especially instructive illustration of this contest between "public truth" and "individual truth," between "codified versions of the facts" and experientially knowing "the facts." A fictional biopic about an indefatigable truth-seeker, *The Man Who Shot Liberty Valance* closes its flashback frame (Nadel, *Containment* 194–95) by affirming the regulatory power of emergent mass media, the manufacturers of "public opinion" (Lippmann 8, 11, 25, 29, 125; Schumpeter 149; Habermas 89, 236). The hero—an accomplished statesman as well as a quixotic reporter and teacher, an agent of both curiosity and literacy played by Jimmy Stewart (Nadel, *Containment* 199)—learns a lesson at the end of the movie, at the end of a rich, varied, and outwardly successful life. The reporter interviewing him, who personifies the regulation of curiosity and the manufacture of public opinion, famously describes his charge, to codify and moralize facts, as follows: "When the legend becomes fact, print the legend."

In contrast to such popular biopic homages to Promethean inquirers, late-century biopics such as Oliver Stone's *JFK*, Danny DeVito's *Hoffa*, and Emilio Estevan's *Bobby* no longer provide "a platform for solo heroics" (O'Brien, *Phantom* 76). In these movies *Gotterdammerung* trumps *Bildung* with the protagonists appearing as the objects of inquiries rather than as subjects who inquire or as committed agents of curiosity. The conflict between such cinematic transformations of subjects into objects and movies that validate inquirers as heroes reflects more nebulous tensions between appeals to apparently "idle curiosity" in Hollywood movies and what supposedly passes for the primary point of interest for most lay moviegoers: "narrative situation . . . what happens . . . plot" (Richards 86, 88, 90).

II

Reds, Warren Beatty's 1982 biopic about the quixotic bohemian Bolshevik John Reed, and *Zelig*, Woody Allen's parodic mirror image of *Reds* a year later, finessed this tension between inquiring heroes and heroes as objects of others' inquiries. Both movies shifted between biographic narrations and talking-head "explanations." These explanations, from both witnesses and experts, purportedly illuminated the protagonist's significance but just as often had the effect of stressing their elusiveness.

Beatty's most famous talking head (or maybe the second most famous, after George Jessel) was novelist Henry Miller. Beatty blended Miller's notorious celebrity, his marginal relevance to the Reed saga, and his habit on screen of punctuating provocative pronouncements—like "people fucked back then just as much as they do now. We just didn't talk about it as much"—with a contentiously tentative rhetorical question: "Don't' ya' know?" These moves underscore how *Reds*, like *Zelig*, subscribed to—or at least exploited—the then-ascendant *Zeitgeist*—or conceptual "placeholder" (Mitchell 318) broadly termed postmodernism. Miller's question and his questionable relevance to the narrative couldn't but encourage skeptical resistance to the kind of "master narrative" implicit in contrasting the way "people talked" then and the way "people talk now" while equating behavior "back then" and "now." The "master narratives" at stake in these movies include Freudianism, Marxism, Miller's programmatic satyriasis, early twentieth-century legends of *la vie bohemienne* and revolutionary derring-do.

While cuing skepticism and undermining familiar master narratives, Beatty and Allen were also making the more conventional move of exploiting the reassuring and often edifying stock Hollywood biopic entertainment formula. With this device Allen and Beatty exploited one familiar Hollywood brand, the old-fashioned biopic as a source of "intellectual fantasy" (Mamet, *Bambi* 124), while keeping open the more challenging marketplace of ideas. The talking-head interpolations in both movies function as a kind of linear master-shot keeping all possible explanations on screen and in the audience's frame of reference. The oscillation between these interview excerpts and the conventional main narrative "breaks whatever spell" the talking-head "close-up work" has "evoked" (Huston 476).

With the release in 2007 of *I'm Not There*, Todd Haynes at once elaborated and extended Allen's and Beatty's moves to fracture and recuperate the "plain biopic" formula (Lane 174). *I'm Not There* features six actors playing different avatars of Bob Dylan, without ever naming or referring to him. These narratives cast the spells Huston notes not only as narratives but with some thirty dubbed-over songs: covers, actual Dylan recordings, and lip-synching performances (G. Marcus 73). These songs obliquely counterpoint the narratives and echo the title by reminding moviegoers that the whole biography isn't there—or here—and by cuing endless reinterpretations of both the facts and significance of Dylan's career (G. Marcus 77). With these cues, Haynes repeatedly breaks the many "spells" Dylan cast—as "the voice of a generation," a reclusive artist, last hope of "authentic" folk-singing, Fender-wielding traitor, spiritual Proteus, or reincarnation of Kerouac or James Dean. These cues include intermittent talking-head witness commentary reminiscent of *Reds* and *Zelig* and, more recently, of Martin Scorsese's 2005 Dylan documentary *No Direction Home* and Christopher Guest's 2003 Peter, Paul, and Mary spoof documentary *A Mighty Wind*.

Both laudatory and dismissive reviews treated Haynes's approach to the biopic formula by calling attention to his intellectual aspirations: Haynes was conducting a "historical inquiry" (A. O. Scott, "Another"), composing "an essay" that derives "its intellectual force from the idea of Bob Dylan" and the "emotional depth" of his songs (Hoberman, "Like"), and busying moviegoers with trying to weigh "the burden of cultural meaning" (Lane 173). Like *Zelig* and *Reds*, *I'm Not There* distills a trait Geoffrey O'Brien ascribes broadly to late-century Hollywood movies. They stir the moviegoer's need for explanations but endlessly defer gratifying it, maintaining a climate in which "new explanations were needed, and then further ones to explain the explanations" (*Phantom* 75).

III

Like many earlier and more formulaic biopics, *Reds* and *Zelig* play out a psychoanalytic treasure hunt, though not as conclusively as many earlier movies. This Freudian template has become such a Hollywood staple that in 2008 Turner Classic Movies turned it into a regular programming feature (Fristoe). Early in its psychiatrist-week feature, "Introduction to Psych 101," TCM showed Montgomery Clift psychoanalyzing—and liberating—Elizabeth Taylor in Joseph Manckiewicz and Gore Vidal's adaptation of Tennessee Williams's *Suddenly Last Summer*. Apparently a warm-up to Clift's playing the title role three years later in Huston's *Freud*,

Manckiewicz's 1959 drama bookended a Hollywood era during which "Freudianisms" remained "fashionable" (Kehr, "*Furies*").

As this era dawned a generation earlier, Sam Wood's *King's Row* and David O. Selznick's production of Hitchcock's *Spellbound* had already firmly established "vulgar" Freudianism as a Hollywood staple. What Selznick described as his hunch that "both psychoanalysis and Dali were all the rage" (Schatz 388) seems to have provided the impetus. As a result of Selznick's hunch, *Spellbound* has come to stand at the center of "Hollywood's fascination with Freud," especially with the "therapeutic session" as a "device to 'speed plot exposition'" (Trebay). Showing the analysand's "breakthroughs" via flashbacks, prompted by the analyst's command to "look and remember," Hitchcock seems to be associatively punning on Freud's concept of "*screen* memories," a psychic double exposure whereby troubling memories appear at once "resisted" and disclosed.

The star turns in *Spellbound*, by Gregory Peck as the analysand and Ingrid Bergman as his analyst, contributed to the movie's seminal place in Hollywood's Freudian canon. Bergman not only plays an analyst, but, as in *Notorious* a year later, she also plays the characteristic Hitchcock "heroine": A "Pandora . . . who can explore and analyze . . . with greater equanimity" than her male patient, though ultimately appearing as "enigma and threat . . . a symbol of anxiety" (Mulvey, *Fetishism* 64). This apercu of Laura Mulvey's recalls the lines Ben Hecht's *Spellbound* script gives to the Bergman's character's aging old-world mentor (Michael Chekhov): "women make the best psychiatrists" until "they fall in love . . . then they make the best patients" and hence, like Pandora and Eve, fall prey to "the usual female contradictions" (Panofsky, *Pandora* 7–8, 11–12, 113). Because *Spellbound* at once honors and trivializes psychoanalytic inquiry, one critic has disparaged the appeal of this "psychological thriller" as "sentimental," resting almost entirely on "Ingrid Bergman's flimsy Freudian ministrations" (Hardison 145–46). This appeal applies as well to *King's Row*. Both these wartime dramas cast familiar romantic stars—Robert Cummings and Bergman, respectively—as psychiatrists dedicated to uncovering and curing the effect of early trauma, despite or because of their emotional involvement with their patients.

The extent to which major studio releases drew on Freudianism reflects the "profound inspiration" that "psychoanalytic theory" afforded Hollywood "filmmaking in general" (Pomerance, *Eye* 64). This inspiration extends at least to two very different 1980 dramas: Robert Redford's *Ordinary People* and Brian Di Palma's *Dressed to Kill*. By this point the psychoanalytic-sleuthing formula had become so familiar that Mel Brooks parodied it in his 1977 comedy *High Anxiety*.

More broadly a comedy of explanation, *High Anxiety* exposes the inevitable self-interestedness of all explanatory inquiry, targeting a prime product of the knowledge economy: the kind of explanatory authority psychoanalysis once could claim until challenges contemporaneous with Brooks's movie issued from all corners of the cultural landscape—from newly ascendant academic feminists, conservative literary critic Frederick Crews, and chic Continental theorists like the French anti-oedipal provocateurs Giles Deleuze and Felix Guattari (J. Bloom, *Gravity* 107–10; Edmundson). Some twenty years before *High Anxiety* MGM released Vincent Minnelli's *The Cobweb*, a "lurid melodrama" (H. Thompson) with the same plot as Brooks's manic comedy. A trailer for *The Cobweb* "promised" to "bare the secrets of the psychiatrist's couch on the screen," spotlighting the mystique and the authority in Hollywood of psychoanalysis as a narrative convention and the moviegoing public's interest in psychotherapy as an explanatory discourse (O'Brien, *Phantom* 72), not simply as one of many healthcare options—imagine marketing a movie as "baring the secrets of the tongue depressor" or "the uretoscope."

Hollywood's most sustained exploration of the promise and foibles of psychoanalysis occurred at the end of the seven-year run of HBO's instant classic *The Sopranos*. This series, which "set the bar very high for anyone who wants to dramatize a therapeutic relationship and raise questions about what therapy is for, and about whether it does any damn good, anyway" (Franklin 78), began with the mobster hero seeking psychoanalytic treatment—talk-therapy and medication—for panic attacks. As the series wound down this plotline ended with his therapist throwing him out of her office, insisting that he needs another kind of treatment and rationalizing that "I don't want to waste your time" with psychoanalysis.

This dramatized failure of psychoanalysis reflects a broader tendency in the relationship between Hollywood intellect and explanatory authority. During the late twentieth century, movie challenges to all kinds of explanatory authority became a staple of popular comedies; hence, Woody Allen's 1979 comedy *Manhattan* shows its Diane Keaton character complaining during a MOMA opening reception about her therapist's warning her against having "the wrong kind" of "orgasm"; two years earlier in *Annie Hall* Allen's on-screen alter-ego announces a merger of two sober purveyors of purportedly sophisticated and rigorously reasoned explanations, products of the storied "New York Intellectuals"—*Dissent* and *Commentary*—into "*Dysentery*." In 1994 Fred Schepisi's *I.Q.* comically showed how easily one could fake even the explanatory authority of a Nobel laureate, a certified genius such as Einstein, and a decade later

Ron Howard showed a similar genius tortured into career failure by corrosive delusions in *A Beautiful Mind*.

IV

The masterwork of Hollywood's most notoriously self-proclaimed intellectual, Orson Welles's *Citizen Kane*, which ranks as Hollywood's greatest product in an American Film Institute poll and according to a broad consensus (May, *Big* 55; C. Roth 79), also depends on and mocks this psychoanalytic-sleuthing formula. Before psychoanalysis lost its scientific stature (P. Cohen), Welles satirized it and by implication explanation industries in general by devising the *Kane* plot around the mystery of Rosebud, only to leave it at once unresolved for the on-screen inquirer and trivialized for the audience as a pat, Freudian cliché. Welles and Herman Manckiewicz's script broadens this critique of customary explanatory paradigms by framing the entire narrative as a reportorial investigation, parodying in the process Time-Life's popular theatrical newsreel series *The March of Time*. Calling into question the explanatory value of both psychoanalysis and journalism, *Citizen Kane* provokes reconsiderations of two of its audience's most influential sources of both information *and* insight. The inquirer in *Citizen Kane* works consequently not as a psychoanalyst, but rather as a reporter, one of Hollywood's favorite inquirer-heroes. The range of bankable leading men playing this kind of inquirer-hero reflects the durability of this formula: Joel McCrea in *Foreign Correspondent*, Humphrey Bogart in *The Harder They Fall*, Gregory Peck in *Gentleman's Agreement*, and Redford as Bob Woodward in *All the President's Men*. Early in the talkie era, Clark Gable "reached the very top" in Hollywood (Basinger 404) by winning an Oscar in 1935 for playing a reporter who started out as an earnest inquirer-hero only to find himself transformed into a reluctantly lovestruck screwball comic suitor in *It Happened One Night*.

V

Detectives have figured as inquirer-heroes most often and most prominently. Hollywood's more ambitious and successful detection-centered research movies include Roman Polanski's *Chinatown* and John Sturges's *Bad Day at Black Rock*. In the first Jack Nicholson plays a detective whose murder investigation turns into a historical mediation on and critique of the politics, especially the land and water battles, that transformed Los Angles into a global metropolis and demographic magnet. In *Bad Day at Black Rock* Spencer Tracy apparently plays a government agent (though

the screenplay never expressly identifies him as one) whose efforts to deliver a posthumous Medal of Honor to the family of a KIA Nisei GI turns
first into a quixotic murder investigation and finally into a critical reflection—the mass media's first—on wartime internment (for the "crime"
of Japanese ancestry) of innocent U.S. citizens. With this move *Bad Day
at Black Rock* does the intellectual work Lippmann called for: analytically
challenging the "moralized and codified version of the facts" that constitutes the "public opinion" and that supports policies like the wartime
Nisei incarceration.

VI

Hollywood developed a permutation of this tradition in the late twentieth
century: a subgenre treating social activists as inquirer-heroes. Over the
past generation two popular biopics featured an Everywoman driven to
heroism by the intrusion of corporate corruption into their domestic se-
curity and the threat environmental degradation posed for them and their
communities. The two movies—Mike Nichols's 1983 *Silkwood* and Steve
Soderbergh's 2000 hit, *Erin Brockovich*—seem to have taken their ideological cue, though not their plotlines, from Norman Ritt's 1979 account of
labor activism, *Norma Rae*. The two later movies complicated this inspiring
plot by transforming their working-class heroines into inquirers, though
Ritt's movie gestured in this direction by having the eponymous heroine
describe her goal as "looking like we know what we're doin' here" and
ensuring that the information she seeks gets "put it in writin'." Just as an
earlier generation of leading men seemed drawn to play reporters, late-
century A-list actresses—Meryl Streep, Julia Roberts, and Sally Field—
took to playing importunately curious civic activists.

   Erin Brockovich bears a family resemblance to more familiar legal thrillers. These familiar legal thrillers, however, tend to emphasize procedural
cleverness, courtroom ritual and theatrics, and the psychological backstory
at the expense of affirming the value and drama of inquiry itself. In traditional legal thrillers, moreover, the eccentricities or virtues—the foibles
and righteousness—of the lawyer heroes often obscure the role of intellect,
as in such star vehicles as *To Kill a Mockingbird*, *Anatomy of a Murder*, *Witness for the Prosecution*, *The Verdict*, and *The Music Box*. Lawyer movies and
trial movies in particular serve to stage spectacles, dramatize vindication,
and simplify causality rather than to stir curiosity and relish inquiry (Custen
186, 192). Writer-director Tony Gilroy's *Michael Clayton*, for example,
shows the eponymous lawyer hero (George Clooney) emerging from his

increasingly fraught Manichean soul-searching to choose, inevitably, to do "the right thing" with each plot twist increasingly burnishing Clayton's virtuosity at winning battles of wits against one-dimensionally corrupt adversaries and gaming the system he fights.

Though understandably compared to *Michael Clayton* and *A Civil Action* (Denby, "*Michael*"), *Erin Brockovich* differs sharply from these conventional legal dramas. *Erin Brockovich* does follow the genre formula by building to a climactic resolution in a courtroom scene. The heroine, however, is *not* the lawyer but a law-firm file clerk. Despite its otherwise conventional plot, *Erin Brockovich* stands as a rarity in the annals of Hollywood intellect: an immediately popular, immensely profitable, and critically acclaimed instance of the compatibility of Hollywood intellect and a readily accessible Hollywood entertainment formula. As the opening credits roll, a prologue establishes the diamond-in-the-rough intellectual *bona fides* of the title character—a former Miss Wichita turned unemployed single mother. A long two-shot in a high-rise medical office shows Erin, apparently during a job interview with a white-coated, graying, and balding man (apparently a physician) sitting in front of a loaded book shelf and a wall of framed degrees. Soderbergh framed Erin with these tokens of intellect and shows her enthusing about her scientific interest in medicine by recalling the "love" of geology she cultivated as a clerk at a construction company. This exchange establishes Brockovich as an "intellectual" according to what may be the most straightforward definition of an intellectual: "someone for whom the life of the mind is emotionally important" (Alvarez 38).

Soon after being rejected for this job, she lands a job as a novice file clerk in a law office. At this point the narrative proper begins. An opportunity Erin stumbles upon at her new workplace sets in motion the movie's inquiry plot. This plot builds on Erin's discovery during her first day on the job, the distinction that makes this otherwise conventional star vehicle such a rarity among popular Hollywood romances. Film editor-theorist Walter Murch calls the seldom-seen, hard-to-film trait that distinguishes *Erin Brockovich* the "intellectual plot" (Ondaatje 165). In a property case file, Erin notices hospital reports about the illnesses of plaintiffs living near the PG&E Hinkley power plant. Since these health data seem out of place in a real-estate transactions file, she points out this apparent misfiling and asks her boss, "Do you mind if I investigate a little further?"

As she begins visiting government offices and examining documents, Soderbergh visually highlights the intensity of her curiosity, the thrill of discovery, by speeding up the narrative tempo while stopping plot progression with a process shot: a rapid-blink sequence of the smoking-gun government records and corporate memos cycling through a photocopier.[1] In a telling plot turn, the increasingly intellectually confident and capable but ever volatile Brockovich storms out of her office when a credentialed expert questions her "research" qualifications and the quality the data she's gathered. Her response—not only can she recite every datum in the files of some seven hundred clients, but she then proceeds to make good on earlier claims about her passion for science by collecting contaminated water samples and teaming up with a university chemist to establish the difference between the molecular structure of the toxic chromium harming her clients and the kind of harmless chromium the defendant claims, mendaciously, to have been using in its offending power plant.

Along with such affirmations of intellect and its progressive rhetorical agenda, *Erin Brockovich* is as much a tried-and-true Cinderella fairytale as was *Pretty Woman*, the "whore with a heart of gold" movie that turned Roberts into "the biggest female movie star in the world" and the "world's most famous actress" (Ascher-Walsh; Basinger 545; Hirshenson 104; Sarkin 298). The denouements in both movies ensure that the heroine becomes the proverbial "girl who has everything": a prince charming (a babysitting biker played by Aaron Eckhart); respect from her educated colleagues (especially her boss played by Albert Finney); surpassing knowledge of the applicable case law, civil procedure, corporate governance, and environmental science; material as well as abstract justice in the form of a $33,000,000 settlement for her clients; and a $2,000,000 bonus for herself. Off-screen, *Erin Brockovich* marked a career milestone for Roberts herself—the point at which she "crossed over into the $20,000,000 pay range" (Sarkin 303). As Cinderella, Roberts's Brockovich embodies the post–Cold War "generation of American intellectuals" that Andrew Ross described as embracing "the uneven development, across a diverse range of social groups and interests . . . the contradictions of living within a capitalist culture . . . and the creativity of consumption" (11).

Susannah Grant's screenplay for *Erin Brockovich* succinctly underscores the compatibility of Hollywood intellect and Hollywood entertainment— of research and glamour. Grant's script shows a riled, inquiring Everywoman as representing "the mass of population" that "comes awake when its curiosity and sensibility and moral responsiveness are aroused" (Shils 291). Puzzling over the career of Otto Preminger, David Denby touches on the importance, for moviemakers and moviegoers alike, of awakening curiosity, when he praises the émigré director and producer as "an inquisitive and urbane fellow who respected the audience's intelligence" ("Balance" 76).

Such "respect" embraces candor as well as literacy. Thus, when Erin's boss wonders about the effectiveness of her research approach, her reply quells any doubts about the compatibility of intellect and curiosity with outrage and sensation:

MASRY (Albert Finney): What makes you think you can just walk in there and find, uh, what we need?

BROCKOVICH: They're called boobs, Ed.

This "explanation" recalls the "appeal to the liberatory body" Andrew Ross deems essential to contemporary intellectual work (11) while harkening back to Dorothy Parker's blunter explanation of what made Clara Bow Hollywood's original "it girl": "*It*, hell. She had *those*" (M. West 6).

This "boobs" explanation also exemplifies "the 'Gap' Theory of Curiosity" that management-marketing gurus Dan and Chip Heath have developed, looking to Hollywood screenplays as a "model of curiosity-generated 'intangible ideas'" in today's marketplace of ideas. The Heaths' theory rests on an understanding, which Brockovich here demonstrates, of the "need to *open* gaps"—or cleavages—"before we close them" and the degree to which "gap theory relies on our ability to point out" in the face of complication "things that people don't know" and "that people"—especially supervisory, professional personnel like Finney's character—"seem to think they know a lot" about (254, 84–85, 57, 88).

Erin's tart "boobs" explanation not only teaches her boss and mentor about sex appeal and the male gaze (Mulvey, *Visual* 20), but also instructs him in the intellectual values of descriptive precision and verbal candor. Overall, *Erin Brockovich* overcomes the obstacle inherent in all Cinderella tales that promise intellectual substance. Like Denzel Washington's *The Great Debaters*, *Erin Brockovich* "transcends its own simplifying and manipulative ploys" (Holden "Leading").

Cumulatively, Roberts's character comes to exhibit the traits that Steve Fuller specified for distinguishing intellectuals from other knowledge workers, including the legal professionals with whom she works:

Experts and censors focus on "only the truth" to preempt disagreement and reinforce their own voices, while intellectuals fixate on "the whole truth" to inject unheard voices potentially capable of resolving disagreement and overturning orthodoxies. . . . The bare possibility—unaddressed, and hence unrefuted—that such other voices exist is sufficient to motivate her inquiries. In this respect, the intellectual unashamedly appeals to the *imagination* as a source of evidence. (54)

A confrontation during a routine adversarial "negotiation," during which the camera moves between the plaintiffs' and defendants' sides of the meeting-room table, demonstrates such an evidence-based appeal to imagination. When a defense attorney justifies her clients' $20 million settlement offer for Brockovich's four hundred clients, she ridicules this "lame ass offer" by pointing out that, unsophisticated as they may seem, her clients can do the math needed to figure out that "$20 million isn't shit." When the attorney reaches for a drink of water from the conference table, Brockovich ends the meeting abruptly by informing the group that the drinking water was "brought in specially for you folks" from one of the contaminated areas. According to Fuller's formulation, the heroine's intellectual triumph in *Erin Brockovich* rests on the realization that "truth is the ultimate conversation stopper" (49).

Soderbergh, Grant, and Roberts's characterization of Brockovich recalls C. Wright Mills's 1958 glorification of the "public intellectual" as a heroic figure: "It is the . . . job of intellectuals to draw [the] line, to say the 'No!' loudly and clearly" (*Causes* 125, 135). The movie repeatedly shows Brockovich making such moves, challenging the often cruel evasions of legalese, the procedural niceties, and the occupational tendency to "deploy technical arguments . . . to absolve" legal professionals and their corporate clients "from the responsibilities of decision-making" (Saluny). Part of a familiar caricature resting on more than a grain of truth, these tendencies often make *the Law* seem more contemptible than majestic. Brockovich's riposte also exposes her corporate antagonists as enemies of intellect because they "retreat to formal trivialities and exact nonsense" when "reason and freedom are being held in contempt, are being smashed" (Mills, *Causes* 125). Mills seemed, moreover, to intimate a blue-collar view of intellectual work with such synonyms for *intellectual* as "cultural workmen" and "intellectual workmen" (127, 133), a view more suitable for Brockovich than for more conventional intellectual characters, on-screen and off.

The success of *Erin Brockovich* in embedding intellect triumphant in a neatly resolved formulaic Hollywood romance has a classic precedent. It figures in John Ford's last hit *The Man Who Shot Liberty Valance*, another nominal lawyer movie. The bookish lawyer from "back East" played by Jimmy Stewart brings not only law and order to a southwest territory on the verge of statehood (with the help of a gruffly altruistic rancher and marksman played by John Wayne), but also opens a makeshift school for illiterates of all ages and assists the local newspaper editor, a dyspeptic and grandiloquent Horace Greely disciple (Edmond O'Brien). These efforts represent the commitment of Stewart's character to bring "civilization" to the open range. In doing so, he also beats out his rival for the hand of his best student, the prettiest and most sensible young woman in town (Vera Miles). His rival (Wayne) grudgingly concedes the power of intellect when he gives up courting the Miles character with a reminder—"you taught her how to read and write"—and a charge—"now give her something to read and write about."

VII

All these movies with inquirer-heroes illustrate the extent to which the figure Parker Tyler called the "agent of curiosity" (197) has long stood at the center of Hollywood movies as a manifestation of Hollywood intellect. Such agents fit Susan Sontag's view of intellectuals as sharing the profession of curiosity (90) in both familiar senses of *profession*: as a calling and activity and as a creed or passion expressly promoted in word and deed.

The twenty-five-year sequence of populist toxic-waste investigation narratives, from *Silkwood* in 1983 to *Erin Brockovich* seventeen years later, to the 2007 *The Simpsons Movie*, pointedly illustrates Hollywood's long-established role in cultural agenda-setting. Critically well-received and reasonably profitable, the earlier movies, essentially blue-collar biopics, drew on news stories—as did *A Civil Action*, a 1999 lawyer movie starring John Travolta. Cartoonist Matt Groening's phenomenally durable and profitable prime-time cartoon series has done similar intellectual work, more diffusely and more durably, over the course of its nineteen-year run. The differences in impact between *The Simpsons* and other headline-ripping movies, though, rests in part on the looser way in which Groening and his collaborators drew on "the news," box-office results, and the explicitness of *The Simpsons Movie*'s *intellectual* agenda.

By 2007 toxic waste—environmental degradation in general—had become so familiar a topic, thanks in part to the earlier Hollywood releases mentioned (as well as such movies as *The China Syndrome* and, more recently, the Oscar-winning documentary *An Inconvenient Truth* in 2006) that Groening's account of composing the script for *The Simpsons Movie* didn't need to cite a particularly tragic news report or screaming-headline incident. He "brought in a newspaper article about a small town facing an environmental nightmare over pig waste. The writers had their movie plot" (Koltnow). Without any on-screen divas or hunks such as Roberts or Travolta (and with Joe Mantegna and Marcia Wallace the biggest stars among *The Simpsons Movie* voices), it grossed $71.9 million domestically and "blew past industry expectations of $45 million" during its weekend opening (Friedman). (Even adjusting for inflation, this animated family comedy dramatically outstripped *Erin Brockovich* with its impressive first-weekend box office of $28 million.) The critical reception of *The Simpsons Movie* included favorable reviews in the *New York Times*, the *Economist*, the *Village Voice*, and the *Wall Street Journal*.

A *Los Angeles Times* reviewer's more mixed assessment pinpoints what makes the movie a milestone in the agenda-setting role of Hollywood intellect. She associates the rhetorical orientation of *The Simpsons Movie* with one character in particular—the Simpsons' precociously intellectual, artistic, and reflective oldest daughter, Lisa—by observing that the film "feels a little like *The Simpsons Movie* Lisa might have written. But it's a strange path for the series' star writers to have chosen—this idea that more existential meant better" (Chocano).

The opening narrative scene—after a visually pyrotechnic, elaborately gag-intensive credit sequence—features Lisa as part of a crowd at an outdoor concert by the band Green Day. When the band interrupts its performance for the lead singer to "preach" against pollution, the crowd suddenly stops applauding and starts hurling garbage at the stage. Lisa turns to the bartender—a series regular—sitting beside her and suggests circumspectly that the singer is "touching on an important issue." He "begs to differ" as he hurls his projectile toward the stage. Lisa's stance here and her character as developed over the course of the series prompted one reporter to identify Lisa as a "martyr to the liberal intelligentsia" (J. Anderson). In making Lisa's perspective and her "martyrdom" so explicit, this exchange sets in motion a plot expressly built around cultural agenda-setting, reflection on timely "issues," and intellectual discussion as central to the ensuing narrative. In this opening scene the writers have also introduced Lisa as their surrogate in calling attention to the role that movies play as they set agendas for public discussion and reflection: their role both in regulating curiosity and in challenging the regulators as well as the uniquely inter-disciplinary "impurity" Pauline Kael claims for the movies as willing and able to embrace "the functions of exploration, anthropology, journalism, of almost any branch of knowledge" ("Trash" 346).

VIII

Curiosity-regulation, which Benedict shows emerging along with its institutionalization during the Enlightenment, and the conflicts curiosity-regulation provokes have an established Hollywood pedigree, perhaps most widely diffused as a B-movie cliché, in the numerous releases with plots turning on the possession of a secret formula and consequent efforts to purloin or suppress it: *Invisible Agent*, an anti-Axis wartime comedy; Disney's Cold War kiddie movie *The Absent-Minded Professor*; a formulaic 1963 Jerry Lewis comedy, *The Nutty Professor* (remade with Eddie Murphy a generation later); and Roger Corman's much-revisited *The Little Shop of Horrors*.

The Prestige, a recent adaptation of Christopher Priest's magician–doppelganger novel of the same title, stages such a conflict and doubles it by leavening the fictional narrative with the historical dispute over the future of electrification. Known to technology buffs as the "war of currents," this subplot features thugs hired by Thomas Edison. A hero played by Mickey Rooney in the 1940 biopic *Young Tom Edison*, "the sage of Menlo Park" figures in *The Prestige* only as a greedy, ruthless venture capitalist bent on sabotaging the work of his "Promethean" competitor Nikola Tesla. Sequestered in a remote mountain laboratory, Tesla has been developing usable electricity and seems on the verge of transmitting electrical power wirelessly when Edison's hirelings roust him out and ruin him.

The Prestige crystallizes the ubiquity of agents of curiosity in Hollywood movies. Typically, agents of curiosity come into conflict with agents of certainty—like the ideologues described in chapter I (Schulberg, *Sanctuary* 64)—and often equate these cognitive monopolists with market monopolists, as in *The Prestige*'s depiction of Edison. "Agents of certainty" appear as villains or at least impediments because, according to the Hollywood intellect consensus, artistic expression and intellectual inquiry, "culture" as a whole, all rest on "applied curiosity" (Hellman 495). Shown repeatedly as subject to regulation and preemption by the constellation of mediating institutions and subinstitutions, the "interpretation industries" and "subinstitutions" David Bordwell has described (*Making* xi, 18–19), curiosity also legitimates—makes necessary—the very regulation it resists. So too, of course, do universities, museums, news media, advertisers, and other merchants of information and sensation in "policing" the range of available images and narratives (Buck-Morss, *Dreamworld* 161).

Just as Hollywood now mimics more overtly "intellectual" practices, more traditionally "intellectual" curiosity-regulators are increasingly "going Hollywood." To promote *Pocahontas*, Disney's 1995 cartoon feature, for example, the studio-sponsored "seminars" in malls "about Native American Culture and animation techniques" (Rosenbaum 10). This habit among commercial outfits, flattering intellect by imitation, ranges from moves by the patron saint of public relations, Edward Bernays, to affect the demeanor of a "professorial . . . freethinker" to the design decision many corporations made late in the twentieth century to establish research "institutes" or turn their headquarters into campuses (Terkel 9; Fussell, *Class* 129).

Conversely, in 2006, the *New York Times*, as America's "paper of record" and perhaps its most esteemed curiosity regulator, announced that it had retained a Hollywood talent agency to help shop film and television projects based on its own articles (Manly; J. Bloom, *Literary* 123–24, 131–42). In 1995 an exhibit at Manhattan's Whitney Museum made a similar accommodation. The exhibit, "Edward Hopper and the American Cinema," demonstrated how far even the most prestigious "fine arts" arbiters of culture and curiosity had come in embracing the equivalence between museum-housed "paintings and movies . . . as both pop-culture icons and works of art" and in recognizing "the cyclical way that" movies and past masters' paintings "have shaped one another" (C. James, "Filmmakers"). J. Hoberman cites Ronald Reagan and Hollywood's "most successful film-maker," Steven Spielberg, to demonstrate how fully Hollywood had by the end of the twentieth century become "the main repository of cultural memory—and authority" ("Film" 531)—at once a theme park and a museum, an arcade and a library, a nightclub and an athenaeum.

For a century now this impurity of motives and the products of such motives—the apparent inability of so many curiosity-regulators and cultural agenda-setters to position themselves definitively either as mercenary or high-minded, formulaic or experimental—has at once chronically fostered and incessantly threatened Hollywood intellect. This fertile instability seems likely to continue roiling the collective life of the mind and the marketplace of ideas for the foreseeable future. Whether Hollywood intellect intervenes in and contributes to the life of the mind or whether it "substitutes for" and lets the movies enervate "national discourse" (J. Hoberman, "Film" 534) remains an open question.

Note

1. A similarly text-intensive process shot evokes the intellectual engagement and turmoil of intellectual passion in the last-season therapy-ending episode of *The Sopranos* when rapidly sequenced close-ups of the pages of the medical journal article that provoke Tony Soprano's therapist to terminate his therapy appear on-screen.

Conclusion: Checking the Gate

*I like being distracted, flattered, tickled, even rather upset—but
I should not mind something more; I should like something
more serious. I should like to be changed by more films, as art
can change one: I should like something to happen when I go to
the cinema.*

—ELIZABETH BOWEN

You always think of everything. That's why I hate you.

—JOAN CRAWFORD AS MARCIA IN *NO MORE LADIES* (1935)

I

As I was beginning to polish *Hollywood Intellect*, early in 2008, I found myself, unexpectedly, treating a topic that was becoming more timely than I
could have hoped for, thanks to the public reaction to a protracted strike
by the Writers Guild against most Hollywood studios. Looking beyond the
questions of profit-allocation that vexed opposing sides in the strike, one
lay observer treated the strike as a conflict over "the value of thought," an
occasion to ask "How much do we value our storytellers?" "How much do
we appreciate those who can make us think by crafting an artful phrase" and
"can draw us into other minds and other realities?" (R. James). This earnest homage to Hollywood from an unlikely source close to home helped
me respond when the inevitable question "What are you working on?"
predictably prompted the rhetorical question "Isn't that an oxymoron?"
whenever I answered with the phrase "Hollywood intellect." I hope the

understanding of what Hollywood does that I set out to elaborate will reassure readers—that the kind of criticism *Hollywood Intellect* conducts—*does* have a *raison d'etre*.

Criticism can do more than feed reviewers and enhance the careers of professors. Since both the reviewer and the professor guilds have claimed me over the years, the imperative of getting beyond self-promotion dogs me whenever I write reviews, articles, and books. Readers of *Hollywood Intellect* know already that the commonplace idea of movies as diversion or escape appeals to me as much as it appeals to anyone else. But when I *hear* movies or television referred to as "*just* entertainment," the adverb *just* stops me dead in my tracks. (Increasingly for me, the whole point of criticism and perhaps of intellectual work in general aims at exorcising the pervasive reliance on *just* and similar modifiers as shortcuts, glib evasions of difficulty, and handy denials of complexity.)

Like many poems and novels, the movies I remember and especially the ones that seem worth watching more than once resist such denials and evasions. They all offer more than *just* one kind of enduring experience. Even movies that prove, for the most part, escapist or diverting at least leave me wondering what I'm escaping from or being diverted from, as well as what I might be escaping into (Robinson 117–18; McMurtry, "Cowboys" 47). Do the literally escapist and self-consciously, even expressly "sentimental" ending and last word in *North by Northwest*, for example, promise only escape from pursuing villains? Or do the Soviet affiliations but American and British guises of these villains promise an escape from Cold War tensions or even the defusing of the threat of "hot war" and the ratification as inevitable of a "free world" victory? Or do the Western (corporate button-down) demeanor and the comic fecklessness of Cary Grant's thrice-wed Roger Thornhill discredit his heroism and therefore the possibility of escape from global conflict and duplicity? Do his last lines—"Come along Mrs. Thornhill . . . I'm sentimental"—hint that anyone bent on repeating such a domestic history and serially succumbing to the same sentiment is allowing "hope" to "triumph over experience," as Samuel Johnson warned? Does such a willfully myopic response foster and embody a broader, public failure to learn from history? However we answer these questions, their very existence provides evidence of Hollywood intellect in action. The way images on screen, dialogue, and narrative sequence combine to raise such questions, to make them at once implicit but obvious, turns Thornhill's apparent escape against moviegoers' escapist temptations to evade these questions.

Annie Hall, a more explicitly self-identifying instance of Hollywood intellect in action, offers an instructive essay addressing these questions about movies as an escape: about what moviegoers are supposedly fleeing by watching seemingly escapist movies, what kind of refuge we're escaping into, and how "liberation" touches us "in the darkness of the movies" (Kael, "Trash" 349). Discussions of this movie often stress the anti-Hollywood iconoclasm of the Woody Allen stand-in, Alvy Singer. Reminders at the beginning and end of the movie that Singer's favorite *film* is Max Ophuls's exhaustive black-and-white documentary about the Nazis' deportation of French Jews, *The Sorrow and the Pity*, reflect his sensibility and bracket the bemusement and contempt Singer expresses toward Hollywood during a brief visit to Los Angeles near the end of his voiceover, first-person story. Nonetheless, Allen complicates this impression by dissociating Singer from stereotypical New York bookishness, the stock alternative to Hollywood glitz, by showing Singer as contemptuous of the legendary "New York intellectuals" ascendant when and where Allen came of age as he is of movie people. When Singer teases his pathologically cerebral second wife that *her* heroes have united with the merger of the two renowned journals, *Dissent* and *Commentary*, to form *Dysentery*, he mentions his preference for the Knicks and sex over her version of intellectual conversation. She counters this blasphemy by advocating censorship and appealing to hackneyed sentiment rather than reason, paradoxically coming to represent a doubly anti-intellectual position: "No jokes—these are friends." In other words, my seemingly "intellectual" community prefers silencing jocular challenges to its self-importance and would rather not address the questions such dissenting commentary might prompt.

Even Singer's grim movie favorite, *The Sorrow and the Pity*, needs protection from indulgent cerebration and verbosity, as an exchange in a movie-theater lobby early in *Annie Hall* illustrates. The exchange begins as Allvy waits in line to see his favorite film yet again. A fellow moviegoer begins to prate loudly about self-indulgence and a lack of cohesion and purity in a new Fellini movie and invokes the authority of the media guru Marshall McLuhan. Much-cited throughout the 1960s, McLuhan had become an icon among the media-savvy by the end of the decade, so much so that, in 1970, *Star Wars* director George Lucas went so far as to treat understanding McLuhan as a mark of autership (J. Lewis 81). At this point, the script directions call for Singer to act "more and more aggravated" and exclaim "What I wouldn't give for a large sock o' horse manure." Asking "aren't you ashamed to pontificate like that?" Singer adds, "the funny part of it is, M-Marshall McLuhan, you don't know anything about Marshall McLuhan's . . . work!" When the pontificator retorts that he teaches a class at Columbia called "TV Media and Culture" to validate his "insights into Mr. McLuhan," Singer brings McLuhan (playing himself) on-screen and into the lobby and instructs McLuhan to "tell him" that "you—you know nothing of my work" and express his amazement that "you ever got to teach a course in anything." As Singer turns toward the camera and muses, "if life were only like this," Allen makes a plea on behalf of the power of fantasy, a reminder in this context that even intellection entails fantasy (Mamet, *Bambi* 124).

Soon after this sequence Allen drives this point home with a Disney interlude, with an animated interpolation showing the three main characters as Disneyesque cartoon figures arguing about "fun." With the narrator's voiceover "if only" sigh, live-action dissolves into a sequence from the animated *Snow White and the Seven Dwarfs* that shows bickering between "the Wicked Queen, resembling Annie" and a cartoon Alvy seated before her. Beyond simply inserting this Disneyesque recap of the movie's plot into the ongoing live action, Allen insists on the possibility of attributing the complexity of live-action depth to cartoon figures. With Alvy recalling his boyhood exposure to Disney cartoons, Allen seems, moreover, to embrace the lasting influence of Disney on his work. The absence in *Annie Hall* of any offsetting interposition of Annie and Alvy's relationship recapped in the style of an Ophuls black-and-white documentary implicitly acknowledges Disney's—Hollywood's—authority and precedence, and the accompanying reminiscence of Alvy's does so explicitly by recalling how "when [his] mother took [him] to see *Snow White*," he "fell for the Wicked Queen" while "everyone fell in love with Snow White." As a corrective to Alvy's, Allen's, and many moviegoers' tenacious residual snobbery, this Disney interlude can also serve as Allen's grudging reminder of Pauline Kael's apercu that seeming "trash gives us an appetite for art" ("Trash" 367)—*The Sorrow and Pity*, for example.

Allen's character-naming and the narrative arc of *Annie Hall* underscore this corrective. Allen names his alter-ego "Singer" while establishing early on that the eponymous Annie, his more fun-loving middlebrow lover-antagonist played by Diane Keaton, *is* a singer. The movie's very title thus makes the singer who goes Hollywood and thrives there its focal point. The closing sequence, moreover, seems implicitly to acknowledge the value of what she represents: "A series of flashbacks following in quick succession while Annie continues to sing" prefaces Allen's closing monologue about how "terrific" Annie is.

In Allen's view serious intellectual engagement with movies needs to produce the *fun* Annie and Alvy had earlier complained about missing. Two years before *Annie Hall* Allen "signified," or riffed, in *Love and Death* on probably the single most remarked-on scene in Ingmar Bergman's oeuvre: Max von Sydow's chess match with Death in *The Seventh Seal*. In a reverential parody (W. Allen), Allen transposes the chess match into a series of teasing encounters with a similarly clad Grim Reaper. Conversing with Bergman, Bergman's audience, and his own audience, Allen sustains the conversation that Bergman, drawing on and drawing out his own signature religious and philosophical preoccupations, inaugurated while introducing what Allen has designated the "definitive" trope for conducting this conversation (Gritten). While Bergman's reputation centers mostly on what he prompts audiences to ponder, both the chess scene and Allen's tribute parody feature games and play as visual and dramatic reminders of the importance of playing, of how the *fun* Annie and Alvy sought complements the intellectual work—reflection and inquiry—in movies that last.

II

Hollywood Intellect has aimed to promote such an understanding of the movies. While Allen was promoting this understanding on screen, several poems from the 1950s by Allen's older contemporary Frank O'Hara did the same kind of cultural work in the house, in the dark, on the audience's side, on behalf of "the soul that grows in darkness" (French, *Faber* 110). Two O'Hara poems from 1957, "Ave Maria" and "An Image of Leda," stress this darkness. This darkness covers moviegoers both in the theater and at home with their families. In a move analogous to Allen's punctuating a comedy with scenes from *The Sorrow and the Pity*, O'Hara shows the nuclear family shadowed by threats of "hatred," going to the movies fraught with fears of disgrace, and both home and the movies as steeped in "cruelty" (110–11, 104). Though renowned for their wit and even by some as comic geniuses, both O'Hara and Allen grapple in their work with a prevailing mid-century intellectual consensus, "the dark account of human nature" and the requisite "ironic disposition" advanced by such influential intellectuals as Reinhold Niebuhr, Lionel Trilling, and Arthur Schlesinger Jr. (Mattson 78–79). By mocking Catholicism with his title "Ave Maria," and thus substituting moviegoing for prayer and Mariolatry, O'Hara moves playfully toward the dark, provocative proposition Steve Erickson recently advanced: "God hates the Movies because the Movies are the evidence of what he's done" (271).

O'Hara evoked and avowed Hollywood intellect not only topically but also procedurally. O'Hara's "To the Film Industry in Crisis" expressly pits the movies, specifically the commercial products of the "Motion Picture Industry" that "I love," against the elite media customarily associated with intellectual work: "lean quarterlies and swarthy periodicals," such as *Dissent* and *Commentary* as they figured in *Annie Hall*, and "experimental theater in which Emotive Fruition is wedding Poetic Insight" (84). In "Fantasy" O'Hara's speaker spends twenty lines addressing the kinds of Cold War geopolitics that comprised much of *Dissent*'s and *Commentary*'s stock-in-trade by arguing with *Northern Pursuit*, a World War II sabotage thriller starring Errol Flynn, only to conclude with contradictory assertions about the absolute value of freedom and the absolute silencing power of authority:

> I'm glad that Canada will remain
> Free. Just free, that's all, never argue with the movies. (302)

O'Hara's playful eagerness here to bear the statesman-philosopher's burden shows how a movie—virtually any movie—can provides an occasion to address broad questions of liberty and nationality, conceptual and semantic questions about whether *freedom* has the kind of straightforward meanings that everyday sloganeering ascribes to the word, and even more vexing questions about discursive authority—about who gets to claim *the last word* in the public sphere or the marketplace of ideas. If *Hollywood Intellect* has accomplished what I set out to accomplish, then these questions—the *question* of who gets the last word or even of whether any word can be the last word—must serve as the book's last word.

Works Cited

Agee, James. *Agee on Film: Reviews and Commentary* (1958). Boston: Beacon Press, 1964.

Ajami, Fouad. "The Clash." *New York Times Book Review*, January 6, 2008: 10.

Allen, Richard. *Hitchcock's Romantic Irony*. New York: Columbia University Press, 2007.

Allen, Woody. "The Man Who Asked Hard Questions." *New York Times*, August 12, 2007: 2–9.

Alpert, Hollis. "*SR* Goes to the Movies." *Saturday Review*, March 31, 1962: 26.

Alvarez, Al. "On the Edge." Review of *A Treatise of Civil Power* by Geoffrey Hill. *New York Review of Books*, May 29, 2008: 37–39.

Anderson, Benedict. *Imagined Communities: Reflections on the Origin and Spread of Nationalism* (1983). London: Verso, 1991.

Anderson, John. "Homer's *Odyssey* to *The Simpson's Movie*." *Newsday*, July 22, 2007. www.newsday.com/features/printedition/ny-ffmov5298298jul22,0,4619959 .story.

Anonymous. "Just the Other Day by John Collier and Iain Lang" (review). *Spectator*, November 18, 1932: 714.

Aron, Raymond. *The Opium of the Intellectuals*. Trans. Terence Kilmartin (1955). New York: Norton, 1962.

Ascher-Walsh. "Cinematheque Honoree Roberts Embodies 'Magic' Something." *Hollywood Reporter*, October 12, 2007. www.hollywoodreporter.com/hr/ content_display/film/features/e3iafd724b50c2b4b1177307b5406198a02.

Atkinson, Michael. "Anna Karina and the American Night" *Believer*, March/April 2008: 3–6.

———. "Houses of the Unholy." *Village Voice*, October 24/30, 2001. www.village voice.com/film/0143,atkinson,29323,20.html.

Atlas, James. "The Ma and Pa of the New York Intelligentsia." *New York Magazine*, September 25, 2006. nymag.com/news/media/21344/.

Auden, W. H. *The Collected Poetry of W. H. Auden*. New York: Random House, 1945.

Aufderheide, Pat. "Horse Races." *In These Times*, June 28, 1998: 24.

Austin, Thomas, and Martin Barker, eds. *Contemporary Hollywood Stardom*. London: Arnold/Hodder Headline Group, 2003.

backstory 2: Interviews with Screenwriters of the 1940s and 1950s. Edited by Patrick McGilligan. Berkeley: University of California Press, 1991.

Bai, Matt. "America's Mayor Goes to America." *New York Times Magazine*, September 9, 2007. www.nytimes.com/2007/09/09/magazine/09Giuliani-t.html.

Baker, Nicholson. *Human Smoke: The Beginnings of World War Two, the End of Civilization*. New York: Simon & Schuster, 2008. www.simonsays.com/content/book.cfm?tab=1&pid=616619&agid=2.

Bakshy, Alexander. "The 'Talkies.'" In Lopate, *American Movie Critics*, 45–47.

Baldwin, James. *Going to Meet the Man*. New York: Dial/Dell, 1965.

———. *Notes of a Native Son* (1963). Boston: Beacon Press, 1985.

———. *One Day When I Was Lost: A Scenario Based on Alex Haley's The Autobiography of Malcolm X* (1972). New York: Dell/Laurel, 1992.

———. *Tell Me How Long the Train's Been Gone*. London: Joseph, 1968.

Bankhead, Tallulah. "The World's Greatest Musician." *Ebony*, December 1952. home.earthlink.net/~tgrillo/satchmo.htm.

Baraka, Amiri. *Dutchman and The Slave*. New York: Morrow/Quill, 1971.

———. "Revolution: The Constancy of Change: An Interview with Amiri Baraka." *Black American Literature Forum* 16, no. 3 (Autumn 1982): 87–103.

———. *The Sidney Poet Heroical in 29 Scenes*. New York: Amiri Baraka, 1979.

———. *The System of Dante's Hell*. New York: Grove Press, 1965.

Barker, Martin. "Star Controversies." In Austin and Barker, *Contemporary Hollywood Stardom*, 255–70.

Barrionuevo, Alexi. "A Filmmaker and a Challenger of Brazil's Conscience." *New York Times*, November 22, 2007: A3.

Barry, Iris. "A Tomorrow Grown out of Today's Fears." *Herald Tribune*, May 7, 1933: 6.

Basinger, Jeanine. *The Star Machine*. New York: Knopf, 2007.

Bayard, Louis. "The Wild, Unpredictable and Never-ending Business of Turning Books into Movies." *Washington Post*, March 5, 2006: TO8.

Bayard, Pierre. *How to Talk About Books You Haven't Read*. Trans. Jeffrey Mehlman. New York: Bloomsbury, 2007.

Bazin, Andre. *What Is Cinema II* (1971). Trans. Hugh Gray. Berkeley: University of California Press, 1972.

Bell, Clive. *Civilization and Old Friends* (1928/1956). Chicago: University of Chicago Press, 1973.

Bell, Daniel. "Daniel Bell and the Information Age." 1973. www.skagitwatershed.org/~donclark/history_knowledge/bell.html.

Bellow, Saul. *Seize the Day* (1956). New York: Penguin, 1996.

Benhabib, Seyla. "The Intellectual Challenge of Multiculturalism and Teaching the Canon." In Garber et al., *Field Work*, 1–17.

Benedict, Barbara. *Curiosity: A Cultural History of Early Modern Inquiry.* Chicago: University of Chicago Press, 2002.

Benjamin, Walter. *Illuminations.* Trans. Harry Zohn. New York: Schocken, 1969.

Berger, John. *A Painter of Our Time* (1958). London: Writers and Publishers Publishing Cooperative, 1976.

Berman, Marshall. *All That Is Solid Melts into Air.* New York: Verso, 1983.

———. "Faust in the 60's." In *The Sixties: Art, Politics, and Media of Our Most Explosive Decade*, edited by Gerald Howard, 495–504 (1982). New York: Paragon House, 1991.

Bernstein, Harry. *The Invisible Wall.* New York: Ballantine, 2007.

Bernstein, Matthew. *Walter Wanger: Hollywood Independent.* Minneapolis: University of Minnesota Press 1994.

Billingsley, K. L. "Best Witness." *Heterdoxy* (February 1999). www.udel.edu/History/garymay/hist221/Billingsley%20Best%20Witness.doc.

Bird, David. "Janet Gaynor Is Dead at 77: First 'Best Actress' Winner." *New York Times*, September 15, 1984: 1:30.

Birnbaum, Norman. "In Memoriam: Partisan Review." *Chronicle of Higher Education*, May 9, 2003. chronicle.com/weekly/v49/i35/35b01401.htm.

Biskind, Peter. *Easy Riders, Raging Bulls: How the Sex-Drugs-and-Rock-'n'-Roll Generation Saved Hollywood* (1998). London: Bloomsbury, 1999.

Bloom, Harold. *A Map of Misreading* (1975). New York: Oxford University Press.

Bloom, James. *Gravity Fails: The Comic Jewish Shaping of Modern America.* Westport, Conn.: Praeger, 1983.

———. *Left Letters: The Culture Wars of Mike Gold and Joseph Freeman.* New York: Columbia University Press, 1992.

———. *The Literary Bent: In Search of High Art in Contemporary American Writing.* Philadelphia: University of Pennsylvania Press, 1997.

———. "The Occidental Tourist: The Counterorientalist Gaze in Fitzgerald's Last Novels." *Style* 35, no. 1 (2001). www.encyclopedia.com/doc/1G1-97074174.html.

Blum, Howard. *American Lightning: Terror, Mystery, Movie-making and the Crime of the Century.* New York: Crown, 2008.

Blume, Harry. "Spiegelman Lips: Interview with Art Spiegelman." *Boston Book Review* (1995). www.bookwire.com/bbr/interviews/art-spiegelman.html.

Bohlen, Celestine. "Kenneth Clark, Art Historian, Author of *Civilisation*, Dies." *Washington Post*, May 22, 1983: C8.

Boorstin, Daniel. *The Americans: The Democratic Experience* (1973). New York: Vintage, 1974.

———. *The Image* (1961). New York: Vintage, 1987.

Bordwell, David. *Making Meaning: Inference and Rhetoric in the Interpretation of Cinema.* Cambridge, Mass.: Harvard University Press, 1989.

———. *The Way Hollywood Tells It.* Berkeley: University of California Press, 2006.

Bordwell, David, and Kristin Thompson. *Film Art: An Introduction,* fifth ed. New York: McGraw-Hill, 1997.

———. *Film History: An Introduction,* second ed. Boston: McGraw-Hill, 2003.

Bourdieu, Pierre. *Distinction: A Social Critique of the Judgment of Taste.* Trans. Richard Nice. Cambridge, Mass.: Harvard University Press, 1984.

Bowen, Elizabeth. *The Heat of the Day* (1948). New York: Penguin, 1962.

———. "Why I Go to the Cinema." In Davy, *Footnotes to the Film,* 202–20.

Boygoda, Randy. "Bright Lights Big Speeches: RE and the Perils of Publicity." Review of *Ralph Ellison: A Biography* by Arnold Rampersad. *Harpers* (May 2007): 93–98.

Bramann, Jorrn. "*Barton Fink.*" *The Educating Rita Workbook* (1994). faculty.frostburg.edu/phil/forum/Fink.htm.

Braudy, Leo, and Marshall Cohen, eds. *Film Theory and Criticism,* sixth ed. New York: Oxford University Press, 2004.

Bray, Christopher. "Jean-Luc Godard: Portrait of the Weirdo as Director." Review of *Everything Is Cinema* by Richard Brody. *Daily Telegraph,* June 20, 2008: 25.

Brody, Richard. "Auteur Wars." *New Yorker,* April 7, 2008: 56–65.

Bromell, Nick. *Tomorrow Never Knows: Rock and Psychedelics in the 1960s.* Chicago: University of Chicago Press, 2000.

Brooks, David. "Joe Strauss to Joe Six Pack." *New York Times,* June 16, 2005: A27.

———. "The Segmented Society." *New York Times,* November 20, 2007: A23.

Browne, Nick. *Francis Ford Coppola's Godfather Trilogy.* Cambridge: Cambridge University Press, 2000.

Bruns, Gerald. *The Material of Poetry: Sketches for a Philosophical Poetics.* Athens: University of Georgia Press, 2005.

Buck-Morss, Susan. *The Dialectics of Seeing.* Cambridge: MIT Press, 1991.

———. *Dreamworld and Catastrophe: The Passing of Mass Utopia in East and West.* Cambridge, Mass.: MIT Press, 2000.

Canby, Vincent. "*If . . .* Begins Run: Tale of School Revolt Opens at the Plaza." *New York Times,* May 10, 1968. movies.nytimes.com/movie/review?res=9500 E3D7123DE134BC4852DFB566838267EDE.

———. "Jabberwocky Monster with Heart." *New York Times,* April 16, 1977. movies2 .nytimes.com/mem/movies/review.html?title1=&title2=Jabberwocky%20%28 Movie%29&reviewer=VINCENT%20CANBY&v_id=25665&pdate= 19770416.

———. "*The Wild Bunch.*" In Lopate, *American Movie Critics,* 397–99.

Cather, Willa. "Coming, Aphrodite." In Lopate, *Writing New York,* 419–58.

———. *Early Novels and Stories.* New York: Library of America, 1987.

Catsoulis, Jeanette. "An Actor's Playful Tribute to a Dissident Director." Review of *Never Apologize: A Personal Visit with Lindsay Anderson. New York Times,* August 15, 2008: E16.

Cavanaugh, Tim. "After the Party." *The Rake* (2005). www.rakemag.com/commentary/rakes-progress/after-party.

Chafets, Zev. "The Huckabee Factor." *New York Times Magazine*, December 16, 2007: 68–75, 88, 95–96.

Chambers, Whittaker. *Witness*. New York: Random House, 1952.

Chandler, Daniel. "Notes on the Male Gaze." June 7, 2000. www.aber.ac.uk/media/Documents/gaze/gaze09.html.

Charters, Ann, ed. *The Portable Sixties Reader*. New York: Penguin Classics, 2003.

Chesnutt, Charles W. *The Marrow of Tradition*. Boston: Houghton Mifflin, 1901.

Chocano, Carina. "*The Simpsons Movie*." *Los Angeles Times*, July 27, 2007: E1.

Cieply, Michael. "Scene Stealer: Your Publicist Should Call My Publicist." *New York Times*, February 24, 2008: B1.

Clark, Kenneth. *Civilisation: A Personal View* (1969). New York: Harper & Row, 1970.

Cohen, Adam, "Editorial Observer: After 30 Years, the Mood of *Nashville* Feels Right Once Again." *New York Times*, June 6, 2005: A18.

Cohen, Patricia. "Ideas & Trends: Freud Is Widely Taught . . ." *New York Times*, November 25, 2007: 4:6.

Cohen, Stanley. *Folk Devils and Moral Panics: The Creation of the Mods and Rockers*. New York: Routledge, 2002.

Collier, John. *Defy the Foul Fiend*. New York: Knopf, 1934.

———. *Fancies and Goodnights*. Alexandria, Va.: Alexandria Time Reading Special Edition/Time-Life Books, 1965, 1980.

———. *The John Collier Reader*. New York: Knopf, 1972.

———. *Milton's Paradise Lost: Screenplay for a Cinema of the Mind*. New York: Knopf, 1992.

Connolly, Cyril (Palinurus). *The Unquiet Grave*. London: Penguin Books, 1944/1967.

Cook, Robin. "The Special Relationship Has Become a National Delusion." *Guardian*, November 12, 2004: 30.

Corrigan, Timothy. *Film and Literature*. Upper Saddle River, N.J.: Prentice-Hall, 1999.

Courtwright, David. "Movie Review: *The Aviator*." *Journal of American History* 92, no. 3 (2005). www.historycooperative.org/journals/jah/92.3/mr_9.html.

Cowell, Alan. "Blair Says 'Evil Ideology' Must Be Faced." *New York Times*, July 17, 2005: A1.

Cox, Sidney. *Indirections*. New York: Knopf/Borzoi, 1947.

Crafton, Donald. *The Talkies: American Cinema's Transition to Sound, 1926–1931* (1997). Berkeley: University of California Press, 1999.

Crane, Hart. "Chaplinesque." www.poemhunter.com/p/m/poem.asp?poet=35863&poem=432885.

Crisler, B. "*Gunga Din.*" *New York Times*, January 27, 1939. movies2.nytimes. com/movie/review?res=EE05E7DF173FE264BC4F51DFB7668382629EDE.

Crowther, Bosley. "*The Americanization of Emily* Arrives." *New York Times*, October 28, 1964. movies.nytimes.com/movie/review?res=9E02E7D91E3FEE32A 2575BC2A9669D946591D6CF.

———. "*Darling.*" *New York Times*, August 4, 1965. movies.nytimes.com/movie/ review?res=EE05E7DF1739E767BC4C53DFBE66838E679EDE.

———. "*The Four Horsemen of the Apocalypse.*" *New York Times*, March 10, 1962. movies.nytimes.com/movie/review?res=9A06E7DF1238E63ABC4852DFB56 68389679EDE.

———. "*Freud*" (review). *New York Times*, December 13, 1962. movies2.nytimes .com/movie/review?res=EE05E7DF1739E265BC4B52DFB4678389679EDE.

———. "*The Green Pastures*" (review). *New York Times*, July 17, 1936. movies2 .nytimes.com/movie/review?res=9B00E1DB143CE53ABC4F52DFB166838 D629EDE.

———. "*My Favorite Wife*" (review). *New York Times*, May 31, 1940. movies2. nytimes.com/movie/review?res=9E05E6D91531E23ABC4950DFB366838B 659EDE.

Cullen, Countee. "Heritage." 1927. www.english.upenn.edu/~jenglish/Courses/ Spring02/104/Cullen_Heritage.html.

Custen, George *BioPics: How Hollywood Constructed Public History.* New Brunswick, N.J.: Rutgers University Press, 1992.

Czitrom, Daniel. *Media and the American Mind: From Morse to McLuhan.* Chapel Hill: University of North Carolina Press, 1982.

Dargis, Manohla. "Apocalypse Soon: A Mushroom Cloud Doesn't Stall 2008 Electioneering." Review of *Southland Tales. New York Times*, November 13, 2007: E5.

———. "The Folks You Meet on the Border Between Consciousness and Dreams." *New York Times*, December 14, 2007: E13.

———. "Hot Properties." Review of *The Star Machine* by Jeannine Basinger. *New York Times Book Review*, December 30, 2007: 17.

———. "In over Their Heads, with Destiny Looming." Review of *Cassandra's Dream. New York Times*, January 18, 2008: E8.

———. "War May Be Hell But Hollywood Is Even Worse." *New York Times*, August 13, 2008: E1.

Davis, Lennard. "The Man Behind Woody Allen." *Common Review* (Summer 2008). www.thecommonreview.org/spotlight.html.

Davy, Charles, ed. *Footnotes to the Film.* London: Lovat Dickson/Readers Union, 1938.

Dayan, Daniel. "The Tutor Code of Classical Cinema." In Braudy and Cohen, *Film Theory and Criticism*, 106–17.

"De Cabezas Creadoras: El Nacimento de Barton Fink." *Miradas de Cine*, 2002. miradas.net/estudios/2002/05_jcoen/bartonfink.html.

Delbanco, Andrew. "Remarks Delivered at the American Academy of Arts and Sciences, 13 October 2001." *Southern Review* 38, no. 1 (2002): xi–xiii.

Deleuze, Giles. *Cinema 1: The Movement—Image* (1983). Trans. Hugh Tomlinson and Barbara Habberjam. Minneapolis: University of Minnesota Press, 1986.

Demuth, Charles. "Think-Tank Confidential." *Wall Street Journal*, October 11, 2007: A21.

Denby, David. "Critic at Large: Balance of Terror." *New Yorker*, January 14, 2008: 76–82.

———. "Critic at Large: Big Pictures." *New Yorker*, January 13, 2007: 54–63.

———. "*Michael Clayton* and *Into the Wild*." *New Yorker*, October 8, 2007: 100.

———. "Obsessed." *New Yorker*, November 19, 2007: 103–5.

De Stefano, George. *An Offer We Can't Refuse: The Mafia in the Mind of America.* London: Faber, 2006.

Diawara, Manthia. "Black Spectatorship and the Problem of Identification and Resistance." In Braudy and Cohen, *Film Theory and Criticism*, 892–901.

DiBattista, Maria. *Fast-Talking Dames.* New Haven, Conn.: Yale University Press, 2001.

Dickinson, Emily. *The Complete Poems of Emily Dickinson.* Edited by Thomas H. Johnson. Boston: Little Brown, 1960.

Dicum, Gregory. "Foraging/Los Angeles: Intelligentsia Café." *New York Times*, March 9, 2008: Tr6.

Didion, Joan. *After Henry.* New York: Simon & Schuster, 1991.

———. "Letter from Manhattan." *New York Review of Books*, August 16, 1979: 18–9.

———. *Play It As It Lays* (1970). New York: Bantam, 1971.

———. *Slouching toward Bethlehem.* New York: Dell/Delta, 1968.

———. *The White Album.* New York: Bantam, 1979.

"Digital *South Park*" (editorial). *New York Times*, August 28, 2007: A20.

Doherty, Thomas. "Thus Spake Stanley Kubrick." *Chronicle of Higher Education*, August 3, 2007: B10.

Donat, Robert. "Film Acting." In Davy, *Footnotes to the Film*, 16–36.

Douglas, Ann. *Terrible Honesty: Mongrel Manhattan in the 1920s.* New York: Farrar Straus Giroux, 1995.

Dowd, Maureen. "Madness as Method." *New York Times*, October 24, 2007: 19.

Drabble, Margaret. *Jerusalem the Golden* (1967). New York: Popular Library, 1977.

Dreiser, Theodore. *Sister Carrie* (1900). Edited by Donald Pizer. New York: Norton Critical, 1970.

DuBois, W. E. B. *The Souls of Black Folks: Essays and Sketches* (1903). New York: A.C. McClung, 1907.

Dunne, John G. *Monster: Living off the Big Screen* (1997). New York: Vintage, 1998.

Durant, Will and Ariel. *The Story of Civilization, volume 1.* New York: Simon & Schuster, 1950.

Durgnat, Raymond. *Film and Feelings.* Cambridge, Mass.: MIT Press, 1967.

Dyer, Richard. *Heavenly Bodies: Film Stars and Society* (1986). London: Routledge, 2004.

———. *Stars.* London: BFI Publishing, 1979.

Dylan, Bob. *Chronicles: Volume One.* New York: Simon & Schuster, 2004.

Eagleton, Terry. *Ideology: An Introduction.* New York: Verso, 1991.

Ebert, Roger. "*The Last Supper.*" *Chicago Sun-Times*, April 12, 1996. rogerebert.suntimes.com/apps/pbcs.dll/article?AID=/19960412/REVIEWS/604120306/1023.

———, ed. *Roger Ebert's Book of Film: From Tolstoy to Tarantino, the Finest Writing from a Century of Film.* New York: Norton, 1997.

Edmundson, Mark. "Freud and Anna." *Chronicle of Higher Education*, September 21, 2007. chronicle.com/weekly/v54/i04/04b00801.htm.

Edwards, Paul. *A Guide to Films on the Korean War.* Westport, Conn.: Greenwood Press, 1997.

Eisenstein, Sergei. *Film Sense.* Trans. Jay Leda (1938). New York: Harvest/Harcourt, 1970.

Elias, Norbert. *The Civilizing Process* (1939). Trans. Edmond Jephcott. London: Blackwell, 1994.

Eliot, T. S. *Complete Poems and Plays.* New York: Harcourt Brace, 1952.

———. *The Letters of T. S. Eliot, Volume 1: 1898–1922.* Ed Valerie Eliot. San Diego: Harcourt Brace, 1988.

———. *Selected Essays.* London: Faber & Faber, 1951.

———. *The Waste Land.* Edited by Michael North. New York: Norton Critical, 2001.

Elligott, Michelle. Introduction to "Modern Artifacts 3: Tentative And Confidential." *ESOPUS* 9 (FALL 2007): N.P.

Ellison, Ralph. *Flying Home and Other Stories.* New York: Random House, 1996.

———. *Invisible Man* (1952). New York: Vintage, 1995.

———. *Juneteenth* (1999). New York: Vintage, 2000.

Elshtain, Jean Bethke. "Why Public Intellectuals?" *Wilson Quarterly* (Autumn 2001). October 14, 2004. wwics.si.edu/index.cfm?fuseaction=wq.essay&essay_id=4816.

Emerson, R. W. "On the Times." 1841. www.emersoncentral.com/onthetimes.htm.

———. *Emerson's Prose and Poetry.* Edited by Joel Porte and Saundra Morris. New York: Norton Critical, 2001.

Empson, William. *Seven Types of Ambiguity* (1930). New York: New Directions, 1966.

Emshwiller, John, and Melissa Marr. "Lights! Camera! Influence!" *Wall Street Journal*, August 25, 2007: A1.

Erickson, Steve. *Zeroville.* New York: Europa Editions, 2007.

Eszterhas, Joe. *American Rhapsody.* New York: Knopf, 2000.

———. *The Devil's Guide to Hollywood: The Screenwriter as God.* New York: St Martin's, 2006.

Everson, William. *American Silent Film.* New York: Oxford University Press, 1978.

Farber, Manny. *Negative Space.* New York: Praeger, 1971.

Farrell, James. *Literature and Morality.* New York: Vanguard, 1947.

Feeney, Mark. *Nixon at the Movies.* Chicago: University of Chicago Press, 2004.

Fiedler, Leslie. "What Shining Phantom: Writers and the Movies." In Robinson, *Man and the Movies*, 304–23.

Fitzgerald, F. Scott. *The Great Gatsby* (1925). Edited by Matthew Bruccoli. New York: Scribners/Simon & Schuster, 1995.

———. *The Love of the Last Tycoon* (1941). Edited by Matthew Bruccoli. New York: Scribners/Simon & Schuster, 1994.

———. *The Pat Hobby Stories.* New York: Scribners, 1962.

———. *Tender Is the Night.* New York: Scribners, 1934.

Flaherty, Joe. *Managing Mailer.* New York: Coward-McCann, 1970.

Foden, Giles. "Film Adaptations: 50 Books You Must Read." *Guardian Newsprint Supplement*, May 5, 2006: 6.

Foucault, Michel. *The Foucault Reader.* Edited by Paul Rabinow. New York: Pantheon, 1984.

———. *The Use of Pleasure: The History Of Sexuality, Volume 2.* Trans. A. M. Sheridan Smith. New York: Pantheon, 1985.

Franklin, Nancy. "Patience, Patients." *New Yorker*, February 4, 2008: 78–79.

French, Philip, ed. *Faber Book of Movie Verse.* London: Faber & Faber, 1995.

Freud, Sigmund. *Civilization and Its Discontents* (1930). Trans. James Strachey. New York: Norton, 1962.

Friedlander, Paul. *Rock and Roll: A Social History.* Boulder, Colo.: Westview Press, 1996.

Friedman, Jonathan. "Box Office: Bart and Gang Rise to the Occasion." *Los Angeles Times*, July 30, 2007: C1.

Fristoe, Roger. "Introduction to Psych 101." *TCM This Month* (March 2008). www.tcm.com/thismonth/article/?cid=191872.

Frost, Robert. *Poetry and Prose.* Eds. Edward Lathem and Laurance Thompson. New York: Holt/Rinehart Editions, 1972.

Frouda, Christine. *Virginia Woolf and the Bloomsbury Avant-Garde.* New York: Columbia University Press, 2005.

Fuchs, Daniel. *The Golden West: Hollywood Stories.* Boston: Godine, 2005.

Fuller, Steve. *The Intellectual.* Cambridge: Icon Books, 2005.

Fussell, Paul. *Class: A Guide Through the American Status System.* New York: Simon & Schuster, 1983.

———. *The Great War and Modern Memory.* New York: Oxford University Press, 1975.

———. *Samuel Johnson and the Life of Writing.* New York: Harcourt Brace, 1971.

————. *Wartime: Understanding and Behavior in the Second World War*. New York: Oxford University Press, 1989.

Gabler, Neal. *Life the Movie: How Entertainment Conquered Reality*. New York: Knopf, 1998.

Galbraith, John Kenneth. *The Affluent Society*. Boston: Houghton Mifflin, 1958.

Galchen, Rivka. "The Region of Unlikeness." *New Yorker*, March 24 2008: 68–75.

Garber, Marjorie, Rebecca Walkowitz, and Paul Franklin. *Field Work: Sites in Literary and Cultural Studies*. New York: Routledge, 1996.

Gates, Henry Louis. *The Signifying Monkey: A Theory of African American Literary Criticism*. New York: Oxford University Press, 1988.

Gee, Sophie. "Great Adaptations." *New York Times Book Review*, January 13, 2008: 35.

"George Lois: Cultural Provocateur." *New York Public Library Now* (Spring/Summer 2008): 9.

Gerard, Jonathan. "Movie Depicts the Horror of Life Without the Law." *Morning Call*, January 27, 2008: A15.

Gill, Brendan. "The Current Cinema." *New Yorker*, March 31, 1962: 127–28.

Gillespie, Eleanor Ringel. "The Teller of Fantastic Tales Who Lost His Way." *Atlanta Journal-Constitution*, August 26, 2005: IH.

Giovacchini, Saverio. *Hollywood Modernism: Film and Politics in the Age of the New Deal*. Philadelphia: Temple University Press, 2001.

Glyn, Elinor. "*It*." New York: Macauley, 1927.

————. *Romantic Adventure: Being the Autobiography of Elinor Glyn*. New York: Dutton, 1937.

Gold, Michael. *Mike Gold: A Literary Anthology*. Edited by M. Folsom. New York: International, 1972.

Goldman, William. *Adventures in the Screen Trade: A Personal View of Hollywood and Screenwriting* (1983). New York: Grand Central/Hachette, 1989.

————. *Which Lie Did I Tell? More Adventures in the Screen Trade* (2000). New York: Vintage, 2001.

Goldstein, Laurence. *The American Poet at the Movies: A Critical History*. Ann Arbor: University of Michigan Press, 1994.

Goldstein, Laurence, and Ira Konisberg, eds. *The Movies: Texts, Receptions, Exposures*. Ann Arbor: University of Michigan Press, 1996.

Gordon, Andrew. "Smoking Dope with Thomas Pynchon: A Sixties Memoir." In *The Portable Sixties Reader*, 231–38.

Greene, Graham. *Graham Greene on Film*. New York: Simon & Schuster, 1972.

————. "Subjects and Stories." In Davy, *Footnotes to the Film*, 57–70.

Greenspun, Roger. Review of *Panic in Needle Park*. *New York Times*, July 14, 1971: 19.

Grenier, Richard. "Hollywood's Holy Grail." *Commentary* (November 1991): 50–53.

————. "Our Lady of Corruption." *Commentary* (December 1981): 79–83.

Gritten, David. "How Death Gave Cinema a New Life." *Daily Telegraph*, June 30, 2007: Art 16.

Gross, Barry. "What Shylock Forgot." *Journal of Ethnic Studies* 2, no. 3 (1974): 50–57.

Grossman, V. *Life and Fate*. Trans. Robert Chandler. New York: Harper & Row, 1985.

Gunning, Tom. "Modernity and Cinema: A Culture of Shocks and Flows." In Pomerance, *Cinema and Modernity*, 297– 315.

Habermas, Jürgen. *The Structural Transformation of the Public Sphere: An Inquiry into a Category of Bourgeois Society*. Trans. Thomas Burger. Cambridge, Mass.: MIT Press, 1991.

Hagan, John. "Ben Maddow." *Film Reference* (n.d.). www.filmreference.com/ Writers-and-Production-Artists-Lo-Me/Maddow-Ben.html.

Haglund, David. "Slouching Toward Hollywood." *Slate*, June 19, 2007. www .slate.com/id/2170726.

Hansen, Miriam. "The Mass Production of the Senses: Classical Cinema As Vernacular Modernism." *Modernism/Modernity* 6, no. 2 (1999): 59–77.

Hardison, O. B. "The Rhetoric of Hitchcock's Thrillers." In Robinson, *Man and the Movies*, 137–52.

Harrington, E., and A. Abadie. *Faulkner, Modernism, and Film: Faulkner and Yoknapatawpha 1978*. Jackson: University of Mississippi Press, 1979.

Harris, Mark. *Pictures at a Revolution: Five Movies and the Birth of the New Hollywood*. New York: Penguin, 2008.

Haskell, Molly. *From Reverence to Rape*. New York: Holt, 1974.

Heath, Chip, and Dan Heath. *Made to Stick: Why Some Ideas Survive and Others Die*. New York: Random House, 2007.

Hellman, Lillian. *Three: An Unfinished Woman, Pentimento, Scoundrel Time*. Boston: Little-Brown, 1975.

Hertzberg, Hendrik. "Talk of the Town: Basest Instinct." *New Yorker*, July 31, 2000: 23–4.

———. "Talk of the Town: Follow the Leaders." *New Yorker*, December 10, 2007: 41–42.

Hirschberg, Lynn. "Warren Beatty Is Trying to Say Something." *New York Times Magazine*, May 10, 1998: 20.

Hirshenson, Janet, and Jane Jenkins. *A Star Is Found*. Orlando: Harcourt, 2006.

Hitchcock, Alfred. "Direction." In Davy, *Footnotes to the Film*, 3–15.

Hitchens, Christopher. *Unacknowledged Legislation: Writers in the Public Sphere*. New York: Verso, 2000.

Hoberman, J. "The Film Critic of Tomorrow Today." In Lopate, *American Movie Critics*, 528–37.

———. "Like A Complete Unknown: *I'm Not There* and the Changing Face of Bob Dylan on Film." *Village Voice*, November 13, 2007. www.villagevoice .com/2007-11-13/film/like-a-complete-unknown-i-m-not-there-and-the-changing-face-of-bob-dylan-on-film/full.

———. "Unstrung Heroes." Review of *Team America*. *Village Voice*, October 12, 2004. www.villagevoice.com/film/0442,hoberman,57664,20.html.

Hoge, Warren. "Gosford Writer Is Unfazed by Class but Amazed by Fame." *New York Times*, April 4, 2002: E1, E2.

Holden, Stephen. "50 Years, 600 Women Later, True Love." Review of *Love in the Time of the Cholera*. *New York Times*, November 16, 2007: E1.

———. "Leading the Charge to Inspire Underdogs." *New York Times*, December 25, 2007: E1.

Hoyle, Fred. "Introduction." In Collier, *Fancies and Goodnights*, xv–xix.

Hunter, Jefferson. "Poem *Noir* Becomes a Prizefight Film." *Hudson Review* 61, no. 2 (2008): 269–89.

Huston, John. "From an Open Book." In Ebert, *Roger Ebert's Book of Film*, 473–78.

Huyssen, Andreas. *After the Great Divide: Modernism, Mass Culture, Postmodernism*. Bloomington: Indiana University Press, 1986.

Hye, Kenneth. "Ambivalence as a Theme in *On the Waterfront*: An Interdisciplinary Approach to Film Study." *American Quarterly* 31, no. 5 (1979): 666–96.

"*If . . .*" malcolm mcdowell.net, 2008. www.geocities.com/malcolmtribute/if.html.

Isherwood, Christopher. *Prater Violet*. New York: Random House, 1945.

———. "Wake Up, Wake Up." In Sylvester, *The Grove Book of Hollywood*, 364–67.

Itzkoff, Dave. "Two Political Rivals, One Playbook." *New York Times*, March 11, 2009.

Jacoby, Russell. *The Last Intellectuals: American Culture in the Age of Academe*. New York: Basic, 1987.

James, Caryn. "Critic's Notebook: At Wit's End—Algonquinites in Hollywood." *New York Times*, January 8, 1993: C1.

———. "Filmmakers Who Learned of Desolation and Lighting." *New York Times*, June 23, 1995: C1.

———. "Hollywood, Not So Confidential." *New York Times*, February 20, 2004: E1.

James, Henry. *The Art of the Novel*. Edited by R. P. Blackmur. New York: Scribners, 1934.

———. *The Tragic Muse* (1890). New York: Dell/Laurel, 1961.

James, Henry, and Edith Wharton. *Letters*. Edited by Lyall Powers. New York: Scribners, 1990.

James, Jamie. "Masterpiece: Leader of the Pack." *Wall Street Journal*, June 21, 2008: W14.

James, Renee. "Writers Strike Is About the Value of Thought." *Morning Call*, January 13, 2008: A11.

Jameson, Fredric. *The Political Unconscious: Narrative as a Socially Symbolic Act*. Ithaca, N.Y.: Cornell University Press, 1981.

————. *Postmodernism, or, the Cultural Logic of Late Capitalism*. Durham, N.C.: Duke University Press 1991.

Jay, Martin. "Force Fields." *Salmagundi* 143 (Summer 2004): 43–55.

————. "Praise for the Blighted and Blasted." *New Republic*, June 23, 1973: 28–29.

John Milton at 400: A Life Beyond Life. New York: New York Public Library, Astor, Lenox, and Tilden Foundations, 2008.

Jones, Jenny. *The Annotated Godfather: The Complete Screenplay*. New York: Black Dog and Leventhal Publishers/Workman, 2007.

Kael, Pauline. "Circles and Squares." *Film Quarterly* 16, no. 3 (Spring 1963): 12–26.

————. "Movies on Television." In *Grooving the Symbol*, 494–506.

————. "Trash, Art and the Movies." In Lopate, *American Movie Critics*, 337–67.

Kaplan, E. Anne. *Woman and Film: Both Sides of the Camera* (1983). New York: Routledge, 1988.

Kauffmann, Stanley. *A World on Film*. New York: Delta/Dell, 1966.

Kawin, Bruce. "The Montage Element in Faulkner's Fiction." In Harrington and Abadie, *Faulkner, Modernism, and Film*, 103–26.

Kazan, Elia. *Kazan—The Master Director Discusses His Films: Interviews with Elia Kazan*. Edited by Jeff Young. New York: Newmarket, 1999.

Kazin, Alfred. "The President and Other Intellectuals." *American Scholar* 30, no. 4 (1961): 498–516.

Keats, John. *Selected Poems*. New York: Penguin Classics, 2000.

Kehr, Dave "An Appraisal: A Star Who 'Mastered' a New Moral Ambiguity." *New York Times*, March 29, 2008: B7.

————. "Big Important Picture? Sure. But Is It Really the Best?" *New York Times*, January 4, 2009: Arts 10.

————. "New DVDs: *The Furies* and *Solo Sunny*." *New York Times*, June 24, 2008: E3.

————. "New DVDs: Shadows." *New York Times*, February 5, 2008: E4.

————. "New DVDs: Shirley Temple." *New York Times*, April 21, 2008: E4.

Kempton, Murray. *Part of our Time: Some Ruins and Monuments of the Thirties*. New York: Simon & Schuster, 1955.

Keysar, Helene. *Robert Altman's America*. New York: Oxford University Press, 1991.

Khanna, Parag. "Waving Goodbye to Hegemony." *New York Times Magazine*, January 27, 2008: 34–41, 62, 64–65, 67.

Kimmelman, Michael. "A Writer Who Always Sees History in the Present Tense." *New York Times*, November 1, 2007: E1.

King, Barry. "Embodying an Elastic Self: The Parameters of Contemporary Stardom." In Austin and Barker, *Contemporary Hollywood Stardom*, 45–61.

Kinsella, Bridget. "The Triumph of Willard." *Salon*, July 19, 2000. www.salon.com/books/int/2000/07/19/eszterhas/index.html (accessed October 14, 2004).

Kipen, David. *The Schreiber Theory*. Hoboken: Melville Manifestos, 2006.

Kipling, Rudyard. *The Writings in Prose and Verse of Rudyard Kipling, vol. 22*. New York: Scribners, 1904.

Kirkland, Ewan. "'Peter Pan's My Dad': The Man-Child Persona of Robin Williams." In Austin and Barker, *Contemporary Hollywood Stardom*, 243–54.

Kissinger, Henry. "Remarks By Dr. Henry Kissinger at Richard Nixon's Funeral." *Watergate.info*, April 27, 1994. watergate.info/nixon/94-04-27_funeral-kissinger.shtml.

Koch, Howard. "Writer's Roost." In Sylvester, *The Grove Book of Hollywood*, 244–48.

Kohn, Eric. "Why Sammy Won't Run." *Forward*, March 23, 2007. www.forward.com/articles/why-sammy-won-t-run-at-least-not-on-fi/.

Koltnow, Barry. "Don't Have a Cow, Man." *Orange County Register*, July 26, 2000. www.ocregister.com/entertainment/movie-brooks-groening-1786415-characters-simpsons.

Koppes, Clayton, and Gregory Black. *Hollywood Goes to War*. New York: Free Press, 1987.

Kristeva, Julia. "Thinking in Dark Times." *Profession* (2006): 13–21.

Kristol, William. "A Star Is Born?" *New York Times*, September 1, 2008: A17.

Kundera, Milan. "Reflections: *Die Weltliteratur*." *New Yorker*, January 8, 2007: 28–35.

Lahr, John. "Demolition Man." *New Yorker*, December 24 and 31, 2007: 54–69.

Lane, Anthony. "Tangled Up." *New Yorker*, November 26, 2007: 173–75.

Lawrence, D. H. *Studies in Classic American Literature* (1923). New York: Penguin, 1971.

Lawson, John Howard. *Film: The Creative Process*. New York: Hill, 1967.

Lee, Martin, and Bruce Shalin. *Acid Dreams: The Complete Social History of LSD: The CIA, The Sixties, and Beyond*. New York: Grove Press, 1992.

Leibovich, Mark. "In the '60s, a Future Candidate Poured Her Heart Out in Letters." *New York Times*, July 29, 2007: A1.

Leitch, Thomas. *Film Adaptation and Its Discontents: From Gone With the Wind to The Passion of the Christ*. Baltimore: Johns Hopkins University Press, 2007.

Lerer, Seth. *Inventing English: A Portable History of the Language*. New York: Columbia University Press, 2007.

Lerner, Max. *America as a Civilization*. New York: Simon & Schuster, 1957.

Levy, Clifford. "Russia's Knockoff Democracy." *New York Times*, December 16, 2007: 4.

Levy, Emanuel. *Cinema of Outsiders: The Rise of American Independent Film*. New York: New York University Press, 1999.

Lewis, Ethelreda. *Trader Horn* (1927). Two volumes. New York: The Library Guild of America, 1928.

Lewis, Jon. "The Perfect Money Machines." In Lewis and Smoodin, *Looking Past the Screen*, 61–86.

Lewis, Jon, and Eric Smoodin. *Looking Past the Screen: Case Studies in American Film History and Method*. Durham, N.C.: Duke University Press, 2007.

Lewis, R. W. B. *The Poetry of Hart Crane*. Princeton, N.J.: Princeton University Press, 1967

Lewis, Sinclair. *Kingsblood Royal*. New York: Random House, 1947.

Lewis, Wyndham. "Demos Defiled." *Spectator*, June 8, 1934: 892.

———. *Tarr* (1918 and 1928). London: Chatto and Windus/Jupiter, 1968.

Lid, Richard, ed. *Grooving the Symbol*. New York: Free Press/Macmillan, 1970.

Lim, Dennis. "Centenarian Director's Very Long View." *New York Times*, March 9, 2008: AR15, 27.

Lindsay, Vachel. *The Prose of Vachel Lindsay*. Two volumes. Edited by Dennis Camp. Peoria, Ill.: Spoon River, 1988.

Linson, Art. *What Just Happened? Bitter Hollywood Tales from the Front Line*. New York: Bloomsbury, 2002.

Lippmann, Walter. *Public Opinion*. New York: Harcourt Brace, 1922.

Little, Lyneka. "Just Asking: Denzel Washington." *Wall Street Journal*, December 22, 2007: W2.

Longfellow, Henry Wadsworth. *The Writings of Henry Wadsworth Longfellow*. Cambridge, Mass.: Riverside Press, 1886.

Lopate, Philip, ed. *American Movie Critics: An Anthology from the Silents till Now*. New York: Library of America, 2006.

———. *Writing New York: A Literary Anthology*. New York: Library of America, 1998.

Lye, John. "Michel Foucault's 'Nietzsche, Genealogy, History,' A Synopsis." April 30, 2008. www.brocku.ca/english/courses/4F70/geneal.html.

MacLeish, Archibald. *The Irresponsibles*. New York: Duell, Sloan and Pearce, 1940.

Maddow, Ben. "Invisible Man." In *backstory 2*, 157–200.

Maland, Charles. *Chaplin and American Culture: The Evolution of a Star Image*. Princeton, N.J.: Princeton University Press, 1989.

Mamet, David. *Bambi vs. Godzilla*. New York: Pantheon, 2007.

———. *Speed the Plow*. New York: Grove Weidenfeld/Evergreen, 1988.

Manly, Lorne. "Arts, Briefly: *Times* Hires Talent Agency." *New York Times*, August 17, 2006: E2.

March, Joseph Moncure. "One Minute on the Screen—or Two Days on the Lot." *New York Times Magazine*, September 28, 1941: 7, 29.

———. "Shipyard Symphony." *New York Times Magazine*, May 9, 1943: 14.

———. "Star-Gazing in Hollywood." *New York Times Magazine*, October 12, 1941: 10–11, 29–30.

———. *The Wild Party/The Set-Up/A Certain Wildness*. New York: Wheelwright, 1968.

———. "Young Howard Hughes: Reminiscences by a Survivor of Hollywood's Golden Era." Unpublished manuscript, Papers of Joseph Moncure March. Robert Frost Library, Amherst College Box 5/Folder 8.

Marcus, Greil. "Dylan Times Six." *Rolling Stone*, November 29, 2007: 73–77.

Marcus, Laura. *The Tenth Muse: Writing About Cinema in the Modernist Period*. New York: Oxford University Press, 2007.

Marcuse, Herbert. *Eros and Civilization: A Philosophical Inquiry into Freud* (1955). Boston: Beacon Press, 1966.

Martin, Douglas. "Dame Mary Douglas, 86, a Wide-Ranging Anthropologist." *New York Times*, May 22, 2007: B7.

———. "Peter Virtel, 86, Author and Screenwriter Is Dead." *New York Times*, November 6, 2007: B6.

———. "Richard Darman, Aide for Five Presidents, Dies." *New York Times*, January 26, 2008: A15.

Martin, Patricia. *Rengen: Renaissance Generation*. Avon, Mass.: Platinum Press, 2007.

Maslin, Janet. "As the Tides Turned." Review of *Pictures at a Revolution* by Mark Harris. *New York Times*, February 11, 2008: E9.

Mattson, Kevin. "Why We Should Be Reading Reinhold Niebuhr Now More Than Ever: Liberalism and the Future of American Political Thought." *The Good Society* 14, no. 3 (2005): 77–82.

May, Lary. *The Big Tomorrow: Hollywood and the Politics of the American Way*. Chicago: University of Chicago Press, 2000.

———. *Screening out the Past: The Birth of Mass Culture and the Motion Picture Industry*. New York: Oxford University Press, 1980.

McFee, William. "Foreword." In E. Lewis, *Trader Horn, volume 1*, 1–13.

McGrath, Charles. "Meta, Circa 1760: A Movie of a Movie of a Book About a Book." *New York Times*, January 22, 2006: 2:13.

McMurtry, Larry. "Cowboys, Movies, Myths, and Cadillacs: Realism in the Western." In Robinson, *Man and the Movies*, 46–52.

———. "On Rereading." *New York Review of Books*, July 14, 2005: 22.

Mead, Rebecca. "The Literary Life: First at Ninety." *New Yorker*, September 17, 2007: 36.

Mehring, Walter. *The Lost Library*. Translated by Richard and Clara Winston. Indianapolis: Bobbs-Merrill, 1951.

Menand, Louis. "The Horror." Review of *The Ten Percent Plague* by David Hajdu. *New Yorker*, March 31, 2008: 124–28.

Metz, Walter. "Modernity and the Crisis in Truth: Alfred Hitchcock and Fritz Lang." In Pomerance, *Cinema and Modernity*, 74–89.

Micek, John, and Miller, Jeff. "Keynote Speaker Impresses Pennsylvania Delegates." (Allentown) *Morning Call*, July 28, 2004: A3.

Michaels, Walter Benn. *Our America: Nativism, Modernism, and Pluralism*. Durham, N.C.: Duke University Press, 1995.

Mills, C. Wright. *Causes of World War III*. New York: Simon & Schuster, 1958.

———. *Power, Politics, and People: The Collected Essays*. Edited by Irving Louis Horowitz. New York: Oxford University Press, 1963.

Milne, Tom. "The Elusive John Collier." *Sight and Sound* (Spring 1976): 104–8.

Miradas de Cine—Estudio Joel y Ethan Coen—"Barton Fink (1991)." www .miradas.net/estudios/2002/05_jcoen/bartonfink.html.

Mishra, Pankaj. "The Empire Under Siege." *New York Review of Books*, July 15, 2004: 129–30.

Mitchell, W. J. T. *What do Pictures Want: The Lives and Loves of Images.* Chicago: University of Chicago Press, 2005.

Monaghan, Peter. "Coming Together." *Chronicle of Higher Education*, February 8, 2008: B6.

Moody, Rick. *The Diviners.* New York: Little Brown, 2005.

Morgenstern, Joe. "Charlton Heston: Manly, Commanding and Irony-Free." *Wall Street Journal*, April 8, 2008: D8.

———. "Old English Goes New Hollywood." *Wall Street Journal*, November 16, 2007: W1.

Morin, Edgar. *The Stars* (1972). Translated by Richard Howard. Minneapolis: University of Minnesota Press, 2005.

Morrison, Toni. *The Bluest Eye* (1970). New York: Signet/Plume, 1996.

———. *Sula/Song of Solomon/Tar Baby.* New York: Quality Paperback Book Club, 1987.

Moser, Benjamin. "Cemetery of Hope." *Harpers* (January 2008): 67–74.

Mulvey, Laura. *Fetishism and Curiosity.* London: BFI, 1996.

———. *Visual and Other Pleasures.* Bloomington: University of Indiana Press, 1989.

Nabokov, Vladimir. *Speak Memory* (1966). New York: Putnam/Capricorn, 1970.

Nadel, Alan. *Containment Culture: American Narrative, Postmodernism & the Atomic Age.* Durham, N.C.: Duke University Press, 1995.

———. *Invisible Criticism: Ralph Ellison and the American Canon.* Iowa City: University of Iowa Press, 1988.

Navasky, Victor. *Naming Names* (1980). New York: Penguin, 1991.

Nixon, Richard. *RN: The Memoirs of Richard Nixon.* New York: Simon & Schuster/Touchstone, 1990.

North, Michael. *Camera Works: Photography and the Twentieth-Century Word.* New York: Oxford University Press, 2005.

"Notes on Susan: An Exchange." *New York Review of Books*, September 14, 2007. www.nybooks.com/articles/20631.

Nugent, Frank. "*The Raven.*" *New York Times*, July 5, 1935. movies2.nytimes. com/movie/review?res=9804E0D9143FE23ABC4D53DFB166838E629EDE.

Nussimbaum, Lev. *Blood and Oil.* Translated by Elsa Talmey. New York: Simon & Schuster, 1932.

O'Brien, Geoffrey. "A Northern New Jersey State of Mind." *New York Review of Books*, August 16, 2007. www.nybooks.com/articles/20473.

———. *The Phantom Empire.* New York: Norton, 1993.

O'Connor, F. *Three by Flannery O'Connor.* New York: Penguin/Signet, 1983.

Ondaatje, Michael. *The Conversations: Walter Murch and the Art of Editing Film.* Toronto: Vintage Canada, 2002.

Orr, Christopher. "Moral Development." *New Republic/TNR Online,* May 16, 2006. www.tnr.com/doc.mhtml?i=w060515&s=orr051605.

Orr, John. *Cinema and Modernity.* Cambridge: Polity Press, 1993.

Orwell, George. *Collected Essays.* New York: Harvest/Harcourt Brace, 1954.

Otero-Pailos, Jorge. "*Casablanca*'s Régime: The Shifting Aesthetics of Political Technologies (1907–1943)." *Postmodern Culture* 8, no. 2 (1998). muse.jhu.edu/journals/pmc/v008/8.2otero-pailos.html.

Page, Clarence. "Obama's Drama." *Chicago Tribune,* August 1, 2004. www.chicagotribune.com/news/columnists/chi-0408010236aug01,1,4913966.column?coll=chi-news-col.

Paglia, Camille. "My Magical Movie Mystery Tour." *Slate,* June 16, 1999. www.salon.com/people/feature/1999/06/16/movies/.

Pamuk, Ohran. *Other Colors* (2005). Translated by Maureen Freely. New York: Knopf, 2007.

Panofsky, Dora and Ervin. *Pandora's Box: The Changing Aspects of a Mythical Symbol* (1956). New York: Pantheon/Bollingen, 1962.

Panofsky, Ervin. "Style and Medium in Motion Pictures." In Braudy and Cohen, *Film Theory and Criticism*, 289–302.

Parker, Ian. "Somebody Has to Be in Control." *New Yorker,* April 14, 2008: 40–49.

"Parnassus, Coast to Coast." *Time,* June 11, 1956. www.time.com/time/magazine/article/0,9171,862171,00.html.

Paumgarten, Nick. "Talk of the Town: Retrospectives/Cover Guy." *New Yorker,* April 21, 2008: 46–47.

Pease, Allison. "Readers with Bodies: Modernist Criticism's Bridge across the Cultural Divide." *Modernism/Modernity* 7, no. 1 (2000): 77–97.

Perez, Vincent. "Movies, Marxism, and Jim Crow: Richard Wright's Cultural Criticism." *Texas Studies in Literature and Language* 43, no. 2 (2001): 142–68.

Pierson, Frank. "My Battles with Barbra and Jon." *New West,* November 22, 1976. barbra-archives.com/MagazineArchives/streisand_newwest_magazine.html.

Pirandello, Luigi. *Shoot* (1926). Translated by Scott Moncrieff. Chicago: University of Chicago Press, 2005.

Podhoretz, John. "A Bull's Worth." *Weekly Standard,* May 25, 1998: 38.

Poirier, Richard. *The Renewal of Literature: Emersonian Reflections.* New Haven, Conn.: Yale University Press, 1988.

Pomerance, Murray, ed. *Cinema and Modernity.* New Brunswick, N.J.: Rutgers University Press, 2006.

———. *An Eye for Hitchcock.* New Brunswick, N.J.: Rutgers University Press, 2004.

Pound, Ezra. *The ABC of Reading.* New York: New Directions, n.d.

———. "A Few Don'ts by an Imagiste." *Poetry* 1, no. 6 (March 1913): 199–200.

———. "Hugh Selwyn Mauberly." 1917. www.poemhunter.com/p/m/poem.asp ?poem=31460&poet=6621&num=27&total=57.

———. *The Pisan Cantos.* New York: New Directions, 2003.

———. *Selected Literary Essays.* New York: New Directions, 1968.

———. *Translations.* New York: New Directions, 1963.

Preissel, Jeniffer. "Satire and Subversion on the Silver Screen." *Columbia College Today* (November/December 2007): 24–27.

"[Proposal] Nightmare on 53d Street." *Harpers* (January 2008): 20–22.

Pryor, Thomas. "*The Setup.*" *New York Times,* March 30, 1949. movies2.nytimes .com/movie/review?_r=1&res=9F06E2DB133CE23BBC4850DFB56683826 59EDE&oref=slogin.

Rabinowitz, Paula. *Black and White and Noir.* New York: Columbia University Press, 2002.

Radosh, Daniel "The Play's the Thing." *New York Times,* September 28, 2007: A29.

Rampersad, Arnold. *Ralph Ellison: A Biography.* New York: Knopf, 2007.

Raphael, Frederic. *Darling* (1958). New York: Signet/NAL, 1958.

———. *Personal Terms: The 1950s and 1960s.* London: Carcanet, 2001.

Ray, Nicholas. *I Was Interrupted: Nicholas Ray on Making Movies.* Edited by Susan Ray. Berkeley: University of California Press, 1993.

Ray, Robert. *A Certain Tendency of the Hollywood Cinema.* Princeton, N.J.: Princeton University Press 1981.

Rayner, Richard. "Two True Loves." Review of *The Long Embrace* by Judith Freeman. *Los Angles Times,* November 4, 2007: R1, R4, R5.

Rebeck, Theresa. *Free Fire Zone: A Playwright's Adventures on the Creative Battlefields of Film, TV, and Theater.* Hanover, N.H.: Smith & Kraus, 2006.

Reesman, Bryan. "In Search of a Home for Scarlet and Kong." *New York Times,* June 18, 2006: 2:23.

Reeves, Richard. *President Kennedy: Profile of Power.* New York: Simon & Schuster, 1993.

Rich, Adrienne. *The Will to Change.* New York: Norton, 1971.

Rich, Frank. "Forgotten But Not Gone." *New York Times,* January 4, 2009: Wk8.

Richards, Rashna. "The Stuff That Movies Are Made Of." *Arizona Quarterly* 63, no. 4 (2007): 83–118.

Richardson, Robert. *Literature and Film.* Bloomington: Indiana University Press, 1969.

Roach, Joseph. *It.* Ann Arbor: University of Michigan Press, 2007.

Robbins, Harold. *The Dream Merchants.* New York: Knopf, 1949.

Robinson, W. R., ed. *Man and the Movies.* Baton Rouge: Louisiana State University Press, 1967.

———. "The Movies, Too, Will Make You Free." In Robinson, *Man and Movies,* 12–36.

Rodrick, Stephen. "Michael Winterbottom Gets Naked." *New York Times Magazine*. July 3, 2005: 22.

Rosen, Jonathan. "Critic At Large: Return to Paradise." *New Yorker*, June 2, 2008. www.newyorker.com/arts/critics/atlarge/2008/06/02/080602crat_atlarge_rosen.

Rosenbaum, Jonathan. *Essential Cinema*. Baltimore: Johns Hopkins University Press, 2004.

———. *Movie Wars*. Chicago: Cappella, 2002.

Ross, Andrew. *No Respect: Intellectuals and Popular Culture*. New York: Routledge, 1989.

Rossetti, Dante Gabriel, and William M. Rossetti. *The Poetical Works of Dante Gabriel Rossetti*. London: Ellis & Elvey, 1891.

Rosten, Leo. "The Intellectual and the Mass Media: Some Rigorously Random Remarks." *Daedalus* 89, no. 2 (Spring 1960): 333–46.

Roth, Claudia. "Player Kings." *New Yorker*, November 19, 2007: 70–79.

Roth, Joseph. *What I Saw: Reports from Berlin 1920–1933*. Translated by Michael Hoffmann. New York: Norton, 2003.

Roth, Philip. *Exit Ghost*. Boston: Houghton Mifflin, 2007.

———. *The Ghost Writer*. New York: Farrar, Straus, Giroux, 1979.

———. *Goodbye Columbus and Five Short Stories* (1959). New York: Vintage, 1992.

———. *Our Gang*. New York: Random House, 1971.

Ryfle, Steve. "Lessons from a Wise Old Actor." Review of *Life Beyond Measure: Letters to My Great Granddaughter* by Sidney Poitier. *Los Angeles Times*, May 1, 2008: E9.

Sachs, Susan. "A Step Closer to Europe, Proud Turks Hold Off Glee." *New York Times*, October 7, 2004: A12.

Safire, William. "On Language: Hollywords." *New York Times Magazine*, November 11, 2007: 38.

Said, Edward. "The Clash of Ignorance." *Nation*, October 22, 2001: 11–13.

Saluny, Susan. "Michelle Obama Takes to the Trail." *New York Times*, February 14, 2008: A1, 31.

Sarkin, Jane, and Krista Smith. "Mommy's Being Famous Right Now." *Vanity Fair* (December 2007): 298–303, 369–71.

Sarris, Andrew. "Notes on the Auteur Theory." *Film Culture* 62, no. 3 (1962).

Sawhill, Ray. "Books." Review of *The Operator* by Tom King. *Salon*, April 6, 2000. archive.salon.com/books/feature/2000/04/06/geffen/.

Schatz, Thomas. *The Genius of the System: Hollywood Filmmaking in the Studio Era*. New York: Pantheon, 1988.

Schulberg, Budd. *Across the Everglades*. New York: Random House, 1958.

———. "Any Which Way He Could." *American Film* (July/August 1988): 55–59.

———. Budd Schulberg Papers. Manuscripts Division Department of Rare Books and Special Collections, Princeton University Library. Comp. Mary Zaplac and

Karla Vecchia. 2001. 2004libweb.princeton.edu/libraries/firestone/rbsc/aids/ schulberg.html.

———. *Moving Pictures: Memoirs of a Hollywood Prince*. New York: Stein & Day, 1981.

———. *Sanctuary V* (1969). New York: Signet, 1971.

———. "Two Conversations." *Paris Review* 160 (2002): 86–137.

———. *Waterfront*. New York: Random House, 1955.

———. *What Makes Sammy Run* (1941). New York: Vintage, 1990.

———. "The Writer and Hollywood." *Harpers* (October 1959): 133–37.

———. *Writers in America: Four Seasons of Success*. New York: Stein & Day, 1983.

Schultheiss, John. "The 'Eastern' Writer in Hollywood." *Cinema Journal* 11, no. 1 (Autumn 1971): 13–47.

Schuman, Frederick L. "Book Reviews." Review of *Modern Civilization on Trial* by C. Delisle Burns and *Looking Forward* by Nicholas Murray Butler. *American Journal of Sociology* 38, no. 3 (November 1932): 467–68.

Schumpeter, Joseph. *Capitalism, Socialism and Democracy* (1942). New York: Harper/Colophon, 1975.

Schwartz, Delmore. "Views of a Second Violinist: Some Answers to Questions about Writing Poetry." In *Selected Essays of Delmore Schwartz*, edited by Donald A. Dike and David H. Zucker, 24–29. Chicago: University of Chicago Press, 1970.

Schwartz, Vanessa. *It's So French: Hollywood, Paris, and the Making of Cosmopolitan Film Culture*. Chicago: University of Chicago Press, 2007.

Scott, A. O. "Another Side of Bob Dylan and Another and Another." *New York Times*, November 21, 2007: E1.

———. "Francis Ford Coppola, A Kid to Watch." *New York Times*, September 9, 2007: 2:1.

———. "Rage, Fear and Revulsion: At War with War." Review of *Redacted*. *New York Times*, November 16, 2007: E1.

———. "Two Outlaws Blasting Holes in Screen." *New York Times*, August 12, 2007: 2:1.

———. "A War on Every Screen." *New York Times*, October 28, 2007: 2:1.

———. "The Week Ahead—Mar. 2-8: Film." *New York Times*, March 2, 2008: AL4.

Scott, Janny. "In 2000, a Streetwise Veteran Schooled a Bold Young Obama." *New York Times*, September 9, 2007: A1.

Scott-Thomas, Rolfe. "Informal History." *Times Literary Supplement*, October 20, 1932: 760.

Seldes, Gilbert. *The Movies Come from America*. New York: Scribners, 1937.

Shamdasani, Sonu. *Jung and the Making of Modern Psychology: The Dream of a Science*. Cambridge: Cambridge University Press, 2003.

Shils, Edward. "Mass Society and Its Culture." *Daedalus* 89, no. 2 (Spring 1960): 288–314.

Shumway, David. "Authenticity: Modernity, Stardom, and Rock & Roll." *Modernism/Modernity* 14, no. 3 (2007): 527–34.

Simon, John. "On the Kazan Front." Review of *Elia Kazan: A Biography* by Richard Schickel. *New York Times Book Review*, November 27, 2005: 1, 10–11.

Smiley, Jane. *Ten Days in the Hills*. New York: Knopf, 2007.

Smith, Craig. "Revisiting Sgt. York and a Time When Heroes Stood Tall." *New York Times*, June 20, 2006: A3.

Smith, Dinitia. "Novelists Get Back at Hollywood, Mostly Gently." *New York Times*, September 25, 1999.

Smith, Gavin. "A Question of Control." *Film Comment* 28, no. 1 (1992): 28–37.

Smith, Nancy D. "The Real Charlie Wilson." *Wall Street Journal*, December 21, 2007: W10.

Smith, Wendy. "The Big Picture." Review of *Pictures at a Revolution* by Mark Harris. *Chicago Tribune*, February 9, 2008. www.chicagotribune.com/features/booksmags/chi-picturesbw09feb09,1,7808390.story.

Smyth, J. E. *Reconstructing American Historical Cinema*. Lexington: University of Kentucky Press, 2006.

Sontag, Susan. *In America*. New York: Farrar, Straus, Giroux, 1995.

Spengler, Oswald. *The Decline of the West* (1923). Translated by Charles F. Atkinson. New York: Knopf, 1945.

Stead, Christina. *I'm Dying Laughing* (1986). New York: Holt, 1987.

Stein, Gertrude. *Paris, France* (1940). New York: Liveright, 1970/1996.

Stephens, Brett. "Obama and the *South Park* Gnomes." *Wall Street Journal*, May 25, 2009: A17.

Stevens, Wallace. *The Palm at the End of the Mind*. Edited by Holly Stevens (1971). New York: Vintage, 1972.

Stevenson, Richard. "Bush Travels to Georgia to Welcome Home Troops from Iraq." *New York Times*, September 13, 2003: A7.

Stone, Robert. *Children of Light* (1986). New York: Vintage, 1992.

Strauss, Theodore. "The Ghost Creeps, at the Globe." *New York Times*, August 19, 1940. select.nytimes.com/gst/abstract.html?res=F50E17FB385A11728DDDA00994D0405B8088F1D3.

———. "Loew's Criterion Shows Three Faces West, with John Wayne." *New York Times*, August 19, 1940. select.nytimes.com/mem/archive/pdf?res=F5017FB385A11728DDDA00994D0405B8088F1D3.

Stuart, Jan. *The Nashville Chronicles: The Making of Robert Altman's Masterpiece*. New York: Simon & Schuster, 2000.

Sutton, Paul. *Turner Classic Movie/British Film Guide If . . .* London: I.B. Tauris, 2005.

Sylvester, Christopher, ed. *The Grove Book of Hollywood*. New York: Grove Press, 1998.

Tallmer, Jerry. "Screenwriter Budd Schulberg, 90, reminisces on making 'Waterfront'." *The Villager*, November 3–9, 1994. www.thevillager.com/villager_79/screenwriterbuddschulberg.html.

Tanenhaus, Sam. "Requiem for Two Heavyweights." *New York Times*, April 13, 2008: WK1.

Terkel, Studs. *Touch and Go: A Memoir*. New York: New Press, 2007.

Thomas, Desson. "Puppet Masters." Review of *Team America*. *Washington Post*, October 15, 2004: WE33.

Thompson, Howard. "*The Cobweb* at Loew's State." *New York Times*, August 6, 1955. movies.nytimes.com/movie/review?_r=1&res=9D02E3D9103AE53BBC4E53DFBE66838E649EDE&oref=slogin.

Thompson, Kenneth. *Moral Panics*. New York: Routledge, 1998.

Thompson, Luke. "USA-Holes." Review of *Team America*. *Dallas Observer*, October 14, 2004. www.dallasobserver.com/2004-10-14/film/u-s-a-holes/.

Thomson, David. "Cary Grant." In Lopate, *American Movie Critics*, 610–13.

———. "Howard Hawks." In Lopate, *American Movie Critics*, 613–16.

———. *The Whole Equation*. New York: Knopf, 2005.

Tierney, John. "South Park Refugees." *New York Times*, August 29, 2006: A19.

Todorov, Tzvetan. "Letter from Paris." *Salmagundi* 143 (Summer 2004): 3–17.

Torgovnick, Marianne. *Gone Primitive: Savage Intellects, Modern Lives*. Chicago: University of Chicago Press, 1980.

Travers, Peter "*Age of Innocence*." *Rolling Stone*, September 16, 1993: 666.

Trebay, Guy. "Dr. Dippy, Meet Dr. Evil." *New York Times*, January 27, 2008: ST1, 2.

Trilling, Lionel. *The Moral Obligation to Be Intelligent*. New York: Farrar, Straus, Giroux, 2000.

Trimpi, Wesley. "The Meaning of Horace's Ut Pictura Poesis." *Journal of the Warburg and Courtauld Institutes* 36 (1973): 1–34.

"TV Listings." *New York Times*, March 20, 2008: E10.

Tyler, Parker. *The Hollywood Hallucination* (1944). New York: Simon & Schuster, 1970.

Untermeyer, Louis. *From Another World*. New York: Harcourt Brace, 1939.

Updike, John. *In the Beauty of the Lilies* (1996). New York: Fawcett/Columbine, 1997.

———. "Milton Adapts Genesis; Collier Adapts Milton." *New Yorker*, August 20, 1973: 84–86.

Veblen, Thorstein. *The Theory of the Leisure Class* (1899). New York: Dover, 1994.

Vidal, Gore. *Palimpsest: A Memoir*. New York: Random, 1995.

———. "Who Makes the Movies." In Ebert, *Roger Ebert's Book of Film*, 569–80.

Wagner, Bruce. 2003. *Still Holding*. New York: Simon & Schuster, 2004.

Waites, Kathleen J. "Framing the Framed Self: A Reading of Victor Nunez's *Ruby in Paradise*." *Biography* 24, no. 3 (2001): 425–41.

Walkowitz, Rebecca. *Cosmopolitan Style: Modernism Beyond the Nation*. New York: Columbia University Press, 2006.

Walters, Suzanna Danuta. *Material Girls: Making Sense of Feminist Cultural Theory*. Berkeley: University of California Press, 1995.

Wanger, Walter. "Hollywood and the Intellectual." *Saturday Review*, December 5, 1942: 6, 40.

Warshow, Robert. *The Immediate Experience: Movies, Comics, Theater and Other Aspects of Popular Culture*. New York: Doubleday, 1952.

Waugh, Evelyn. *The Loved One* (1948). Boston: Little-Brown, 1976.

———. "Very Egyptian." In Sylvester, *The Grove Book of Hollywood*, 359–61.

Waxman, Sharon "Hollywood's Shortage of Female Power." *New York Times*, April 26, 2007: E1, 7.

Weatherby, W. J. *James Baldwin: Artist on Fire* (1989). New York: Dell/Laurel, 1990.

Weber, Max. "Science as a Vocation." In *Essays in Sociology*, edited by C. Wright Mills and H. H. Gerth, 129–56. New York: Oxford University Press, 1946.

"The Week Ahead." *New York Times*, December 16, 2007: 2:4.

Weideman, John Edgar. *Fanon*. Boston: Houghton Mifflin, 2008.

Weiler, A. H. "Essay on Love: The Savage Eye Bows at Trans-Lux 52d." *New York Times*, June 7, 1960. movies.nytimes.com/movie/review?res=9805E6DC 1F38E333A25754C0A9609C946191D6CF.

Weinberger, Eliot. "Notes on Susan." *New York Review of Books*, August 16, 2007. www.nybooks.com/articles/20494.

Weinraub, Bernard. "Clouds over Disneyland." *New York Times*, April 9, 1995: E1.

West, Mae. *Three Plays by Mae West: Sex, The Drag and Pleasure Man*. New York: Routledge, 1997.

West, Nathanael. *Miss Lonelyhearts & The Day of the Locust* (1933 and 1939). New York: New Directions, 1969.

Wheatcroft, Geoffrey. "Through the Past Darkly." Review of *Reappraisals* by Tony Judt. *New York Times Book Review*, April 20, 2008: 16.

White, Hayden. *Tropics of Discourse: Essays in Cultural Criticism*. Baltimore: Johns Hopkins University Press, 1978.

Widdicombe, Lizzie. "Talk of the Town: Want Ad/Beautiful Minds." *New Yorker*, March 10, 2008: 58, 60.

Wilbur, Richard. "A Poet and the Movies." In Robinson, *Man and the Movies*, 223–26.

Williams, William Carlos. *Collected Poems of William Carlos Williams: Volume II, 1929–1962*. Edited by A. Walton Litz. New York: New Directions, 1986.

Wilson, Edmund. *The Boys in the Back Room*. San Francisco: Colt, 1941.

Wilson, Woodrow. "Final Address in Support of the League of Nations" (September 25, 1919). *The Papers of Woodrow Wilson*. Sixty-nine volumes. Edited by Arthur Link. Princeton, N.J.: Princeton University Press, 1994.

Wolfe, Alan. "Point of View: The Calling of the Public Intellectual." *Chronicle of Higher Education*, May 25, 2001: B20.

Wolff, Cynthia Griffin. "Play It As It Lays: Didion and the Diver Heroine." *Contemporary Literature* 24, no. 4 (1982): 480–95.

Wollen, Peter. *Signs and the Meaning of Cinema* (1969). Bloomington: Indiana University Press, 1972.

Woodress, James. *Willa Cather: A Literary Life* (1987). Lincoln: Bison/University of Nebraska Press, 1989.

Wright, Basil. "Handling the Camera." In Davy, *Footnotes to the Film*, 37–56.

Wright, Richard. *Black Boy* (1945). New York: Harper Perennial, 1998.

———. "Blueprint for Negro Writing." In Wright, *Richard Wright Reader*, 36–49.

———. *Native Son* (1940). New York: Harper Perennial, 1998.

———. *Richard Wright Reader*. Edited by Ellen Wright and Michel Fabre. New York: Harper & Row, 1978.

Yeats, W. B. *The Collected Works of W. B. Yeats, Volume I: The Poems*, second ed. Edited by Richard J. Finneran. New York: Scribner, 1997.

Yehoshua, A. B. *The Lover* (1977). Trans. Philip Simpson. Orlando: Harcourt/Harvest, 1993.

Young, Paul. "The War at Home: Griffith's Intimate Geography of Modern(ist)Warfare." Presented at the Modernist Studies Association Meeting, November 3, 2007.

Yukins, Elizabeth. "An 'Artful Juxtaposition on the Page': Memory, Perception, and Cubist Technique." *PMLA* 119, no. 5 (October 2004): 1247–63.

Zhu, Chungeng. "Ezra Pound's Confucianism." *Philosophy and Literature* 29, no. 1 (2005): 57–72. muse.jhu.edu/journals/philosophy_and_literature/v029/29.1zhu.html.

Index of Names

Index of Movie and TV Titles